KING

KING

Writer:
Joshua Hale Fialkov

Artist:
Bernard Chang

Colorist:
Marcelo Maiolo

Letterer:
Deron Bennett

Cover:
Bernard Chang & Marcelo Maiolo

Editor:
Paul Morrissey

Senior Production Manager:
Jill Taplin

JETCITY
COMICS

KING. The characters and events portrayed in this book are fictitious. Any similarity to real persons, living or dead, is coincidental and not intended by the author. Text copyright © 2016 Velouria Shines, Inc.

Printed in the United States of America.

Published by Jet City Comics, Seattle
www.apub.com

EISBN: 9781503949805 ISBN-10: 1503949990 ISBN-13: 9781503949997

"I Hate Mondays"
CHAPTER ONE

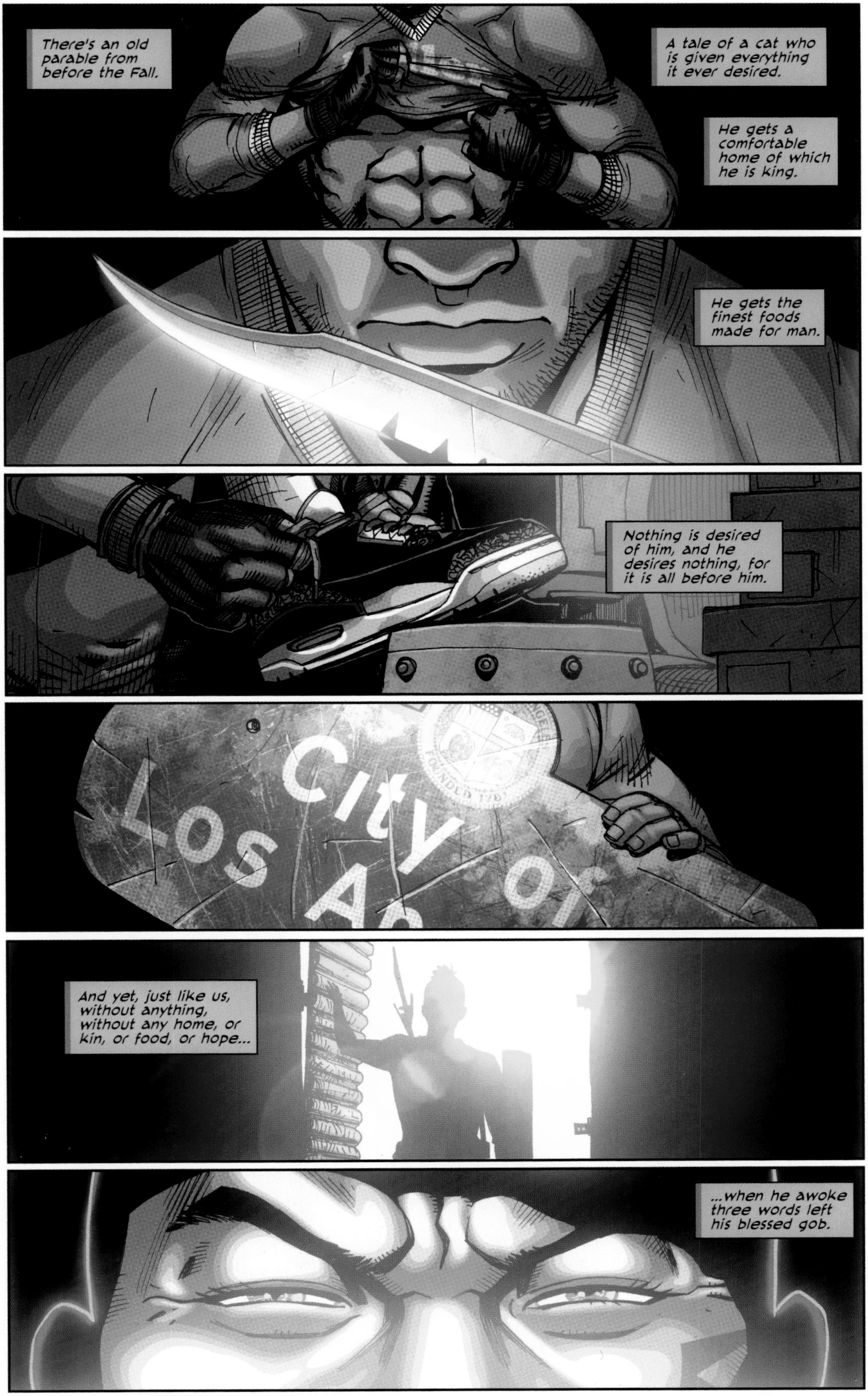
There's an old parable from before the Fall.
A tale of a cat who is given everything it ever desired.
He gets a comfortable home of which he is king.
He gets the finest foods made for man.
Nothing is desired of him, and he desires nothing, for it is all before him.
City of Los An
And yet, just like us, without anything, without any home, or kin, or food, or hope...
...when he awoke three words left his blessed gob.

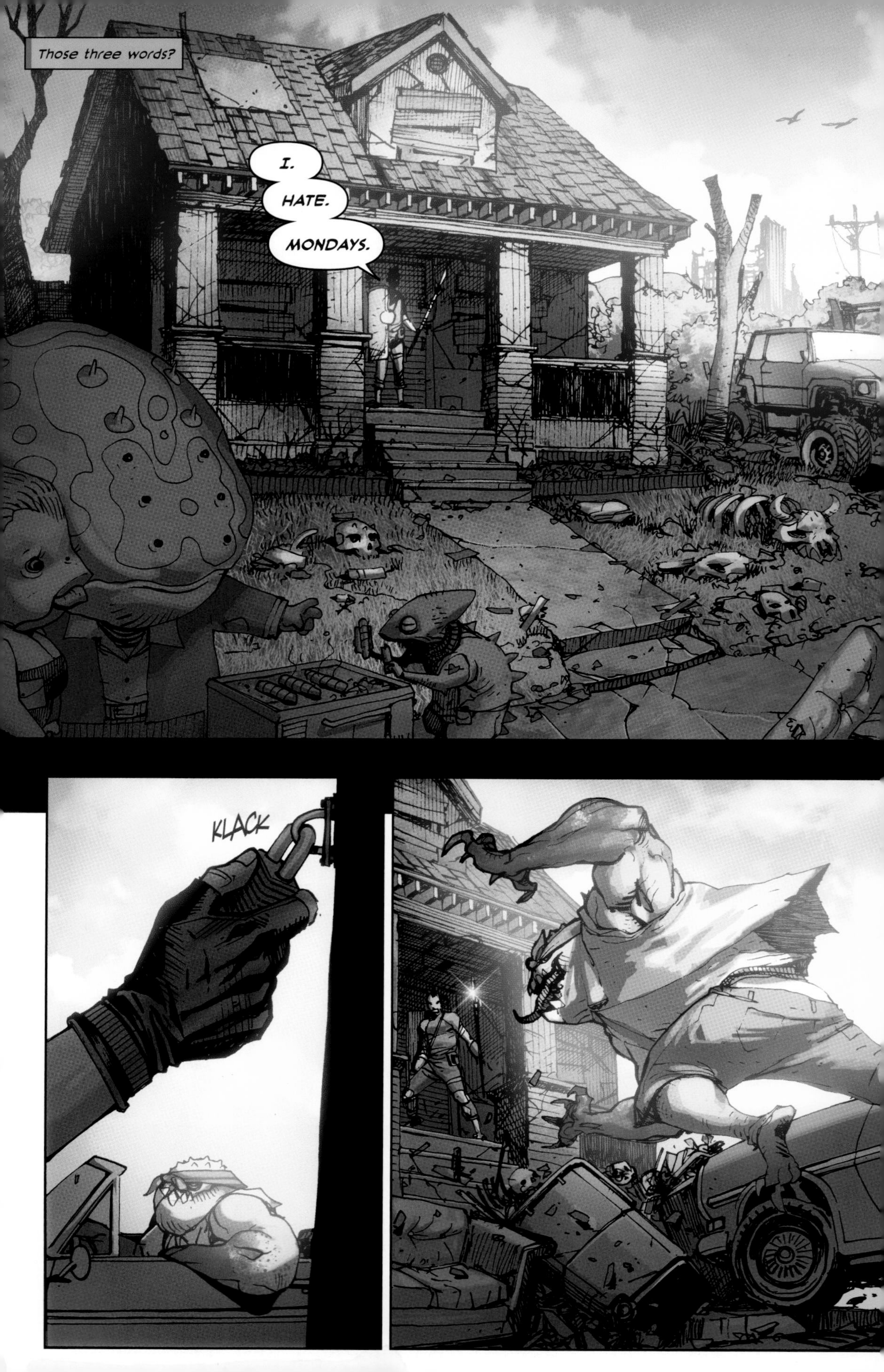
Those three words?
I.
HATE.
MONDAYS.
KLACK

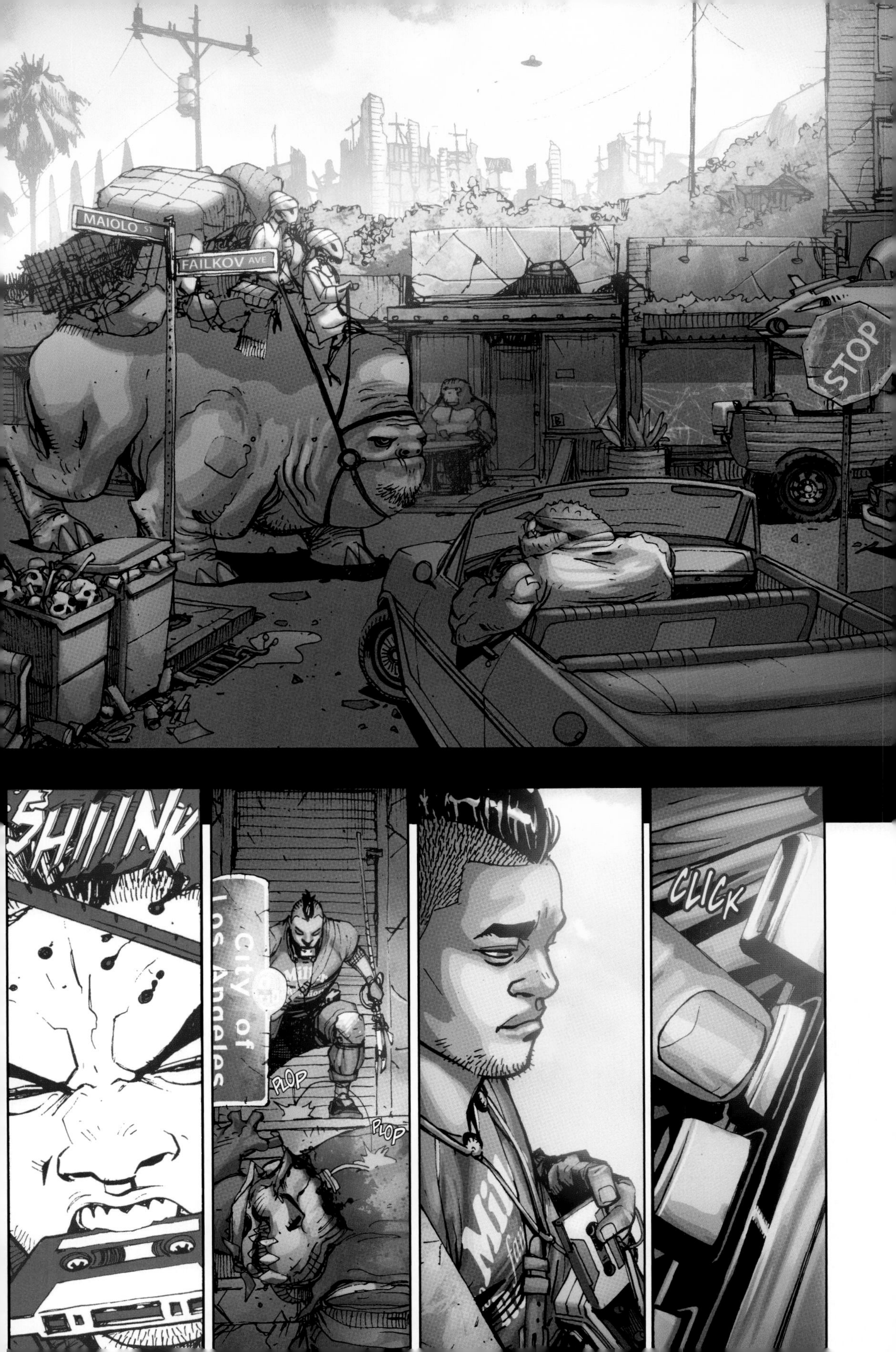

MAIOLO ST
FAILKOV AVE
STOP
SHIIINK
City of Los Angeles
PLOP
PLOP
CLICK

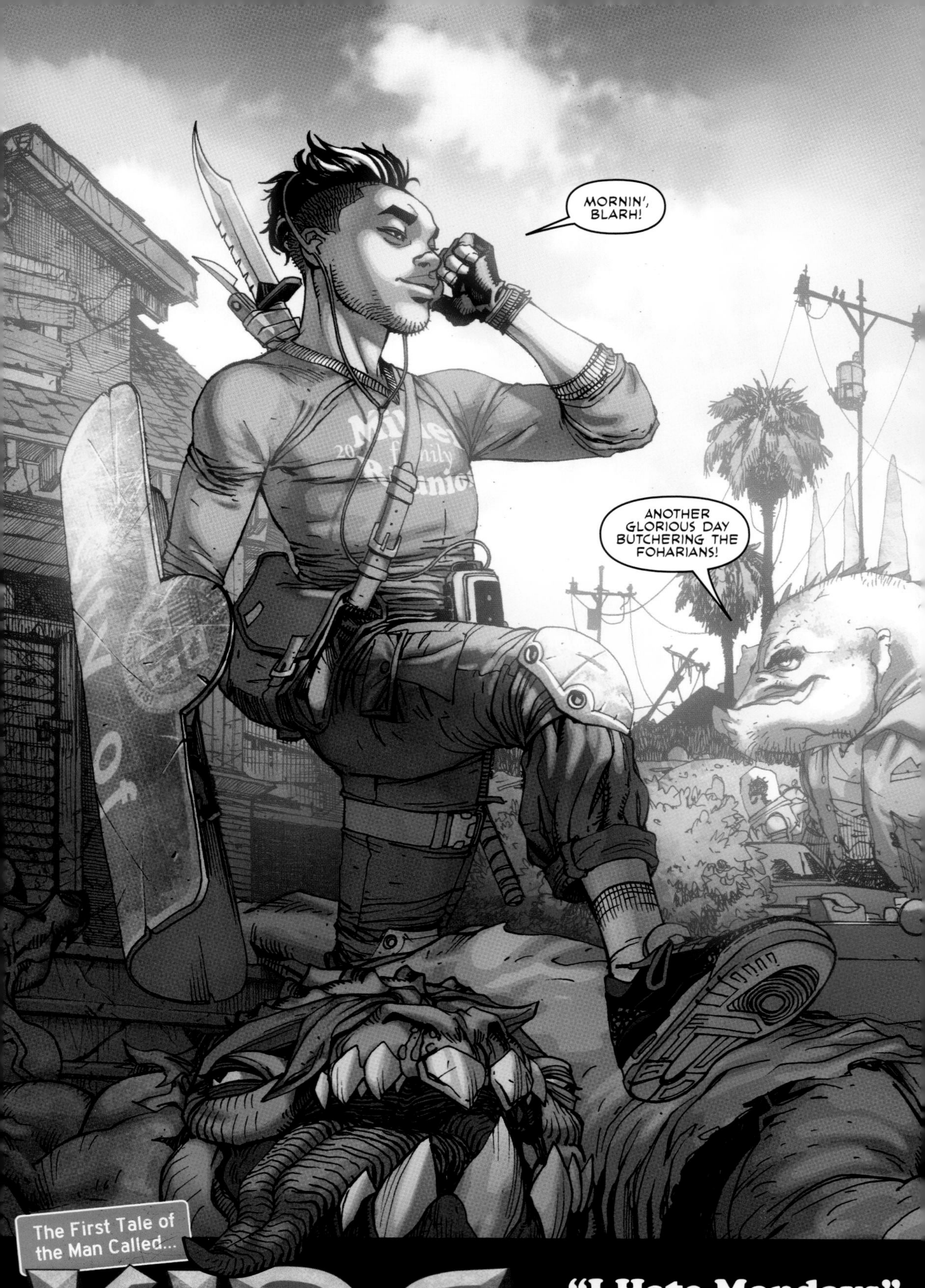
MORNIN', BLARH!
ANOTHER GLORIOUS DAY BUTCHERING THE FOHARIANS!

The First Tale of the Man Called...

KING

"I Hate Mondays"

Writer: JOSHUA HALE FIALKOV Artist: BERNARD CHANG
Colorist: MARCELO MAIOLO Letterer: DERON BENNETT
Cover: BERNARD CHANG & MARCELO MAIOLO

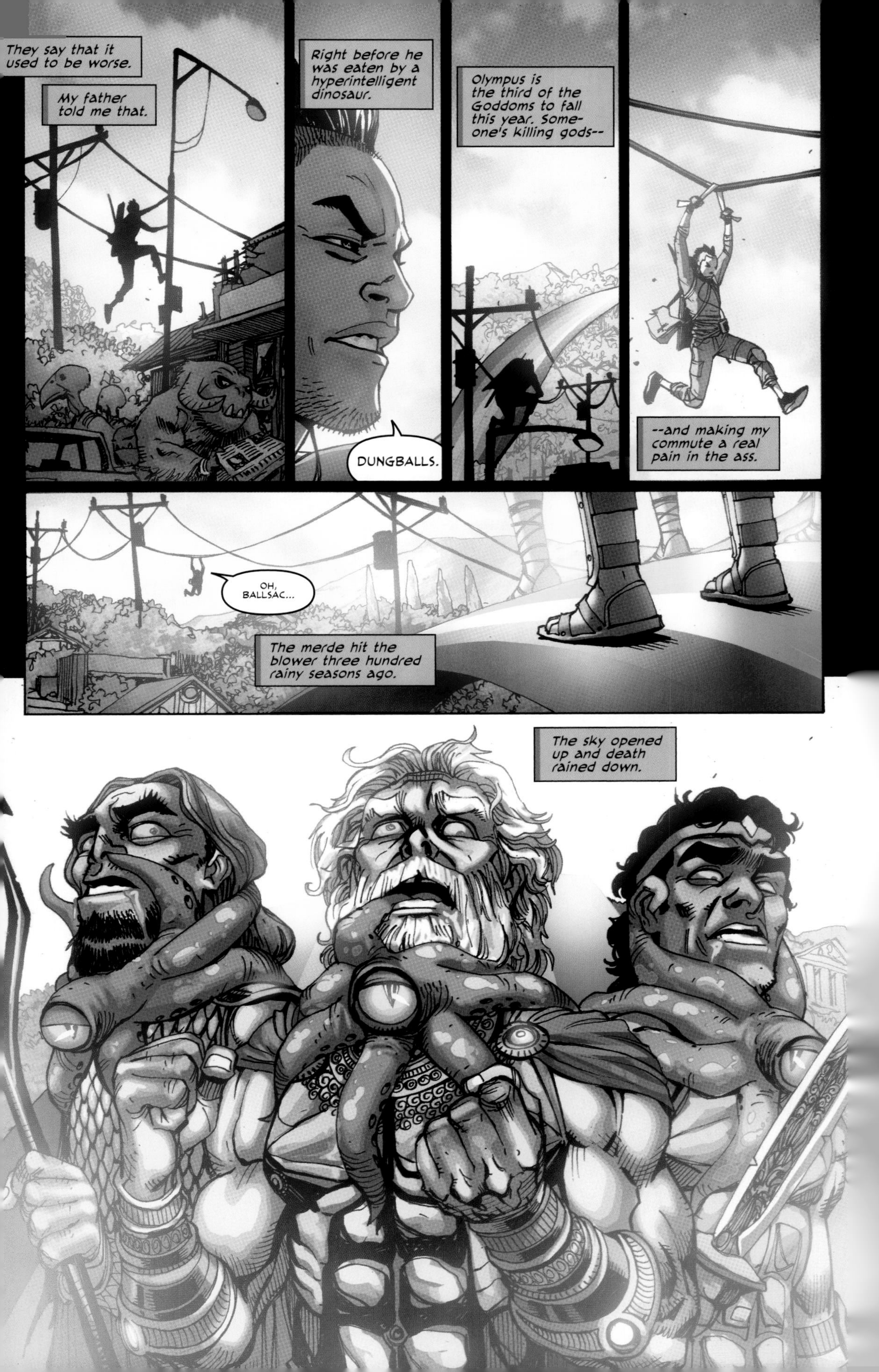

They say that it used to be worse.
My father told me that.
Right before he was eaten by a hyperintelligent dinosaur.
DUNGBALLS.
Olympus is the third of the Goddoms to fall this year. Some-one's killing gods--
--and making my commute a real pain in the ass.
OH, BALLSAC...
The merde hit the blower three hundred rainy seasons ago.
The sky opened up and death rained down.

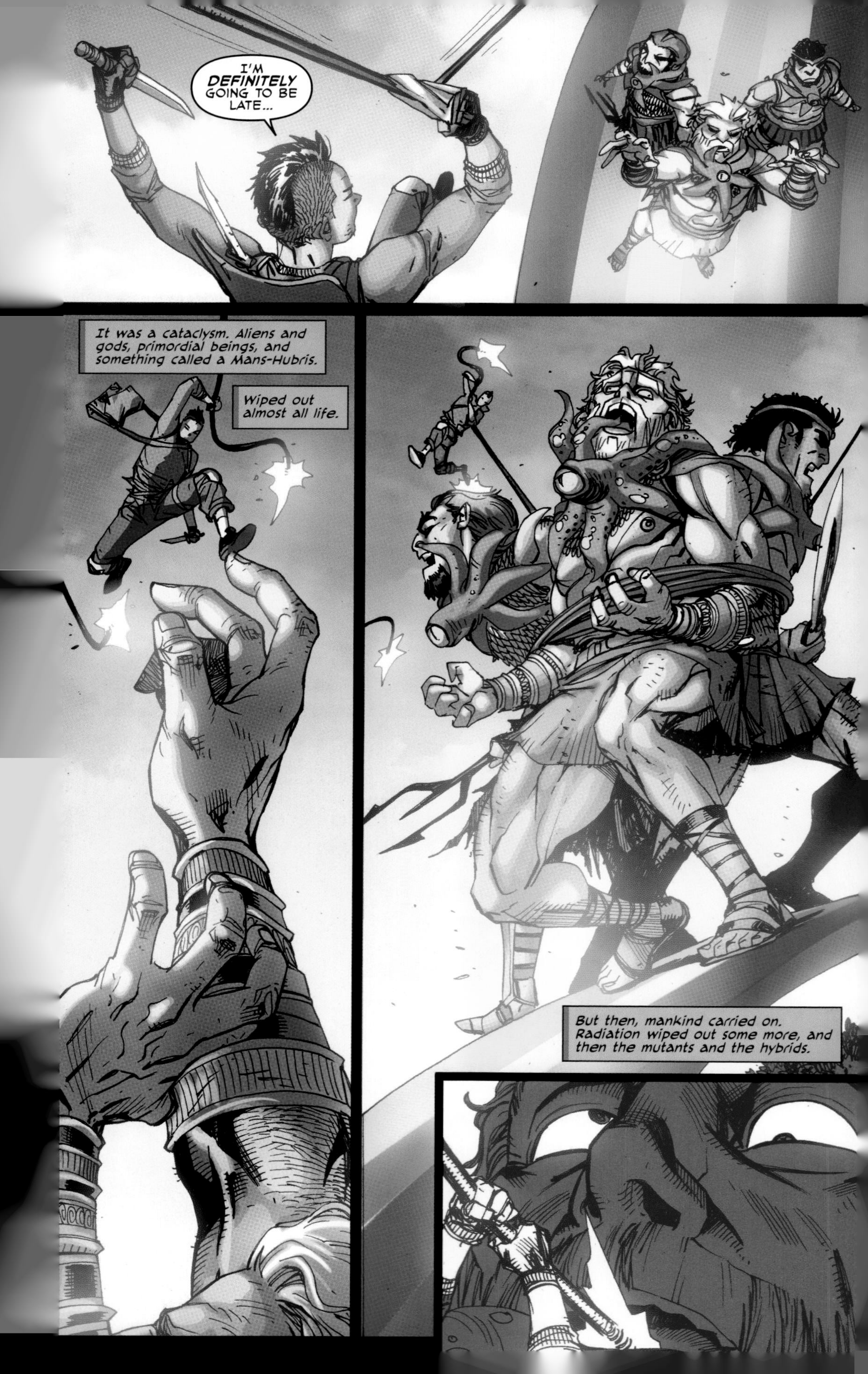
I'M *DEFINITELY* GOING TO BE LATE...
It was a cataclysm. Aliens and gods, primordial beings, and something called a Mans-Hubris.
Wiped out almost all life.
But then, mankind carried on. Radiation wiped out some more, and then the mutants and the hybrids.

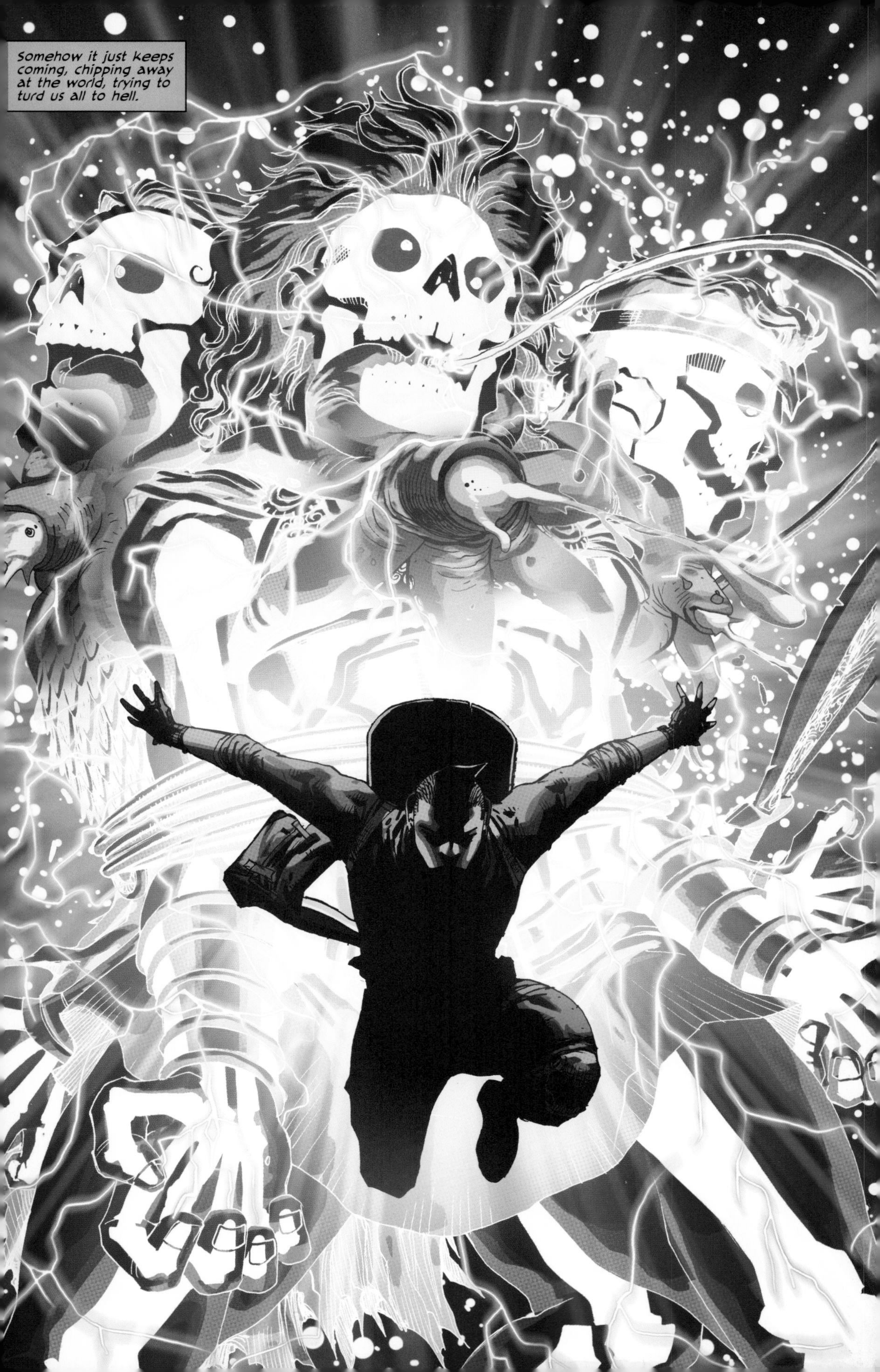
Somehow it just keeps coming, chipping away at the world, trying to turd us all to hell.

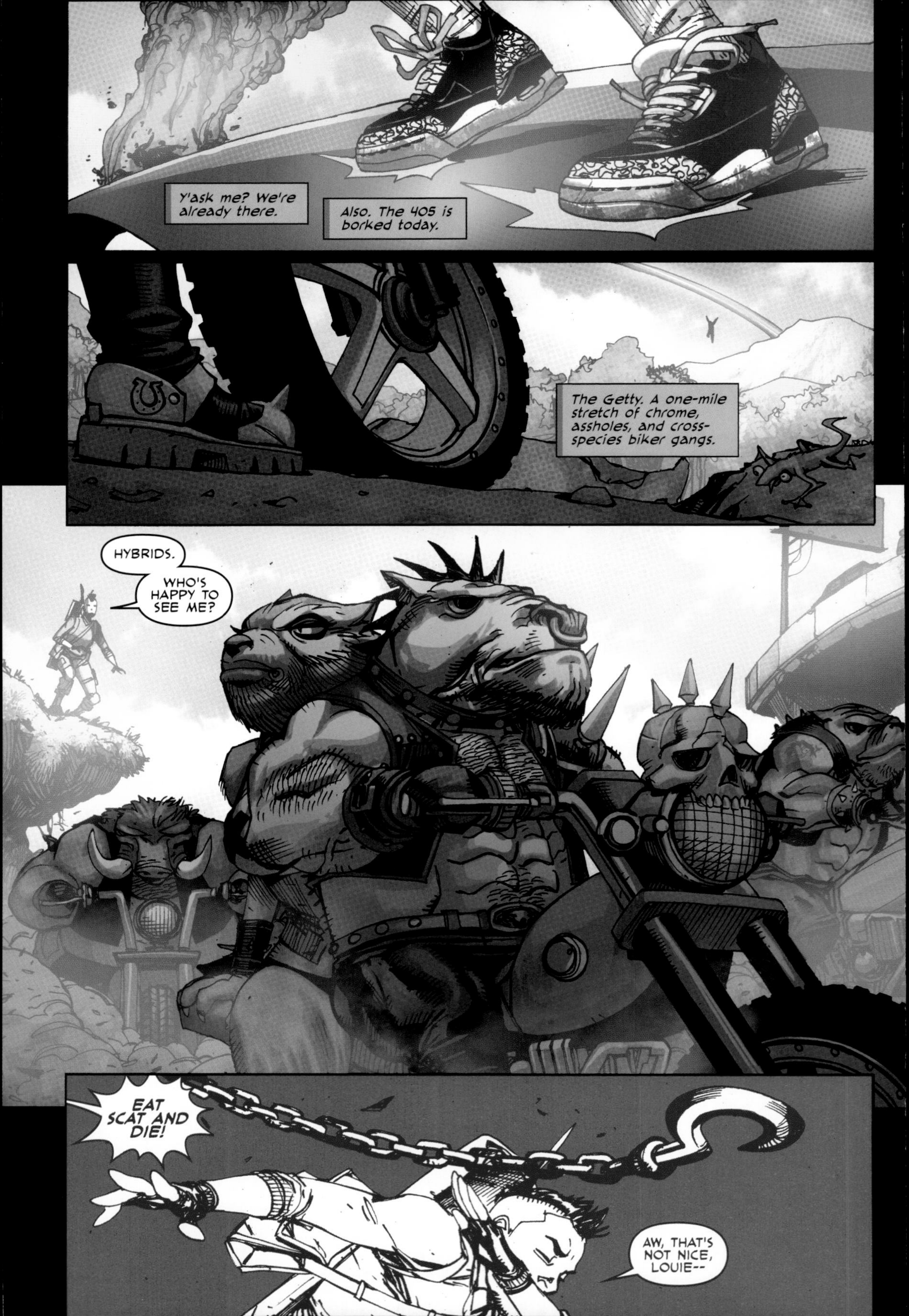

Y'ask me? We're already there.
Also. The 405 is borked today.
The Getty. A one-mile stretch of chrome, assholes, and cross-species biker gangs.
HYBRIDS.
WHO'S HAPPY TO SEE ME?
EAT SCAT AND DIE!
AW, THAT'S NOT NICE, LOUIE--

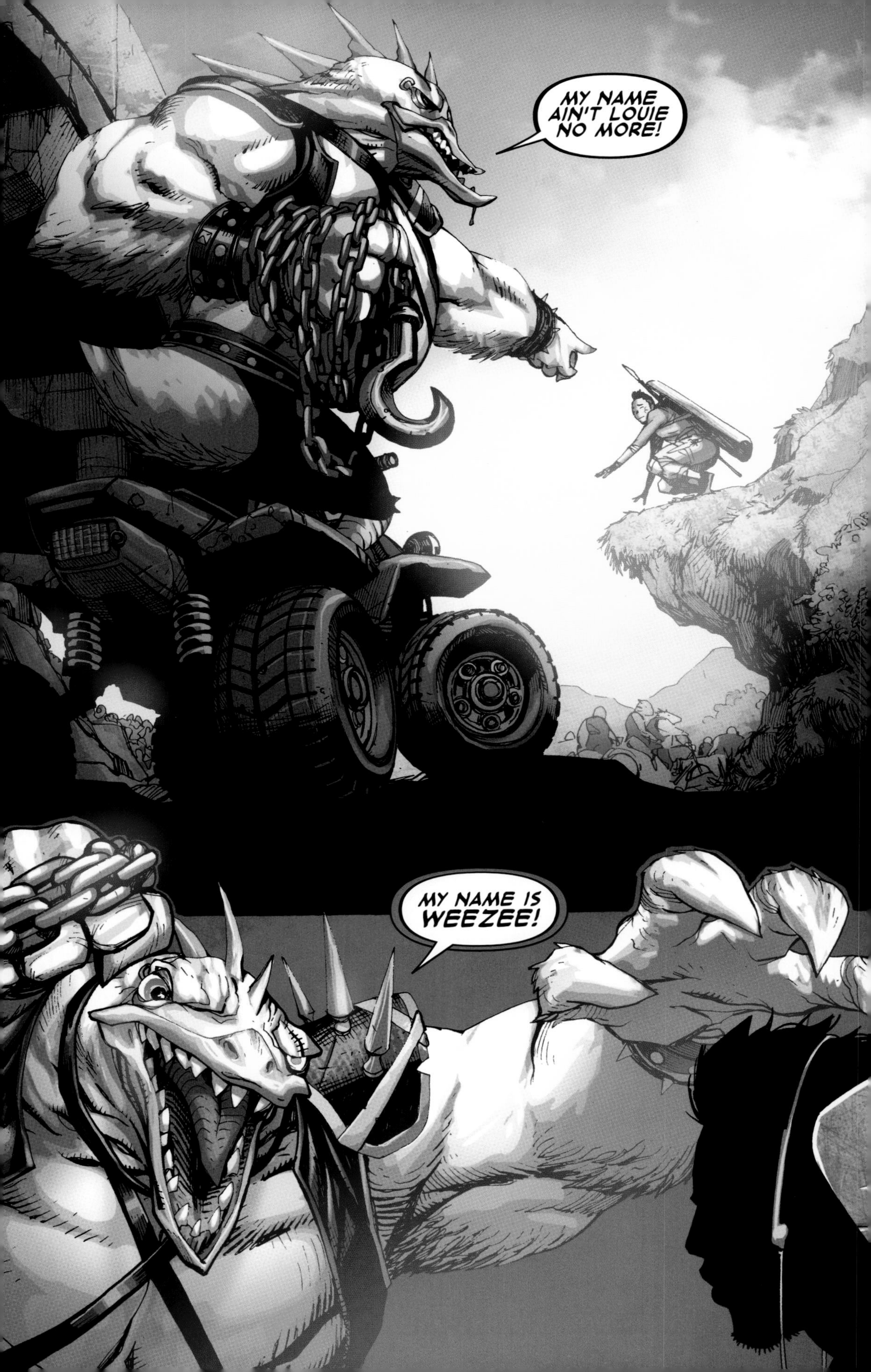
MY NAME AIN'T LOUIE NO MORE!
MY NAME IS WEEZEE!

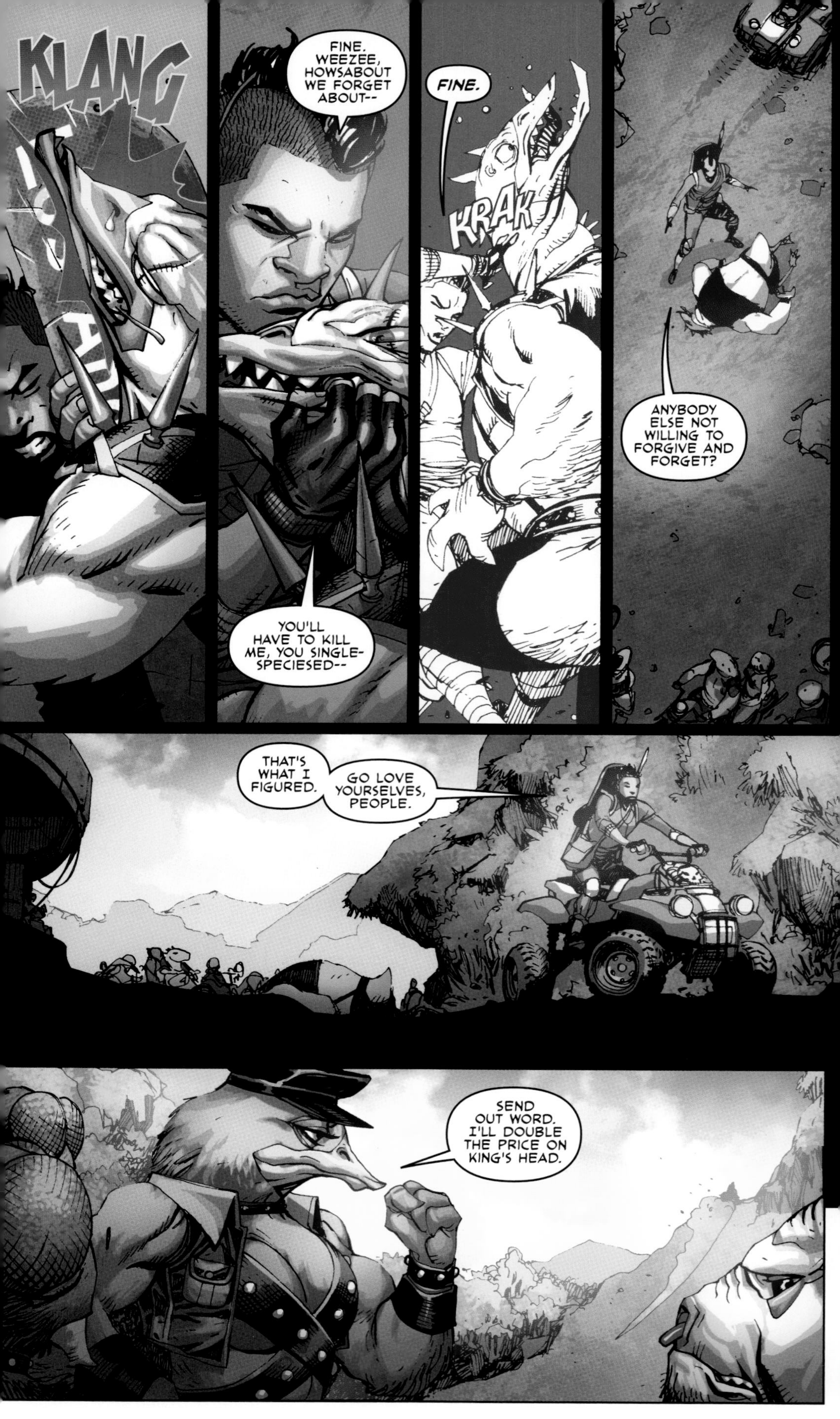
KLANG
FINE. WEEZEE, HOWSABOUT WE FORGET ABOUT--
YOU'LL HAVE TO KILL ME, YOU SINGLE-SPECIESED--
FINE.
KRAK
ANYBODY ELSE NOT WILLING TO FORGIVE AND FORGET?
THAT'S WHAT I FIGURED.
GO LOVE YOURSELVES, PEOPLE.
SEND OUT WORD. I'LL DOUBLE THE PRICE ON KING'S HEAD.

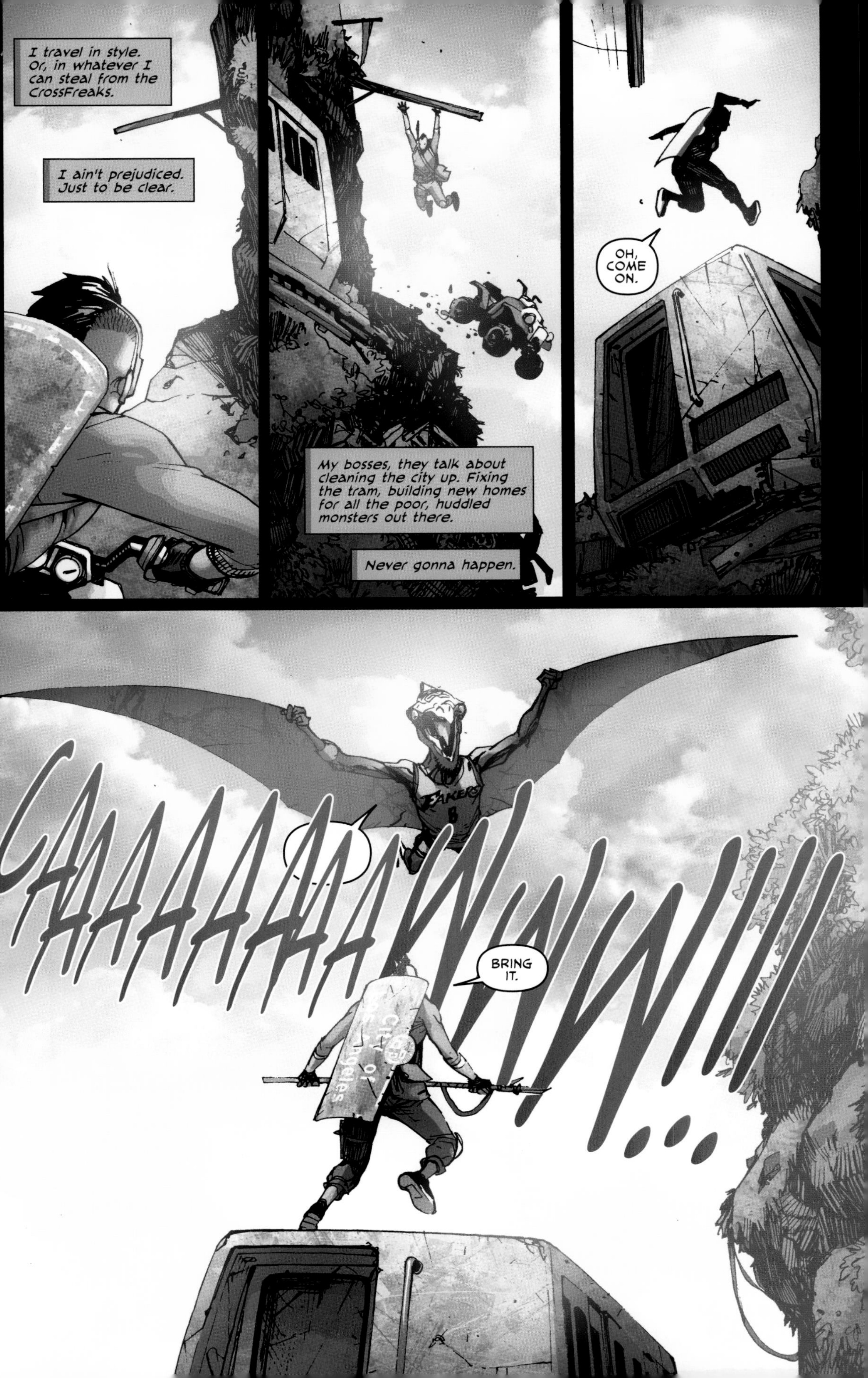
I travel in style. Or, in whatever I can steal from the CrossFreaks.
I ain't prejudiced. Just to be clear.
My bosses, they talk about cleaning the city up. Fixing the tram, building new homes for all the poor, huddled monsters out there.
Never gonna happen.
OH, COME ON.
CAAAAAAAAWWW!!!...
BRING IT.
City of Los Angeles

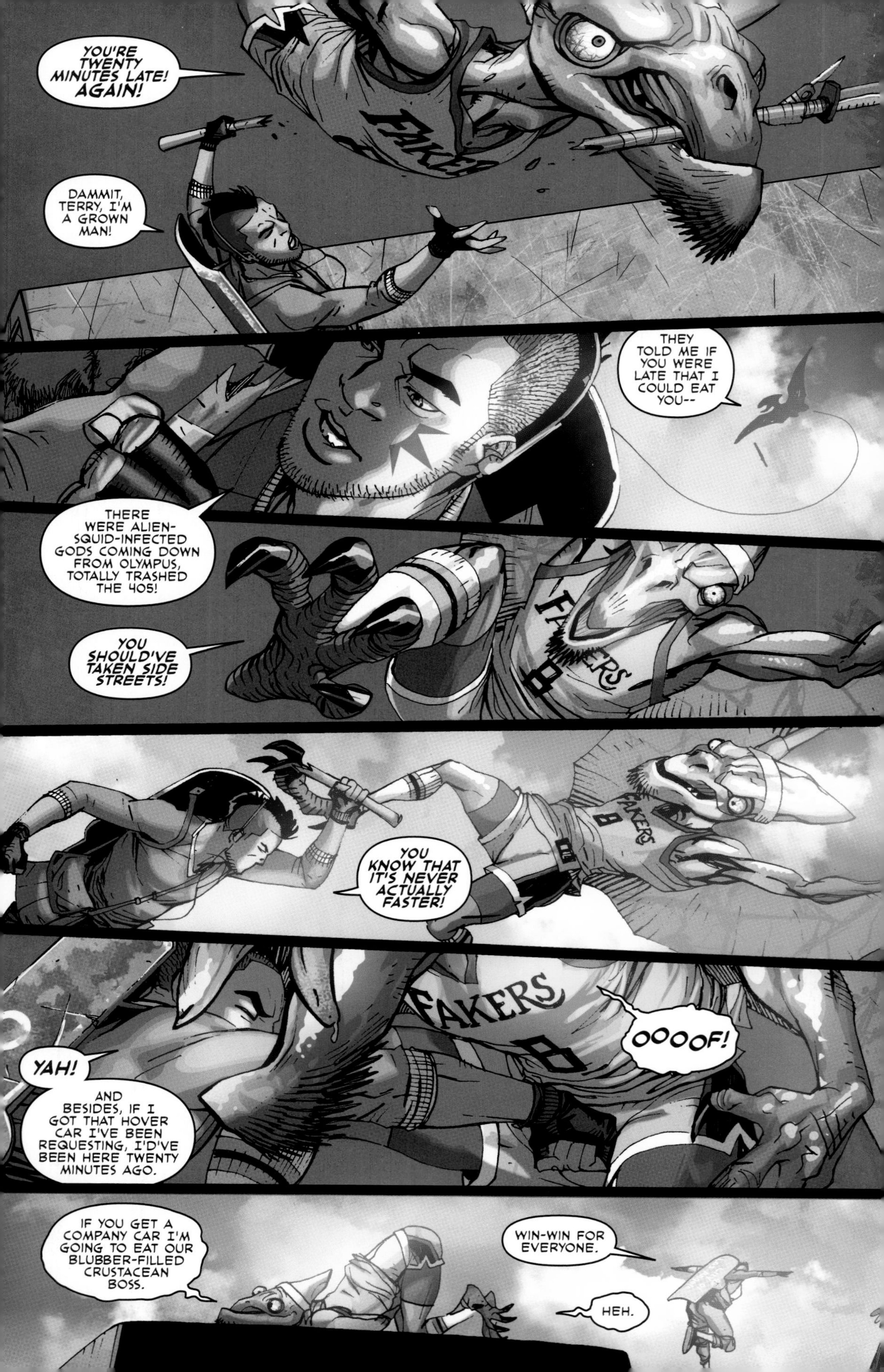
YOU'RE TWENTY MINUTES LATE! AGAIN!
DAMMIT, TERRY, I'M A GROWN MAN!
THEY TOLD ME IF YOU WERE LATE THAT I COULD EAT YOU--
THERE WERE ALIEN-SQUID-INFECTED GODS COMING DOWN FROM OLYMPUS, TOTALLY TRASHED THE 405!
YOU SHOULD'VE TAKEN SIDE STREETS!
YOU KNOW THAT IT'S NEVER ACTUALLY FASTER!
OOOOF!
YAH!
AND BESIDES, IF I GOT THAT HOVER CAR I'VE BEEN REQUESTING, I'D'VE BEEN HERE TWENTY MINUTES AGO.
IF YOU GET A COMPANY CAR I'M GOING TO EAT OUR BLUBBER-FILLED CRUSTACEAN BOSS.
WIN-WIN FOR EVERYONE.
HEH.

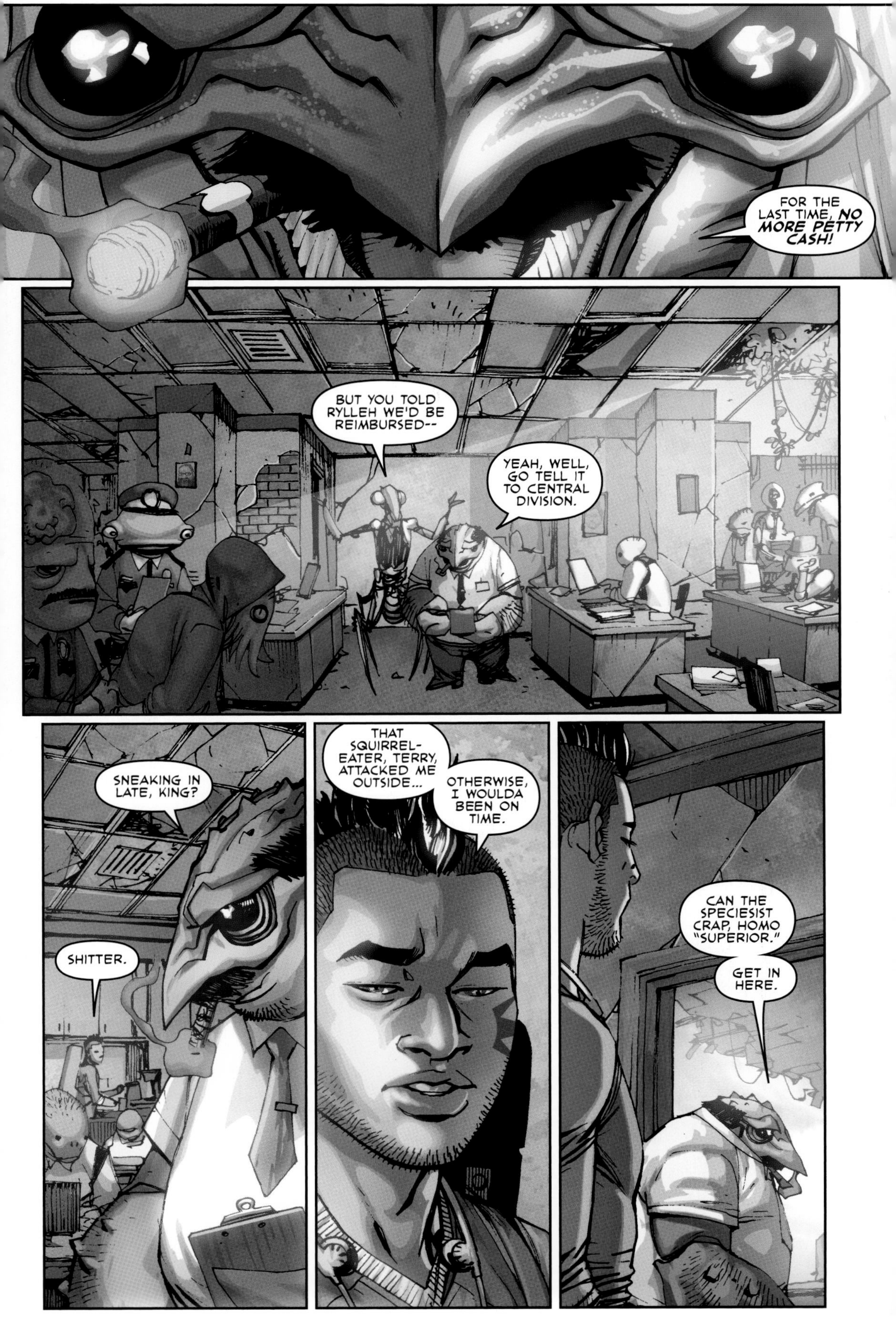

FOR THE LAST TIME, NO MORE PETTY CASH!
BUT YOU TOLD RYLLEH WE'D BE REIMBURSED--
YEAH, WELL, GO TELL IT TO CENTRAL DIVISION.
SNEAKING IN LATE, KING?
SHITTER.
THAT SQUIRREL-EATER, TERRY, ATTACKED ME OUTSIDE...
OTHERWISE, I WOULDA BEEN ON TIME.
CAN THE SPECIESIST CRAP, HOMO "SUPERIOR."
GET IN HERE.

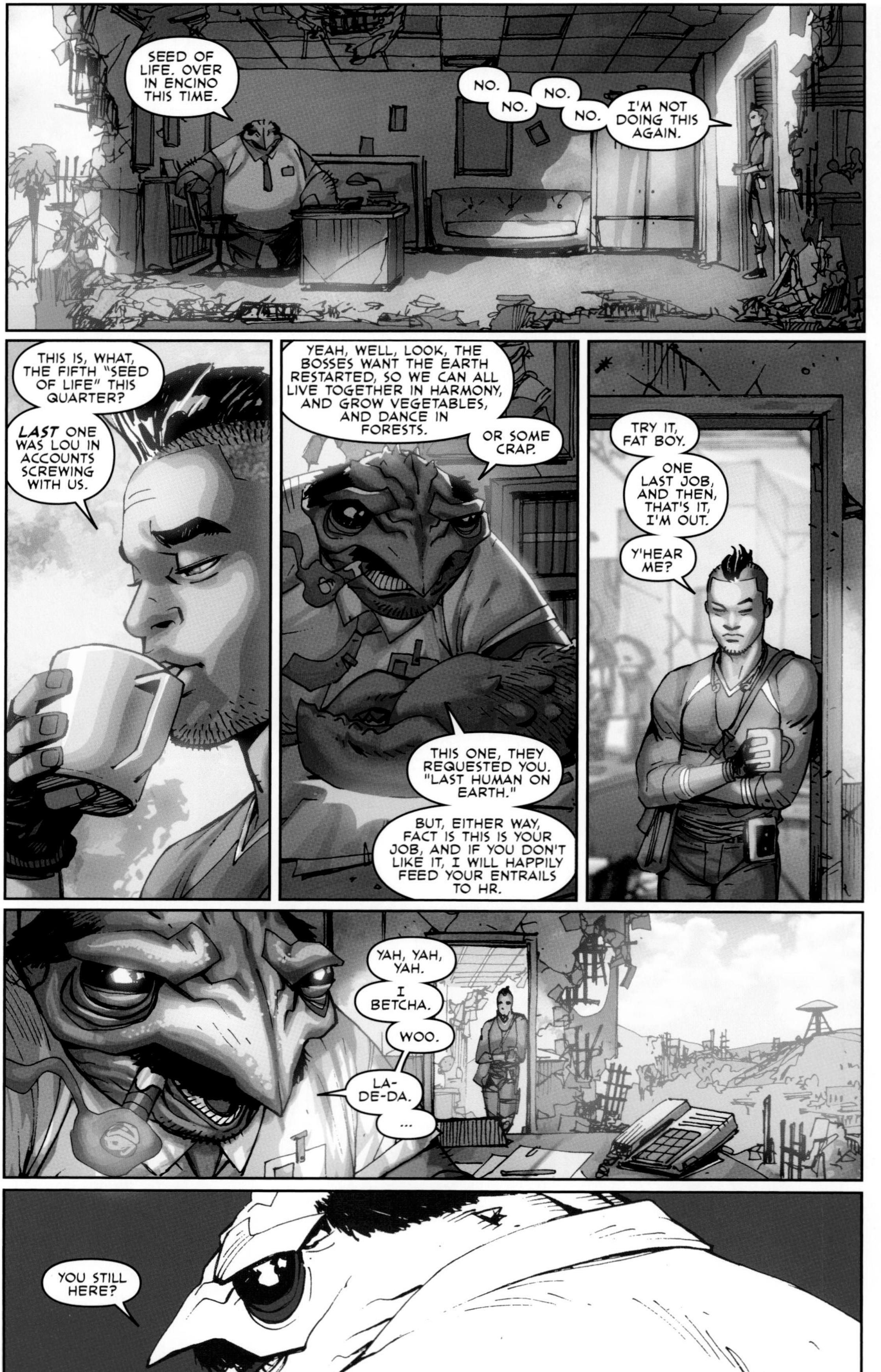
SEED OF LIFE. OVER IN ENCINO THIS TIME.
NO.
NO.
NO.
NO.
I'M NOT DOING THIS AGAIN.
THIS IS, WHAT, THE FIFTH "SEED OF LIFE" THIS QUARTER?
LAST ONE WAS LOU IN ACCOUNTS SCREWING WITH US.
YEAH, WELL, LOOK, THE BOSSES WANT THE EARTH RESTARTED, SO WE CAN ALL LIVE TOGETHER IN HARMONY, AND GROW VEGETABLES, AND DANCE IN FORESTS.
OR SOME CRAP.
THIS ONE, THEY REQUESTED YOU. "LAST HUMAN ON EARTH."
BUT, EITHER WAY, FACT IS THIS IS YOUR JOB, AND IF YOU DON'T LIKE IT, I WILL HAPPILY FEED YOUR ENTRAILS TO HR.
TRY IT, FAT BOY.
ONE LAST JOB, AND THEN, THAT'S IT, I'M OUT.
Y'HEAR ME?
YAH, YAH, YAH.
I BETCHA.
WOO.
LA-DE-DA.
...
YOU STILL HERE?

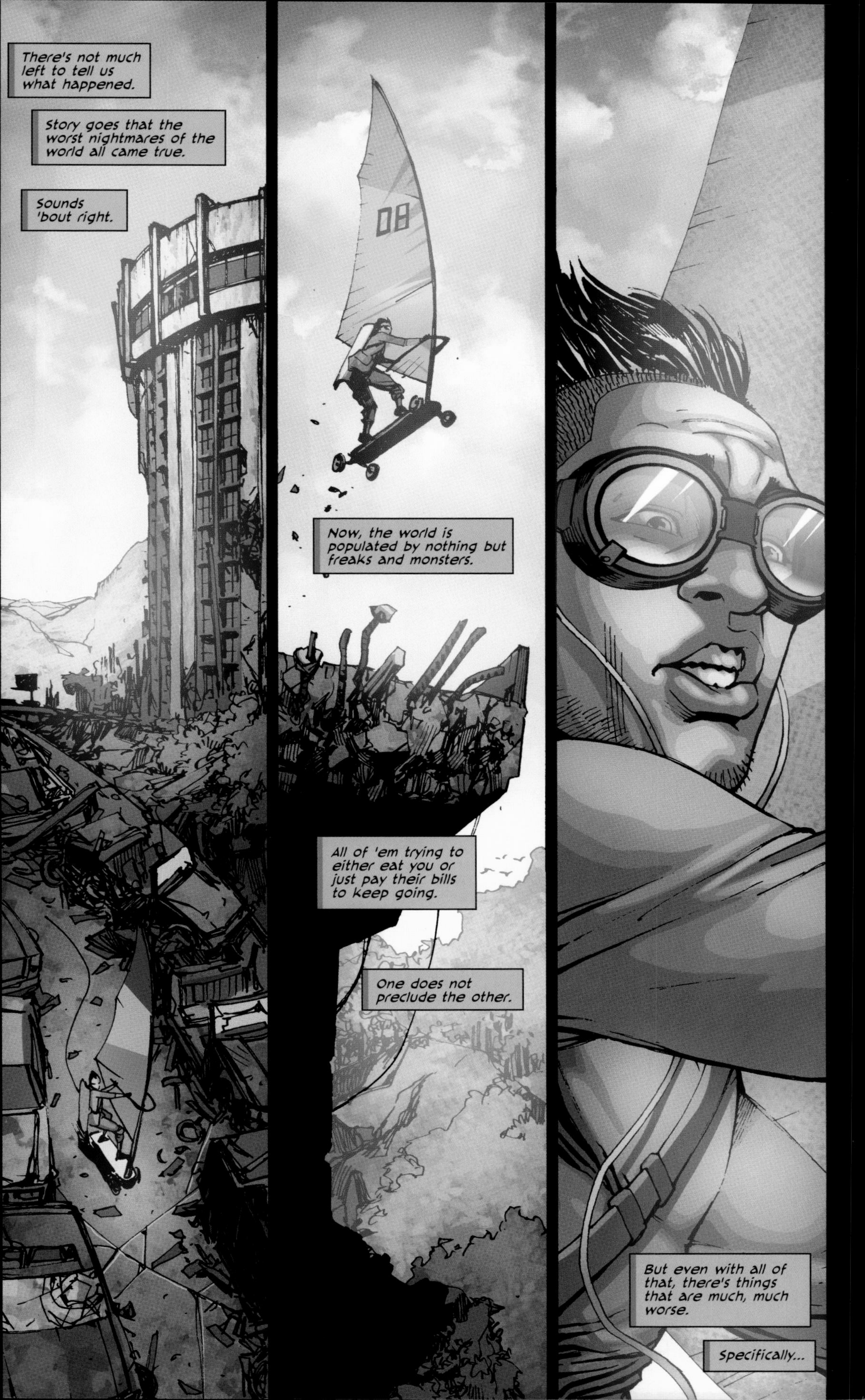
There's not much left to tell us what happened.
Story goes that the worst nightmares of the world all came true.
Sounds 'bout right.
08
Now, the world is populated by nothing but freaks and monsters.
All of 'em trying to either eat you or just pay their bills to keep going.
One does not preclude the other.
But even with all of that, there's things that are much, much worse.
Specifically...

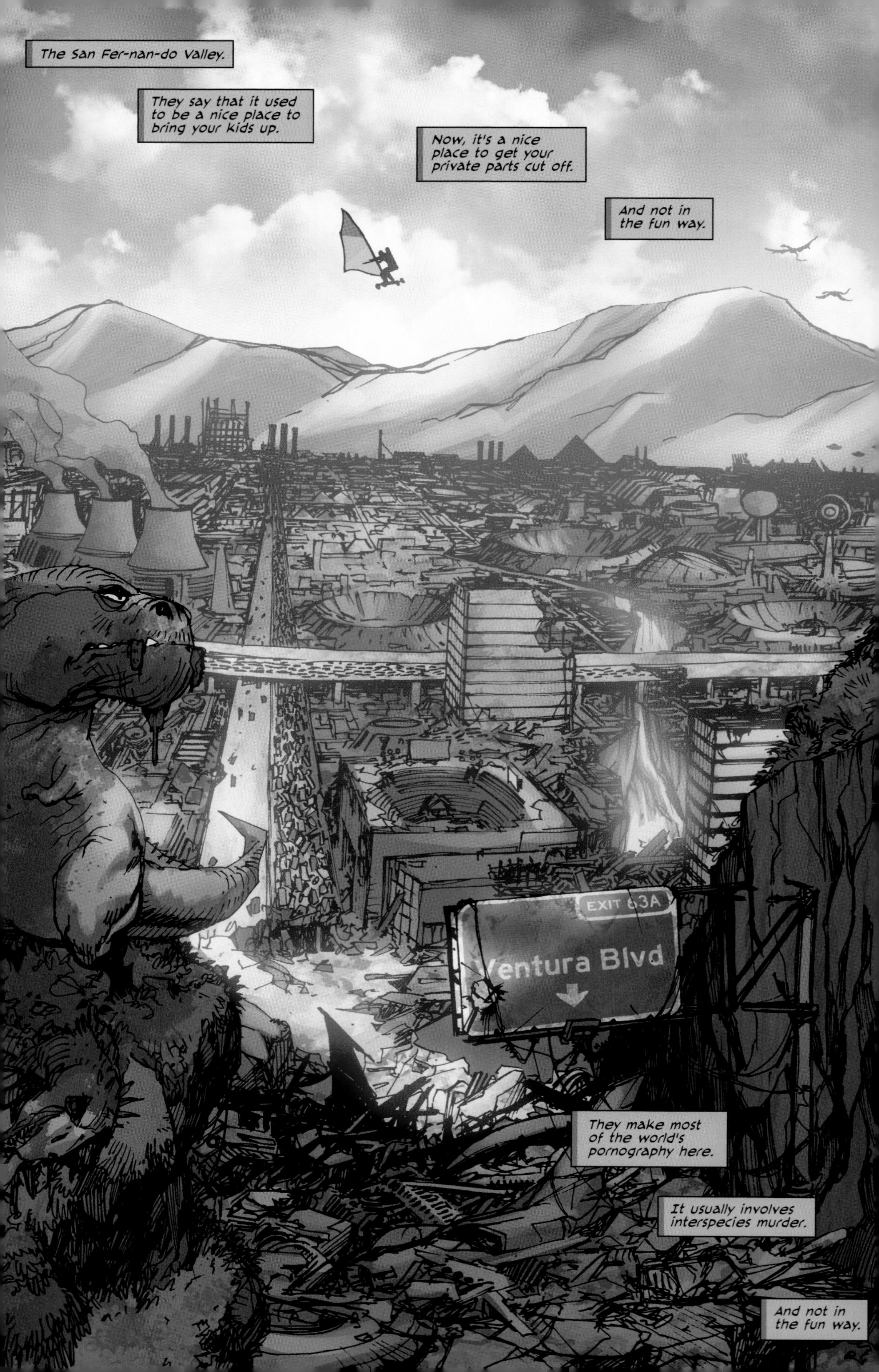
The San Fer-nan-do Valley.
They say that it used to be a nice place to bring your kids up.
Now, it's a nice place to get your private parts cut off.
And not in the fun way.
EXIT 63A
Ventura Blvd
They make most of the world's pornography here.
It usually involves interspecies murder.
And not in the fun way.

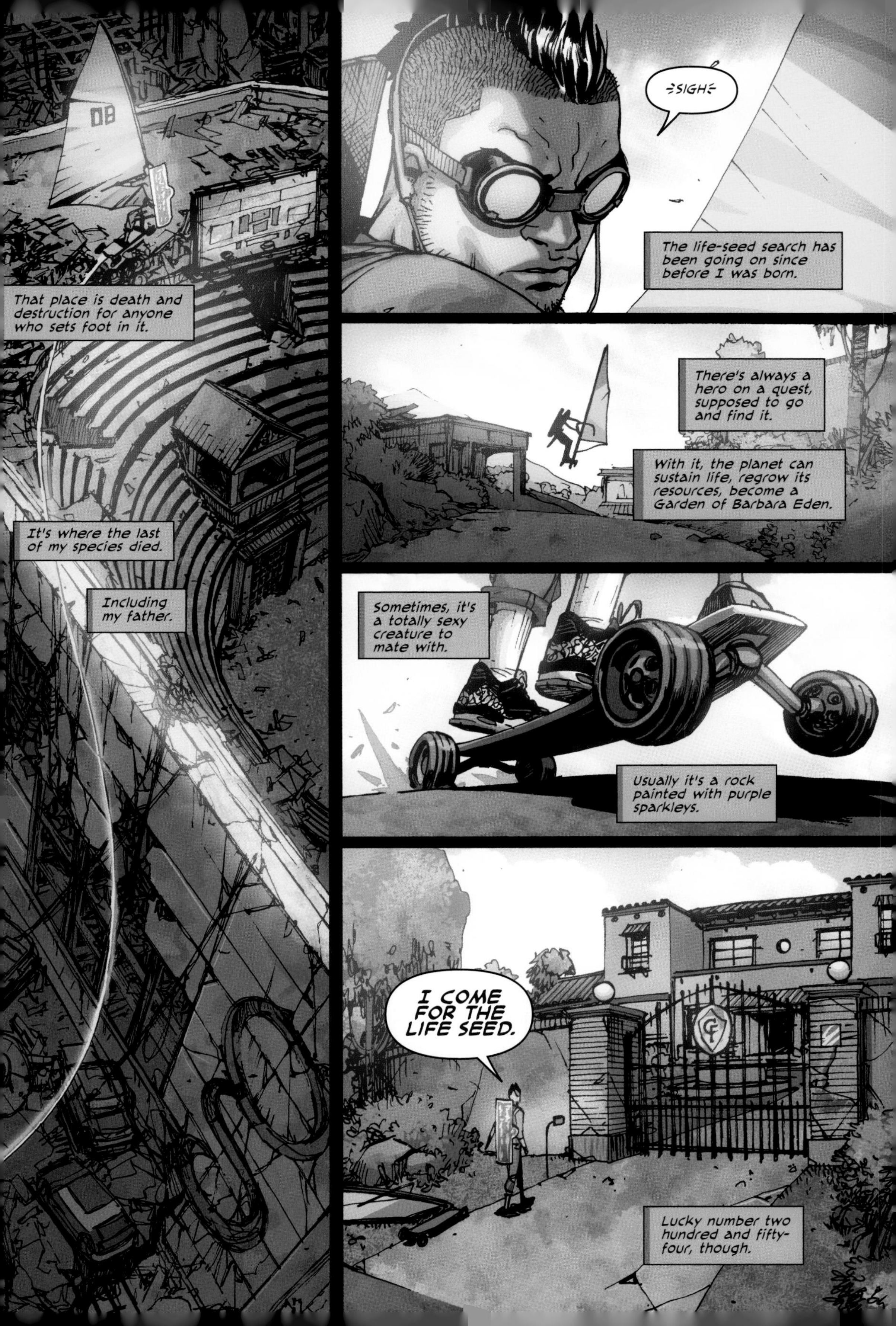
That place is death and destruction for anyone who sets foot in it.
It's where the last of my species died.
Including my father.
≈SIGH≈
The life-seed search has been going on since before I was born.
There's always a hero on a quest, supposed to go and find it.
With it, the planet can sustain life, regrow its resources, become a Garden of Barbara Eden.
Sometimes, it's a totally sexy creature to mate with.
Usually it's a rock painted with purple sparkleys.
I COME FOR THE LIFE SEED.
Lucky number two hundred and fifty-four, though.

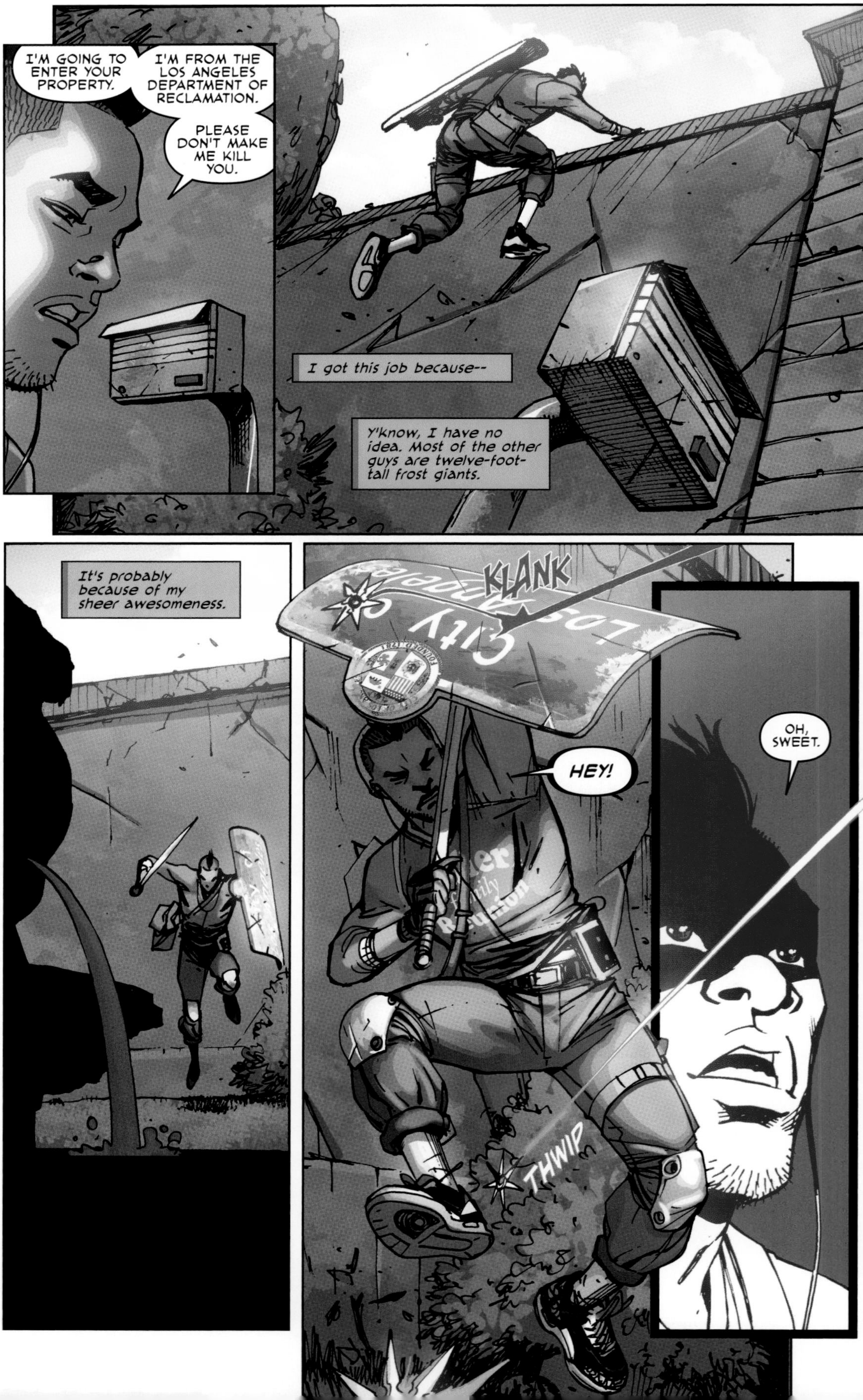
I'M GOING TO ENTER YOUR PROPERTY.
I'M FROM THE LOS ANGELES DEPARTMENT OF RECLAMATION.
PLEASE DON'T MAKE ME KILL YOU.
I got this job because--
Y'know, I have no idea. Most of the other guys are twelve-foot-tall frost giants.
It's probably because of my sheer awesomeness.
KLANK
HEY!
OH, SWEET.
THWIP

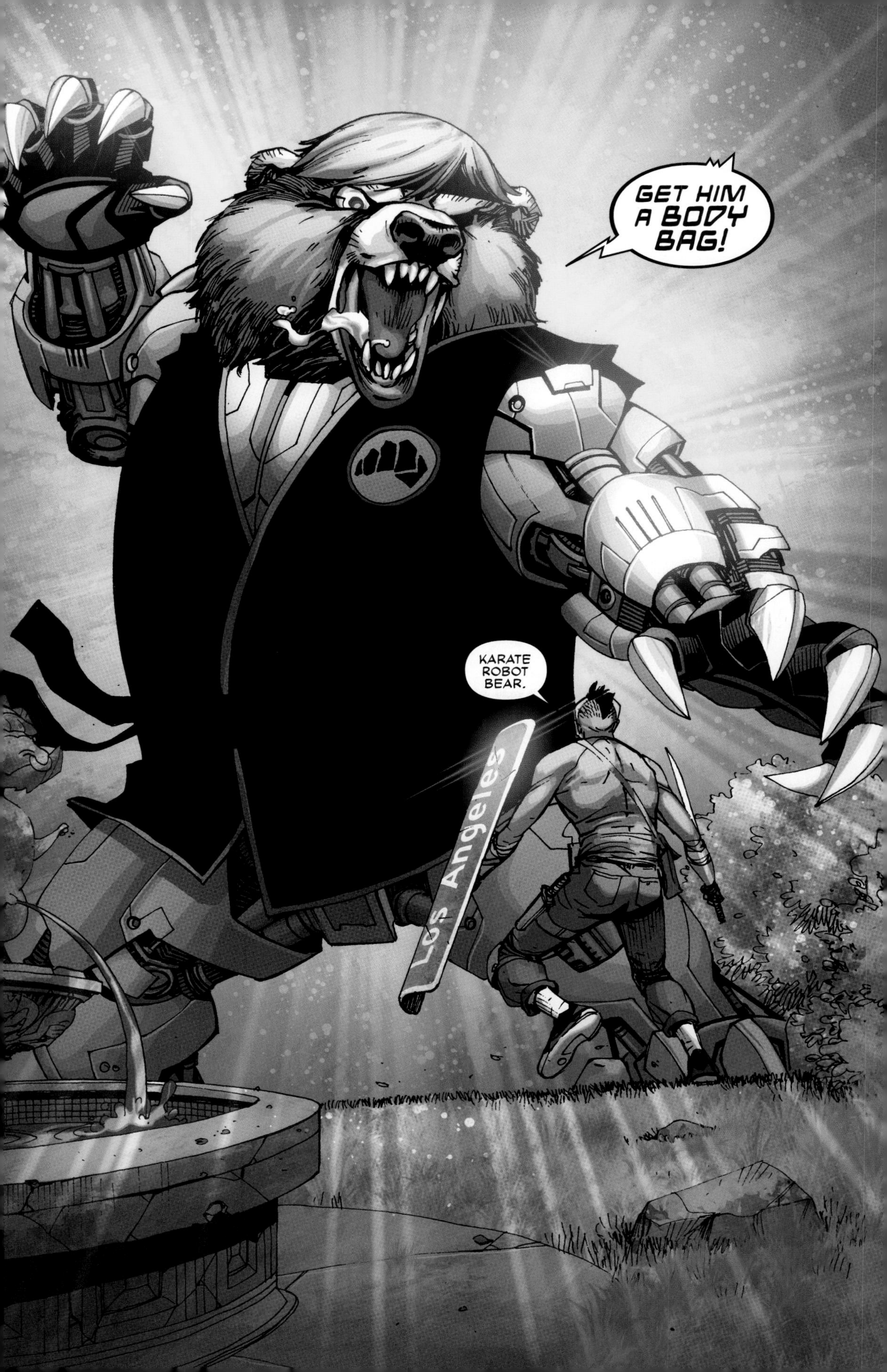
GET HIM A BODY BAG!
KARATE ROBOT BEAR.
Los Angeles

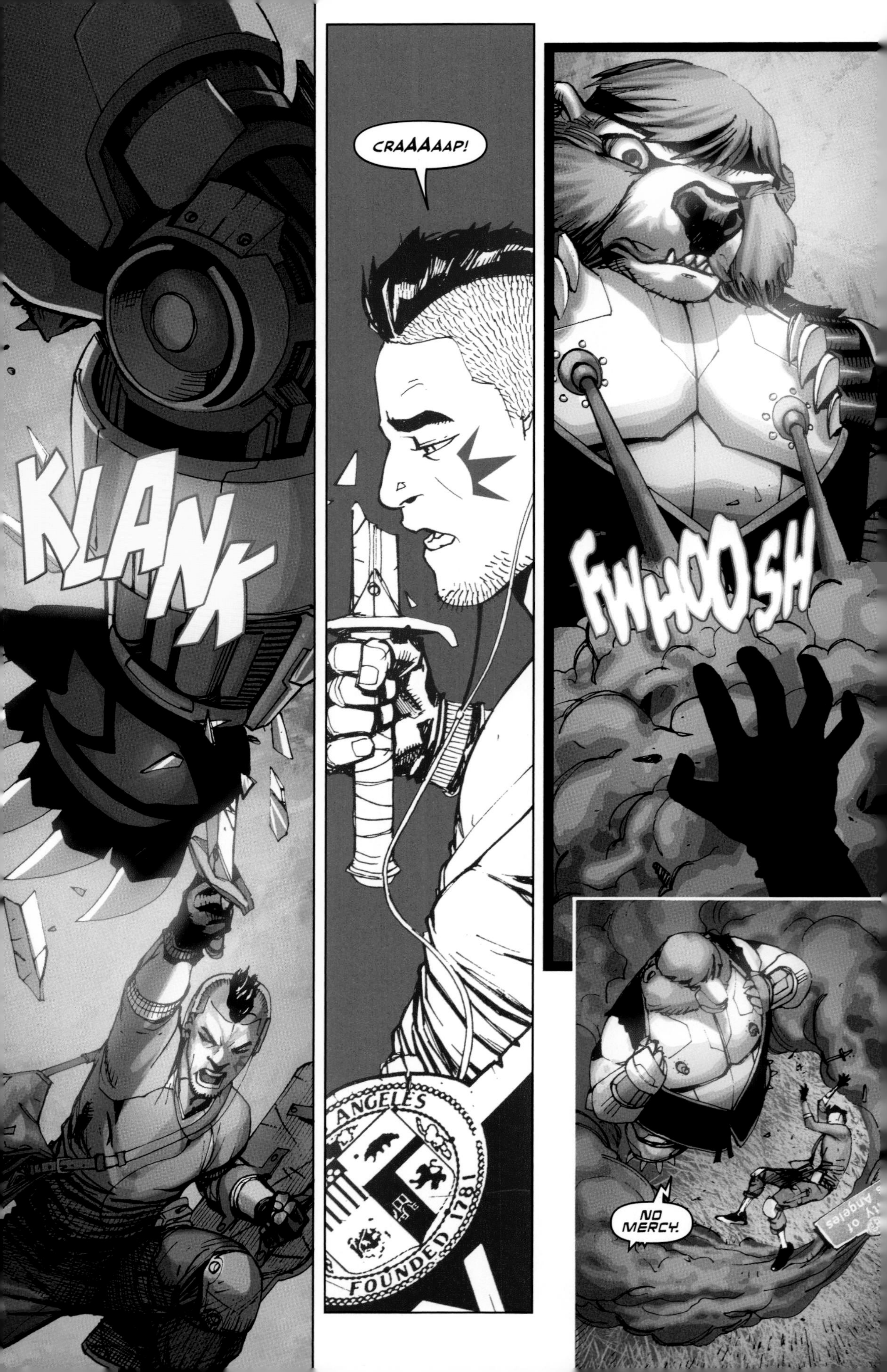
KLANK
CRAAAAAP!
ANGELES
FOUNDED 1781
FWHOOSH
NO MERCY.

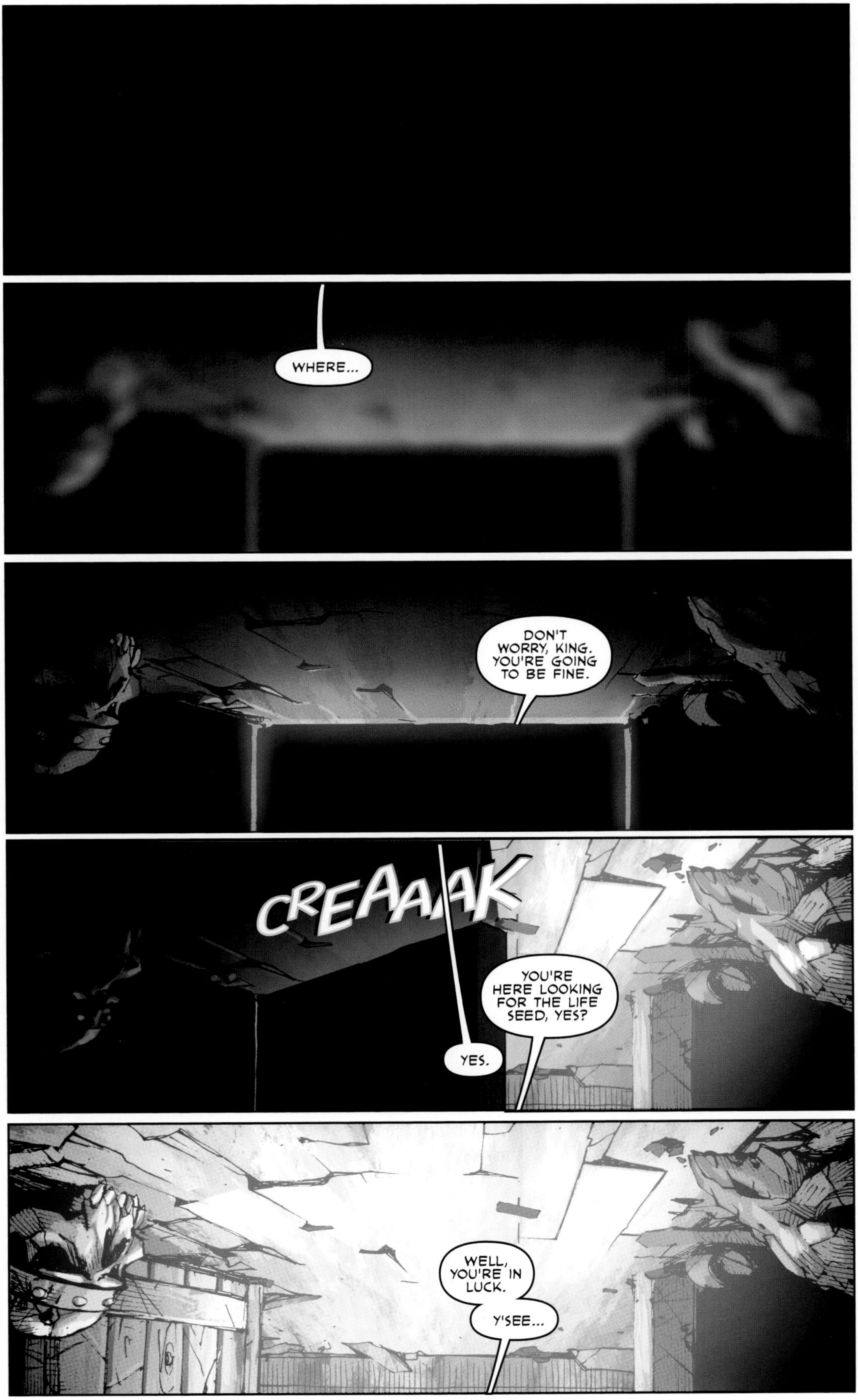
WHERE...
DON'T WORRY, KING. YOU'RE GOING TO BE FINE.
CREAAAK
YOU'RE HERE LOOKING FOR THE LIFE SEED, YES?
YES.
WELL, YOU'RE IN LUCK.
Y'SEE...

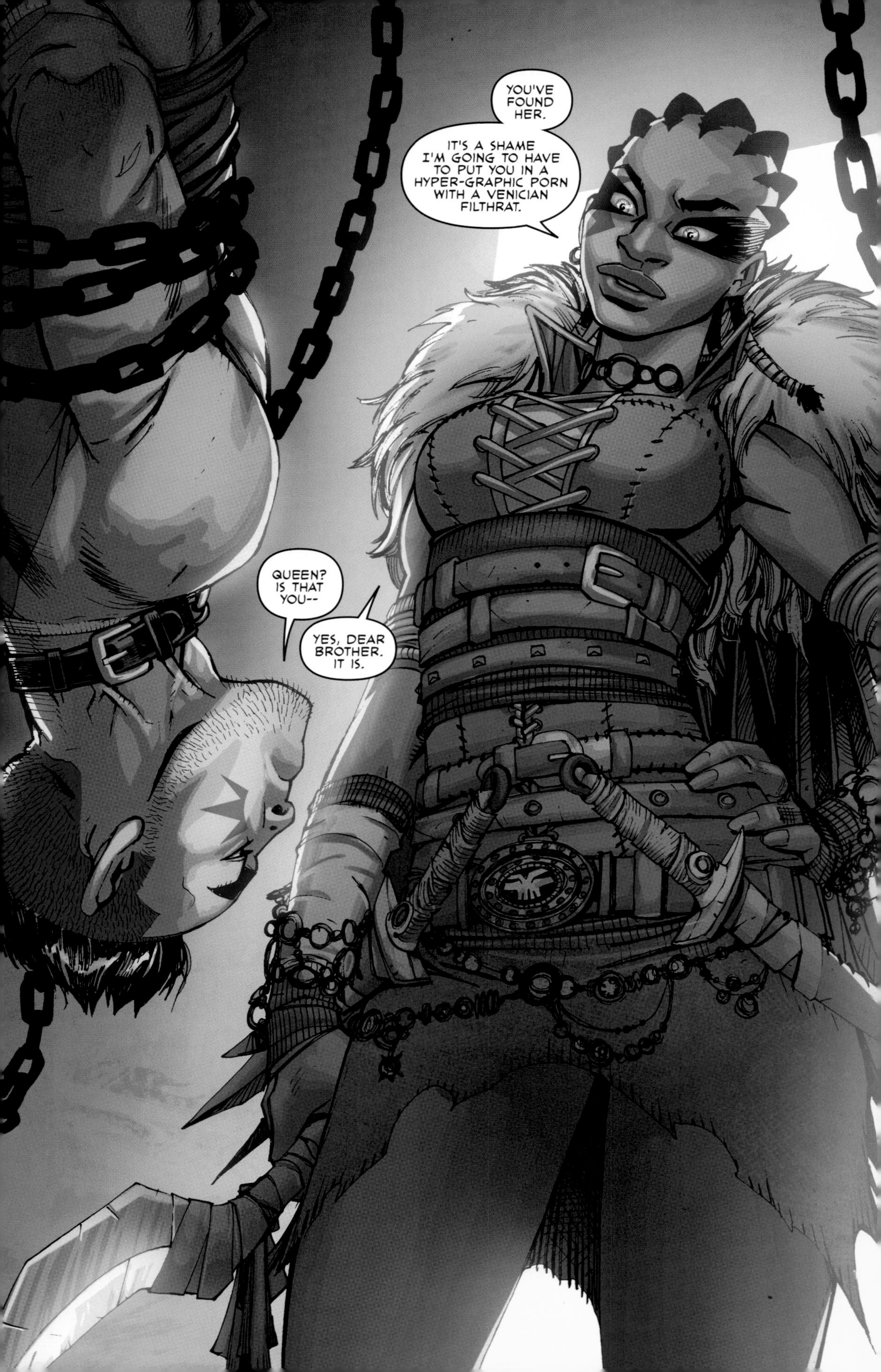
YOU'VE FOUND HER.
IT'S A SHAME I'M GOING TO HAVE TO PUT YOU IN A HYPER-GRAPHIC PORN WITH A VENICIAN FILTHRAT.
QUEEN? IS THAT YOU--
YES, DEAR BROTHER. IT IS.

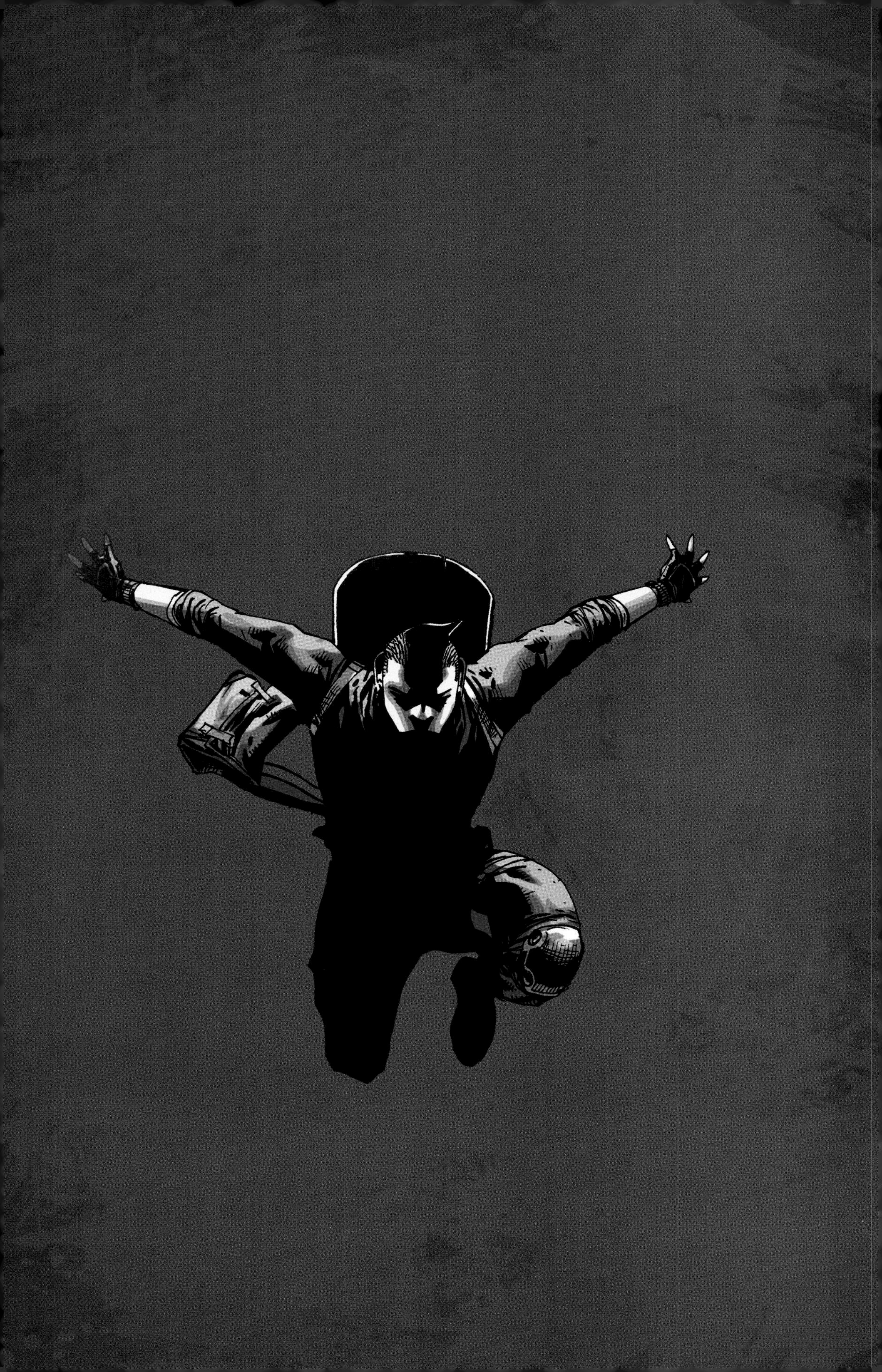

"I Hate Mondays"
CHAPTER TWO

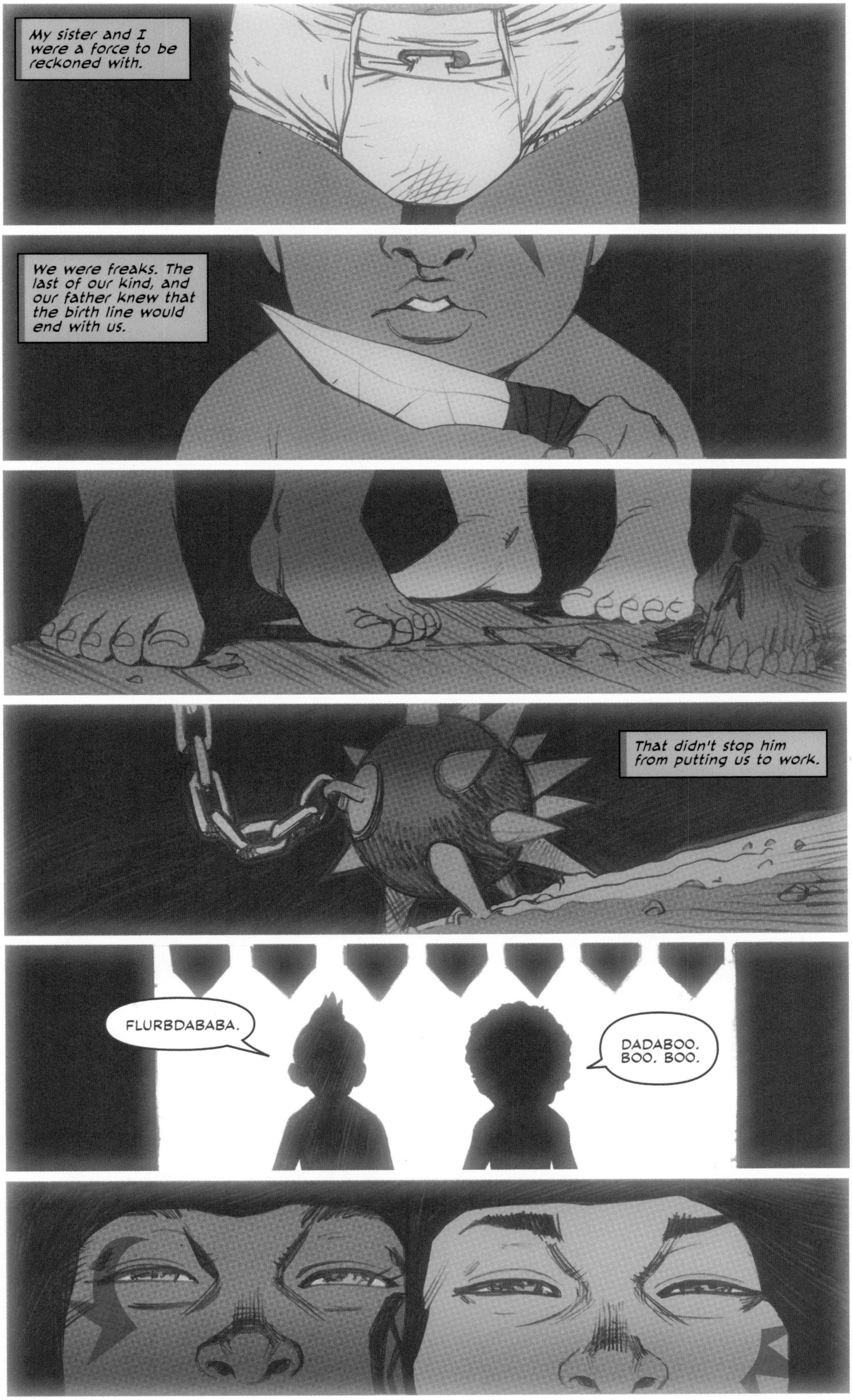
My sister and I were a force to be reckoned with.
We were freaks. The last of our kind, and our father knew that the birth line would end with us.
That didn't stop him from putting us to work.
FLURBDABABA.
DADABOO. BOO. BOO.

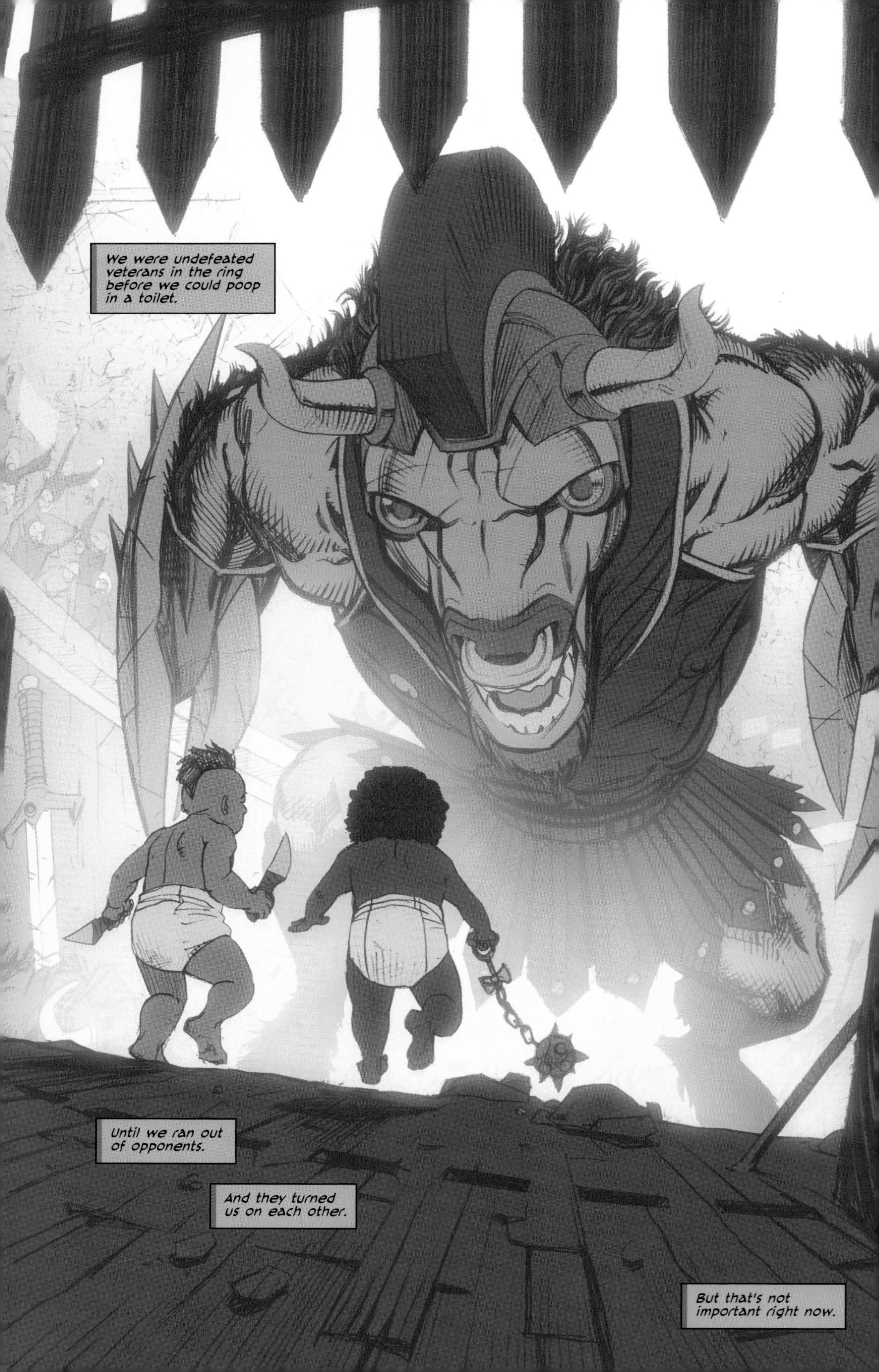
We were undefeated veterans in the ring before we could poop in a toilet.
Until we ran out of opponents.
And they turned us on each other.
But that's not important right now.

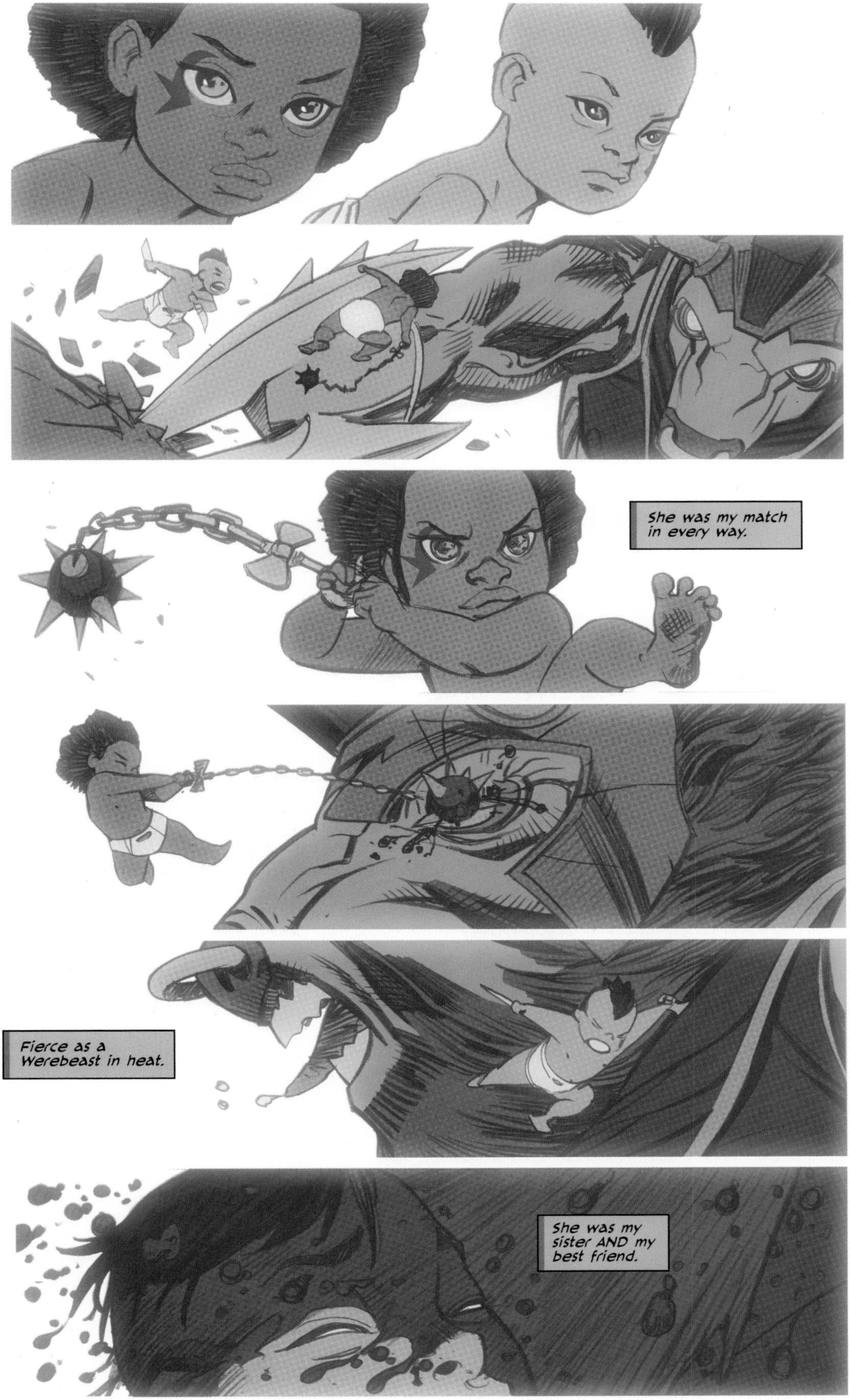
She was my match in every way.
Fierce as a Werebeast in heat.
She was my sister AND my best friend.

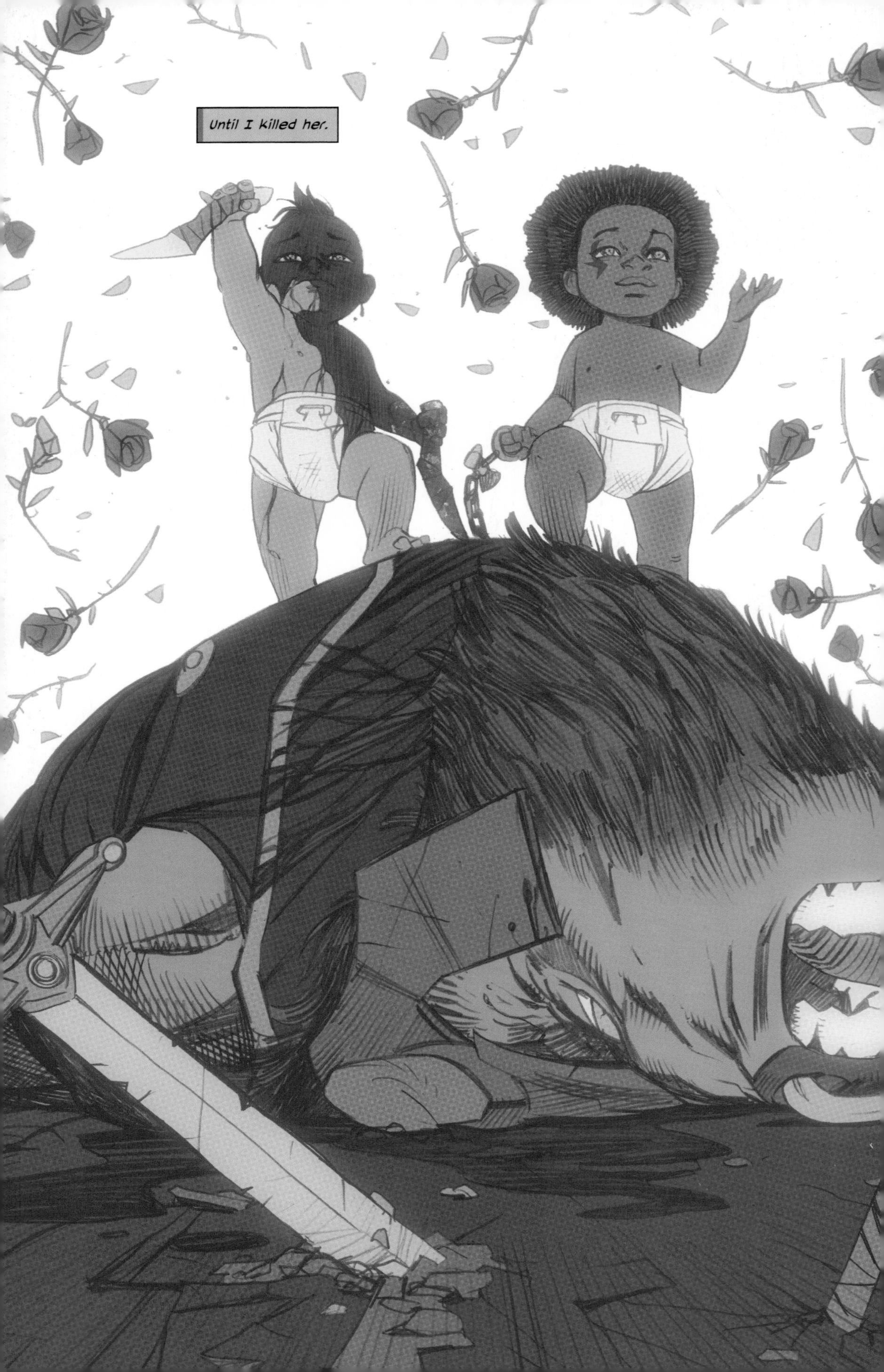
Until I killed her.

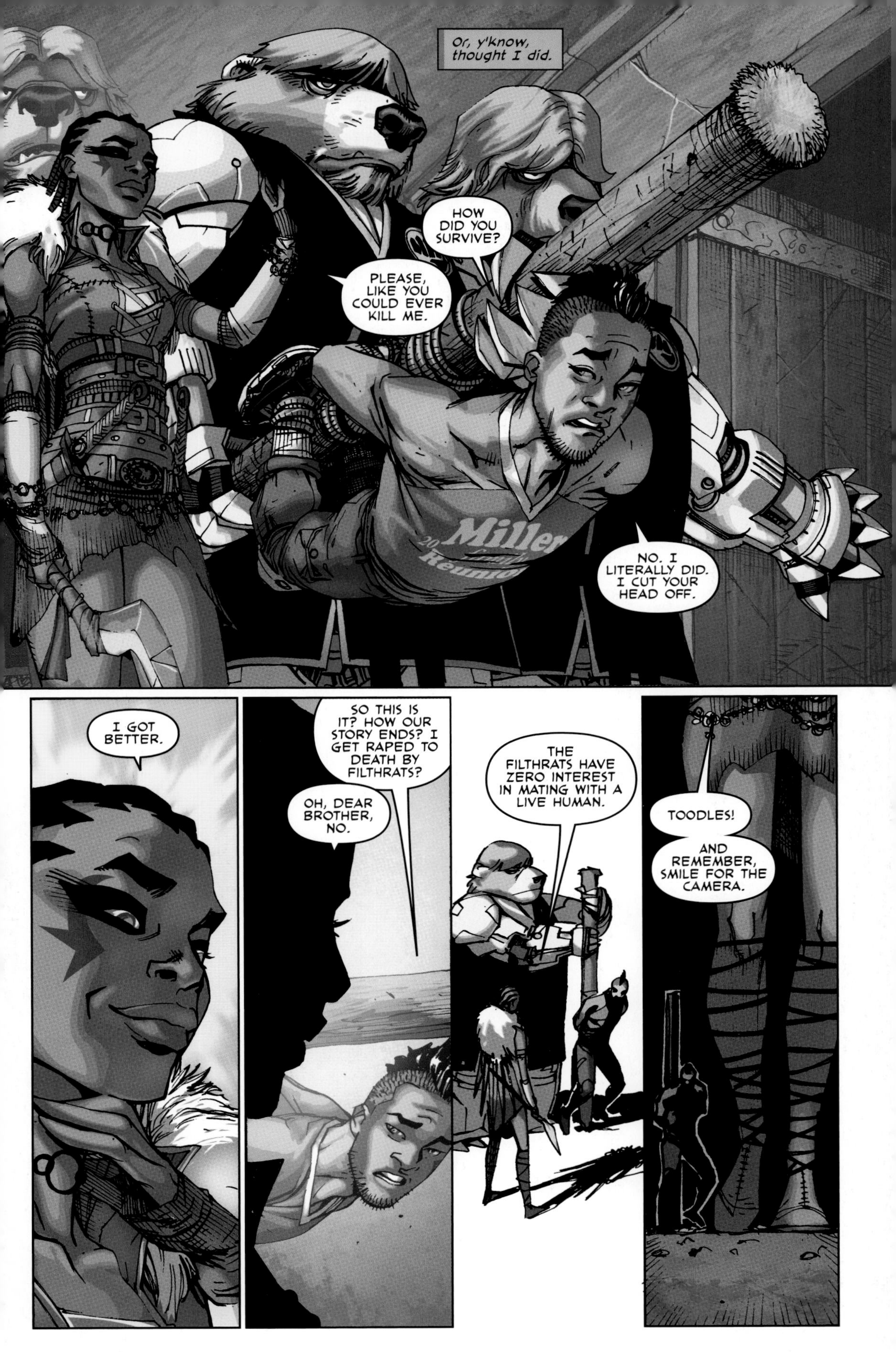
Or, y'know, thought I did.
HOW DID YOU SURVIVE?
PLEASE, LIKE YOU COULD EVER KILL ME.
NO. I LITERALLY DID. I CUT YOUR HEAD OFF.
I GOT BETTER.
SO THIS IS IT? HOW OUR STORY ENDS? I GET RAPED TO DEATH BY FILTHRATS?
OH, DEAR BROTHER, NO.
THE FILTHRATS HAVE ZERO INTEREST IN MATING WITH A LIVE HUMAN.
TOODLES!
AND REMEMBER, SMILE FOR THE CAMERA.

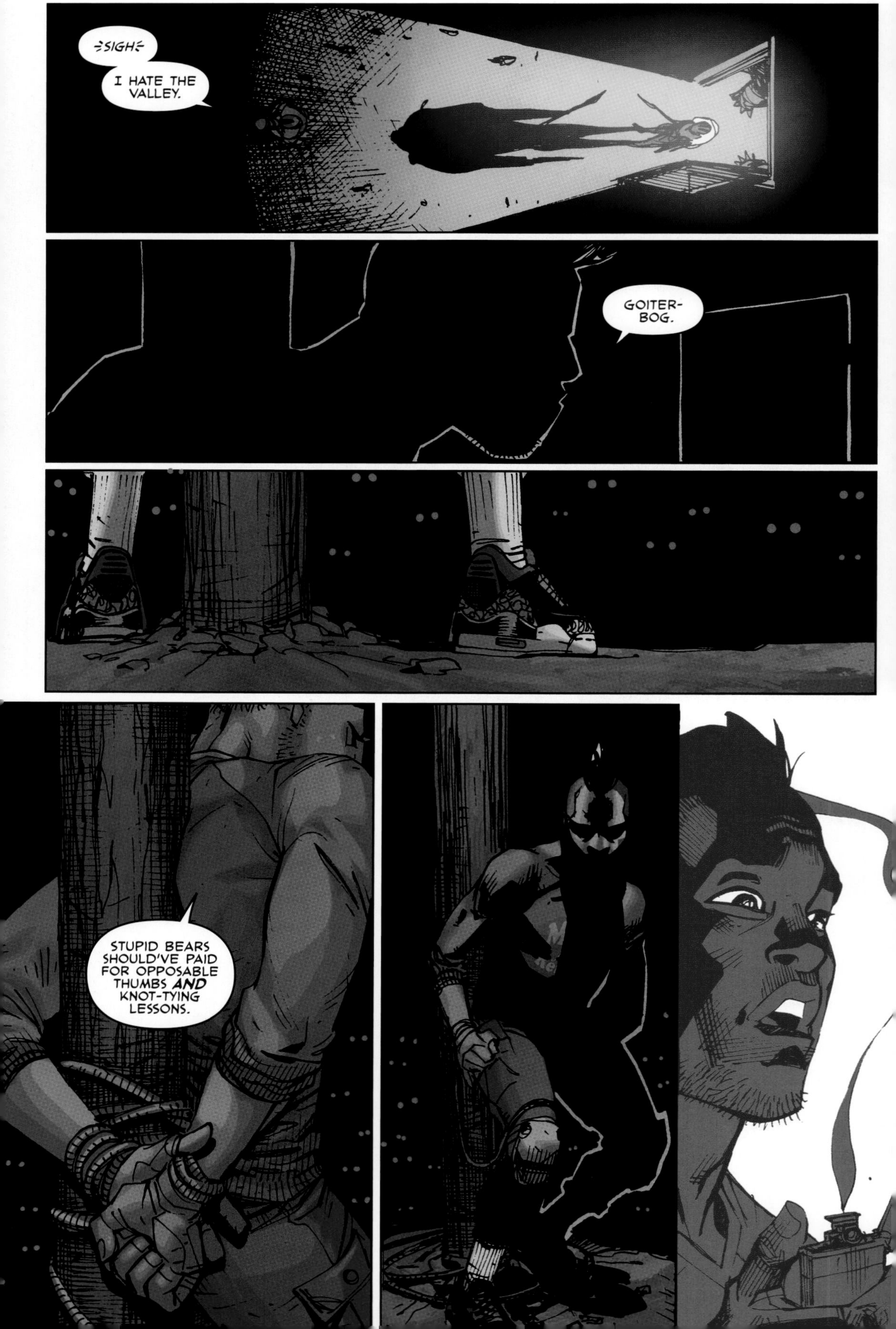

=SIGH=
I HATE THE VALLEY.
GOITER-BOG.
STUPID BEARS SHOULD'VE PAID FOR OPPOSABLE THUMBS ***AND*** KNOT-TYING LESSONS.

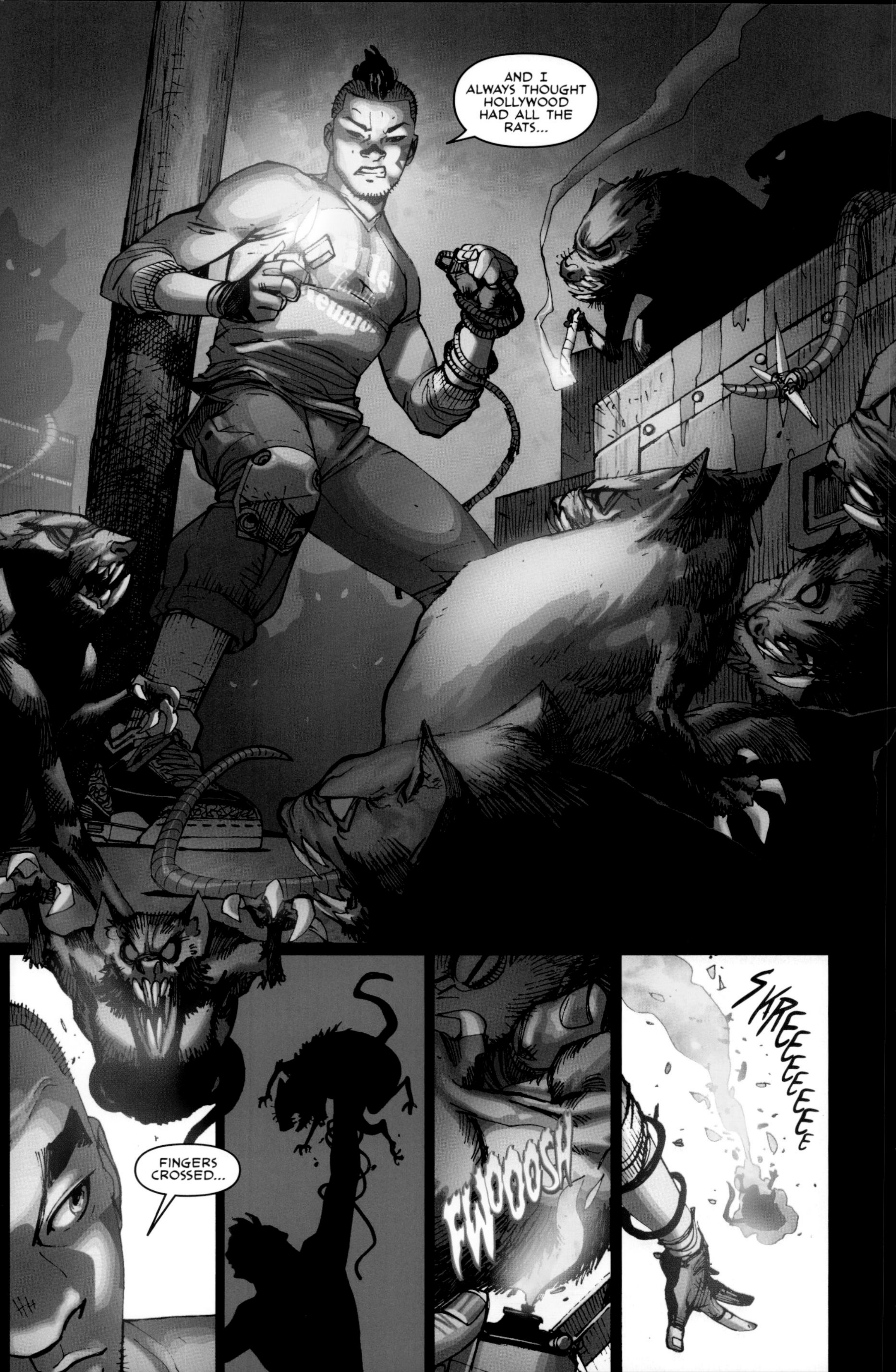
AND I ALWAYS THOUGHT HOLLYWOOD HAD ALL THE RATS...
FINGERS CROSSED...
FWOOOSH
SKREEEEEEE

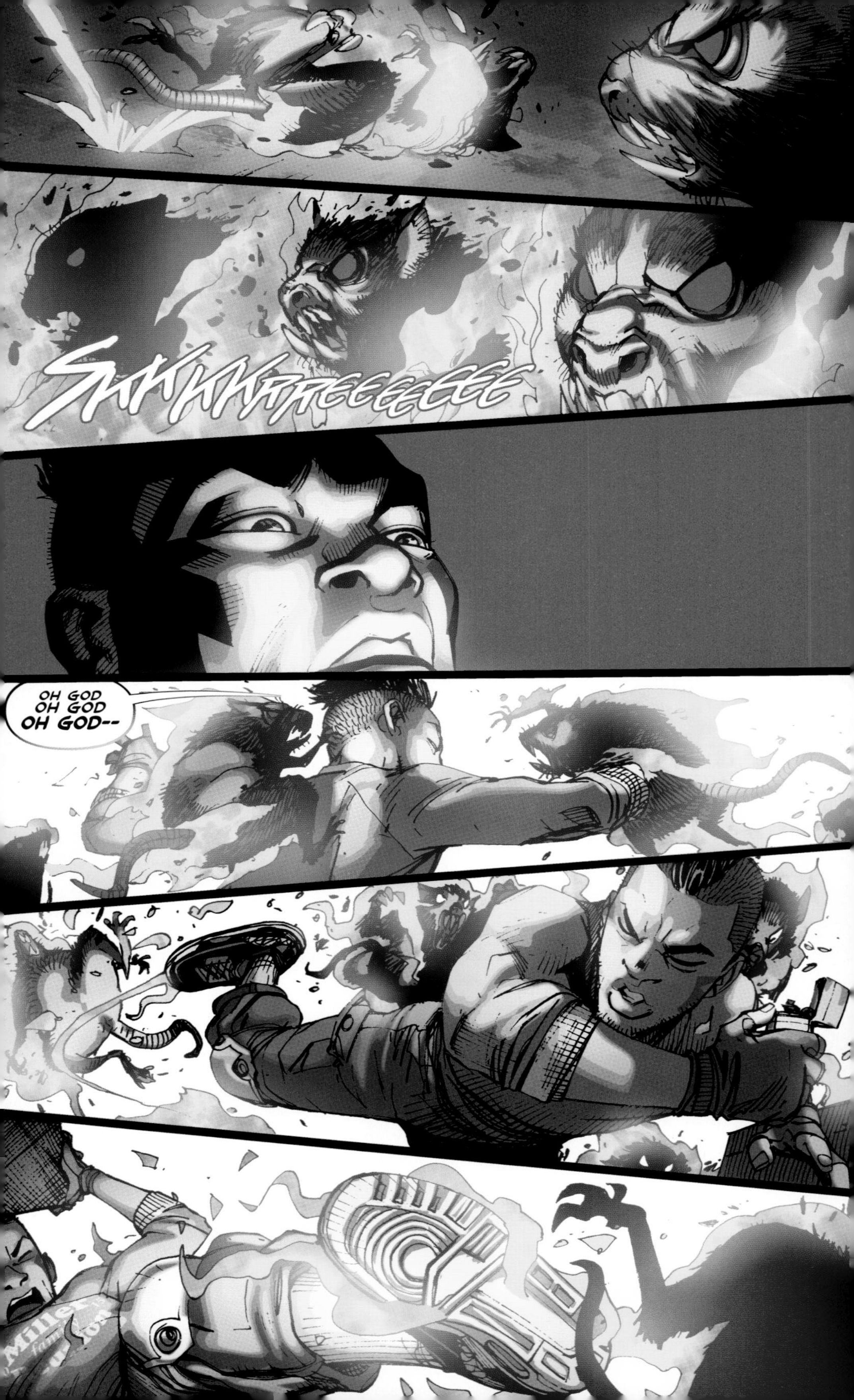
SKKKKRREEEEEEEE
OH GOD
OH GOD
OH GOD--

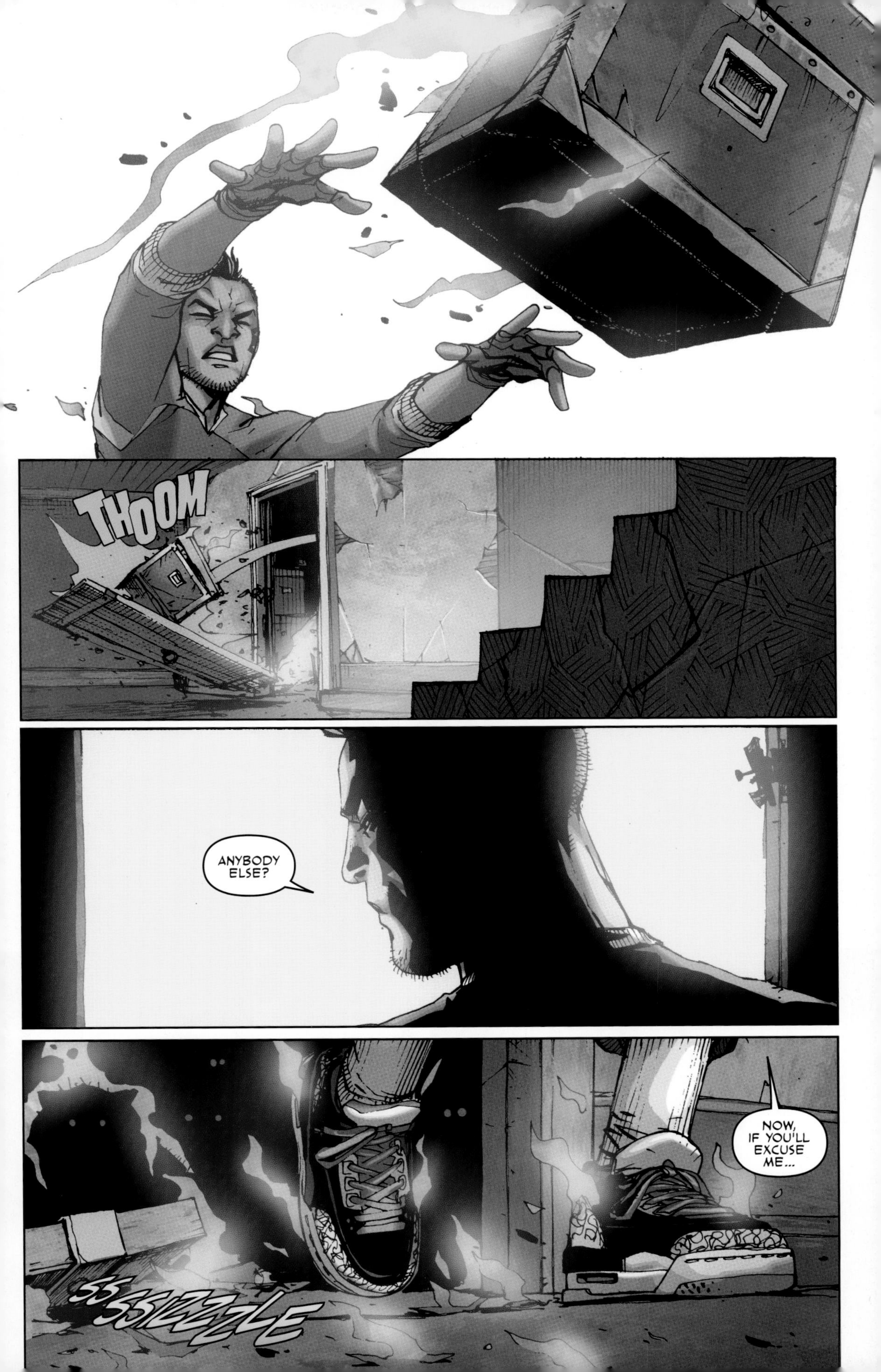
THOOM
ANYBODY ELSE?
NOW, IF YOU'LL EXCUSE ME...
SSSSIZZZLE

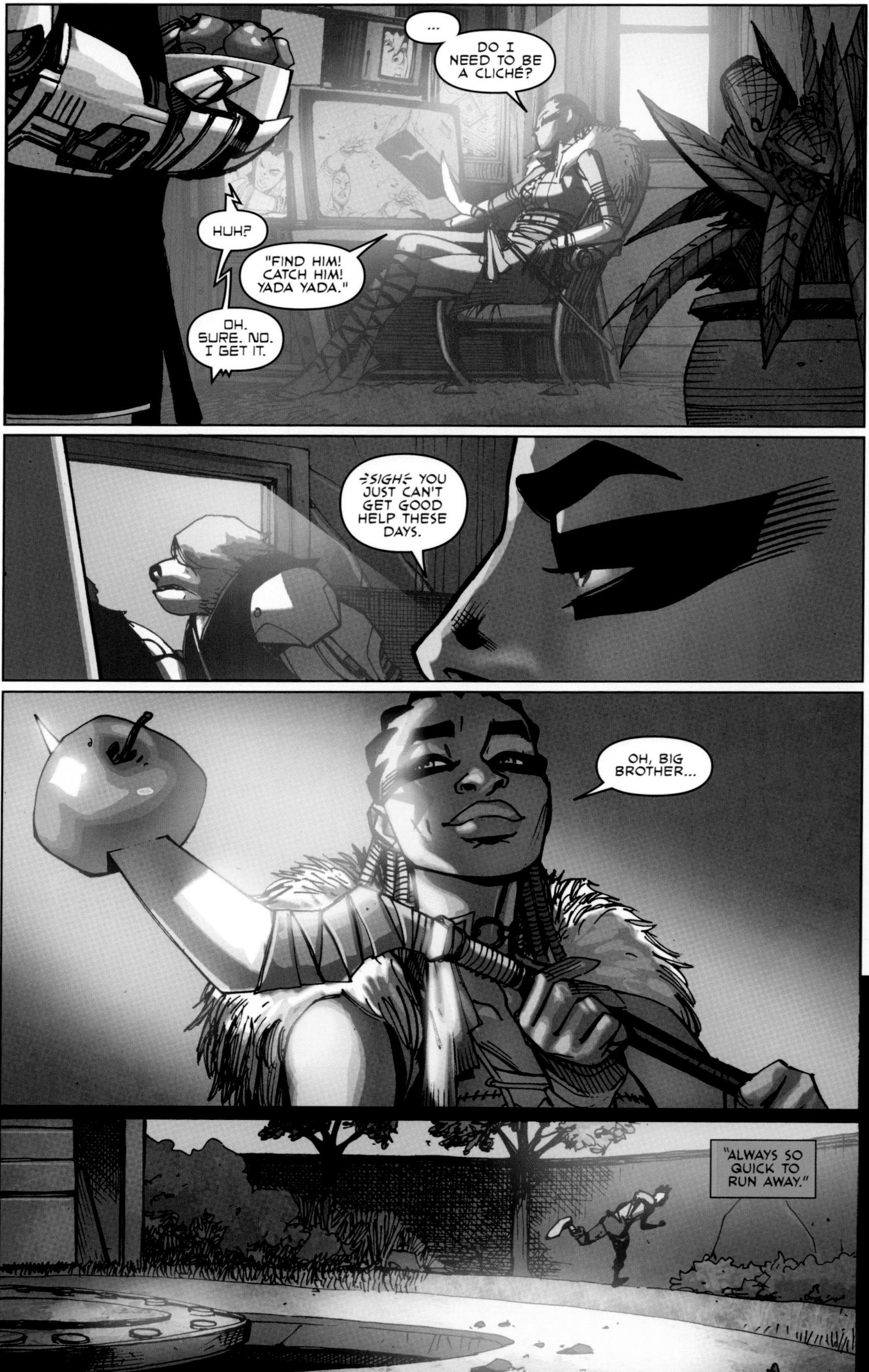
...
DO I NEED TO BE A CLICHÉ?
HUH?
"FIND HIM! CATCH HIM! YADA YADA."
OH. SURE. NO. I GET IT.
SIGH YOU JUST CAN'T GET GOOD HELP THESE DAYS.
OH, BIG BROTHER...
"ALWAYS SO QUICK TO RUN AWAY."

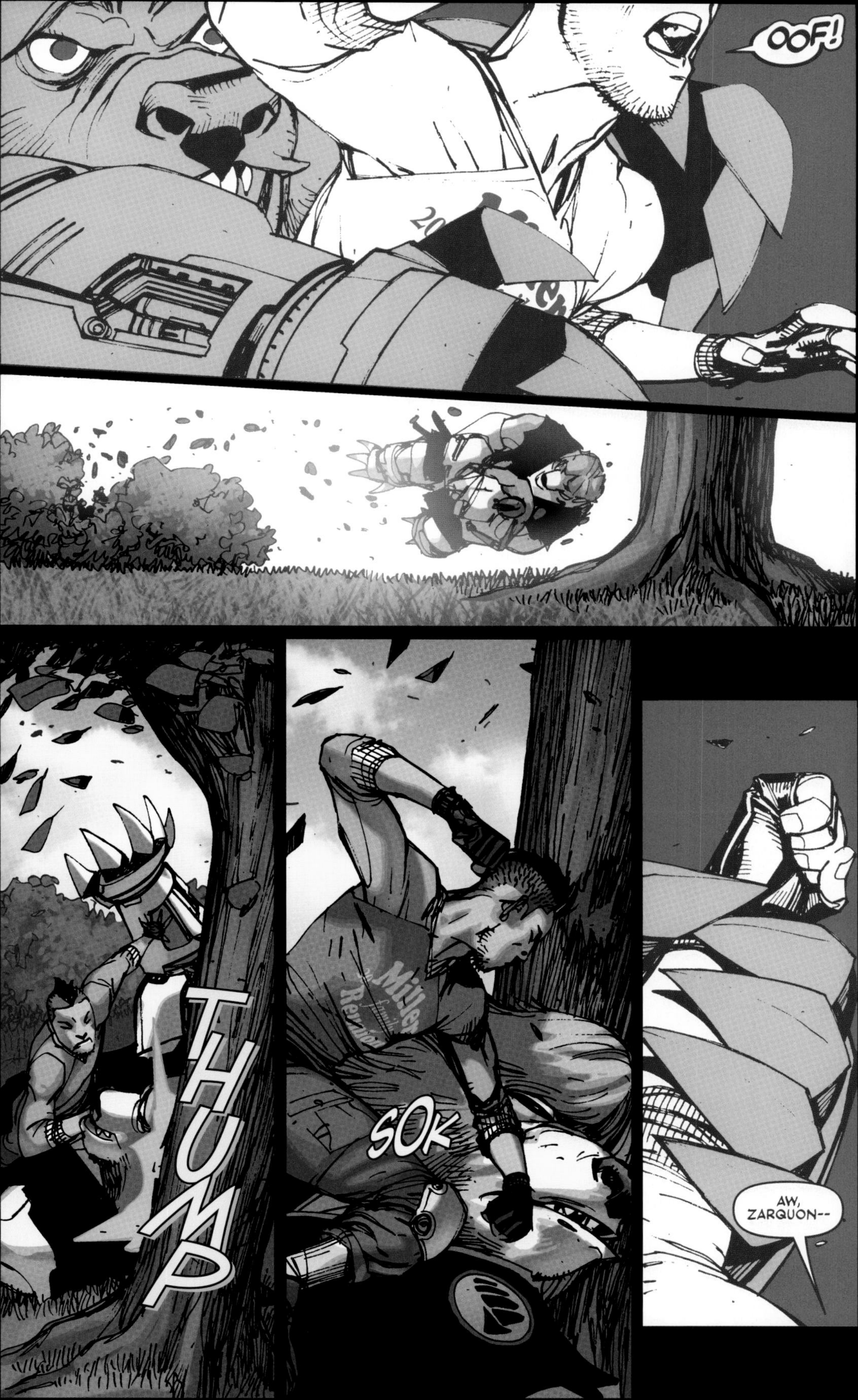
OOF!
THUMP
SOK
AW, ZARQUON--

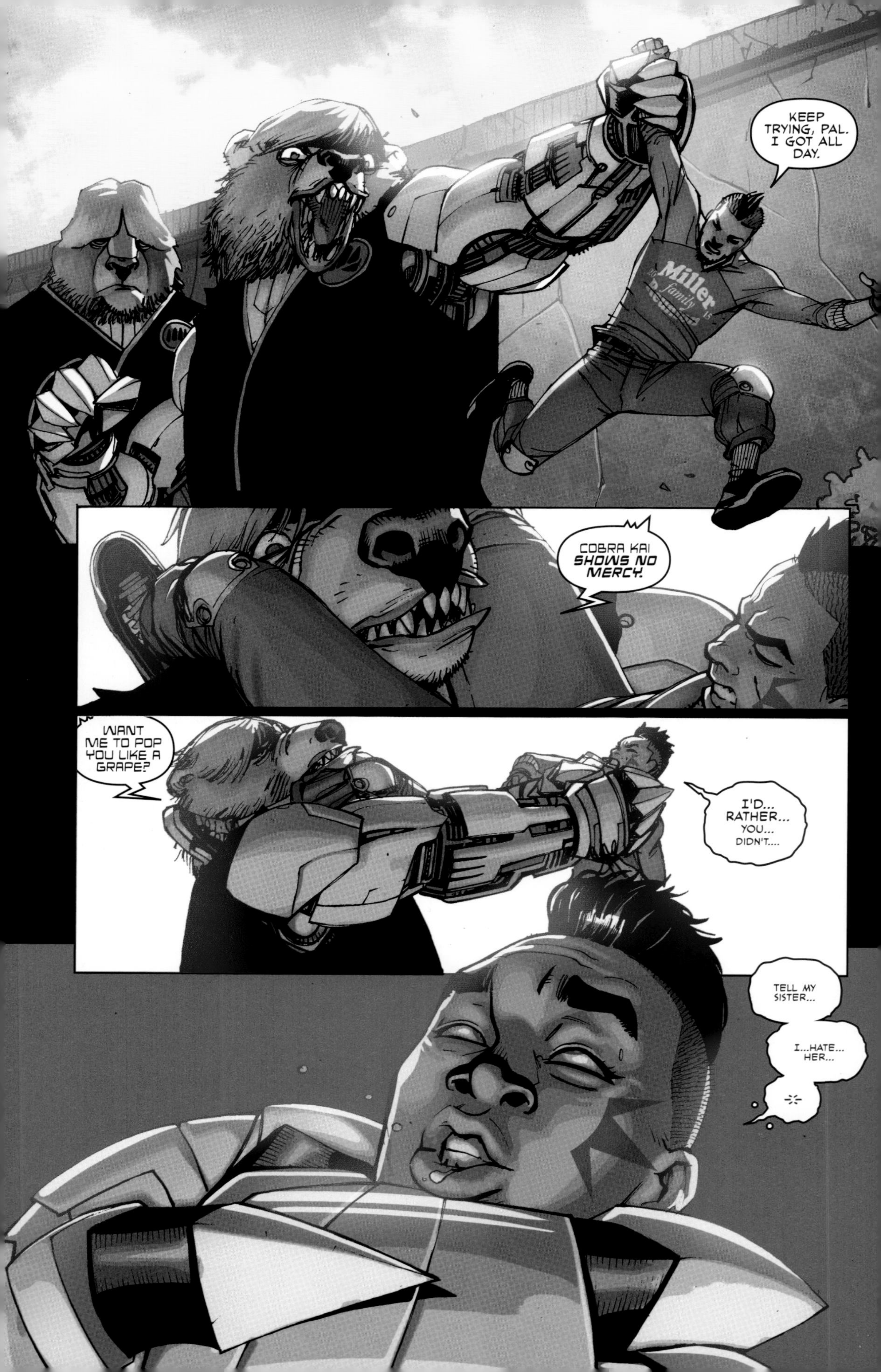
KEEP TRYING, PAL. I GOT ALL DAY.
Miller family reunion 15
COBRA KAI SHOWS NO MERCY.
WANT ME TO POP YOU LIKE A GRAPE?
I'D... RATHER... YOU... DIDN'T....
TELL MY SISTER...
I...HATE... HER...

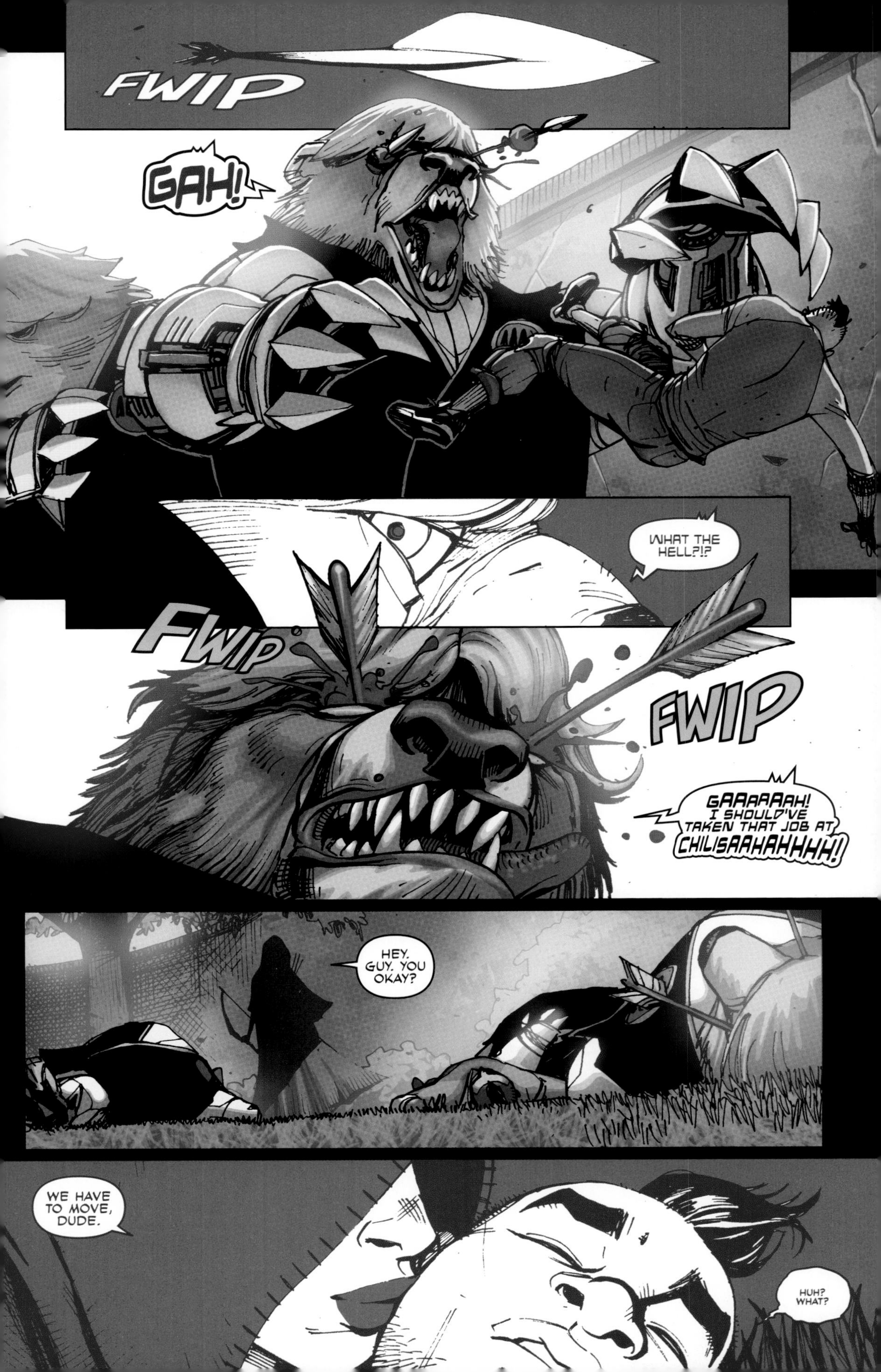
FWIP
GAH!
WHAT THE HELL?!?
FWIP
FWIP
GAAAAAAH! I SHOULD'VE TAKEN THAT JOB AT CHILISAAHAHHHH!
HEY. GUY. YOU OKAY?
WE HAVE TO MOVE, DUDE.
HUH? WHAT?

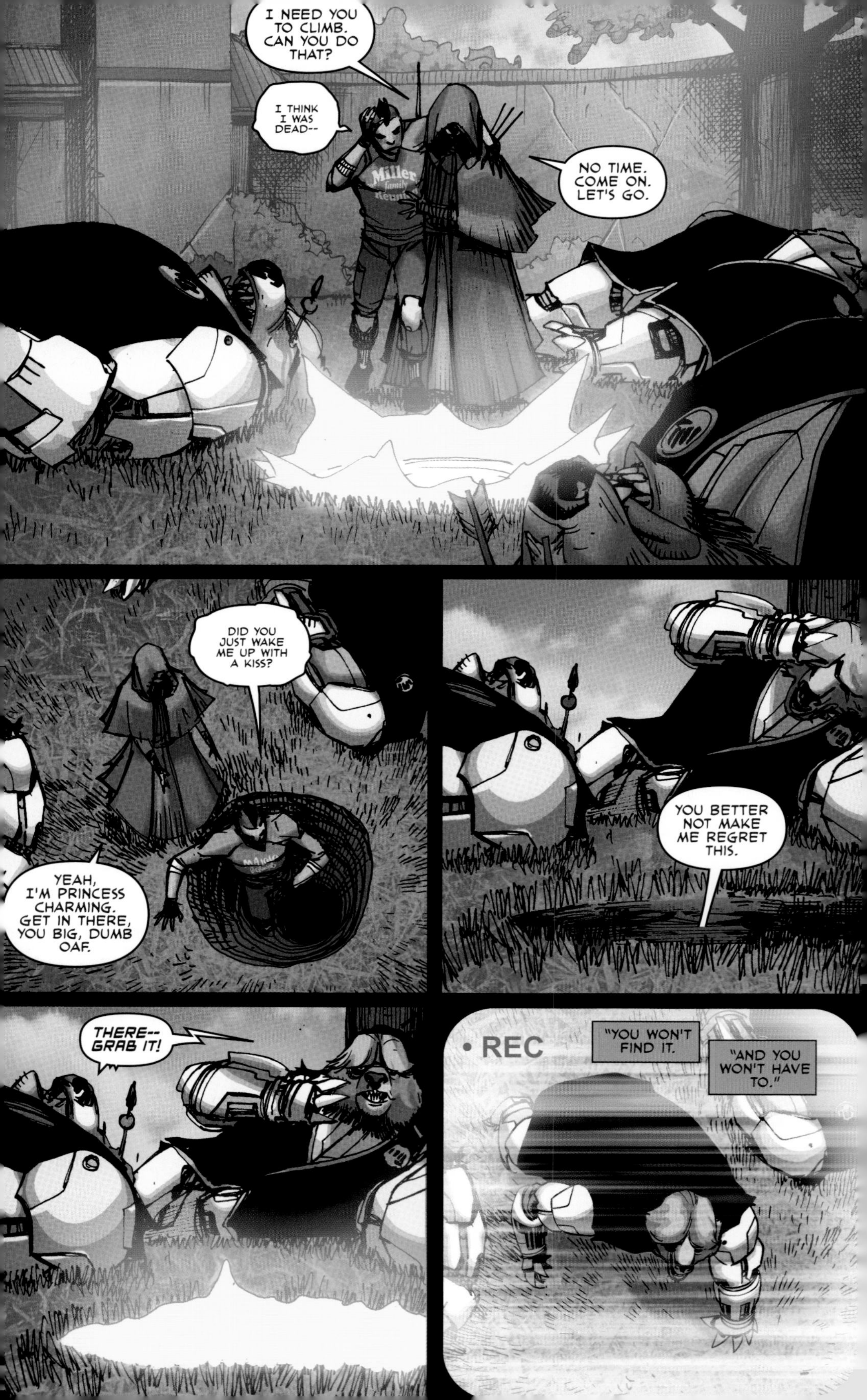
I NEED YOU TO CLIMB. CAN YOU DO THAT?
I THINK I WAS DEAD--
NO TIME. COME ON. LET'S GO.
DID YOU JUST WAKE ME UP WITH A KISS?
YEAH, I'M PRINCESS CHARMING. GET IN THERE, YOU BIG, DUMB OAF.
YOU BETTER NOT MAKE ME REGRET THIS.
THERE-- GRAB IT!
• REC
"YOU WON'T FIND IT.
"AND YOU WON'T HAVE TO."

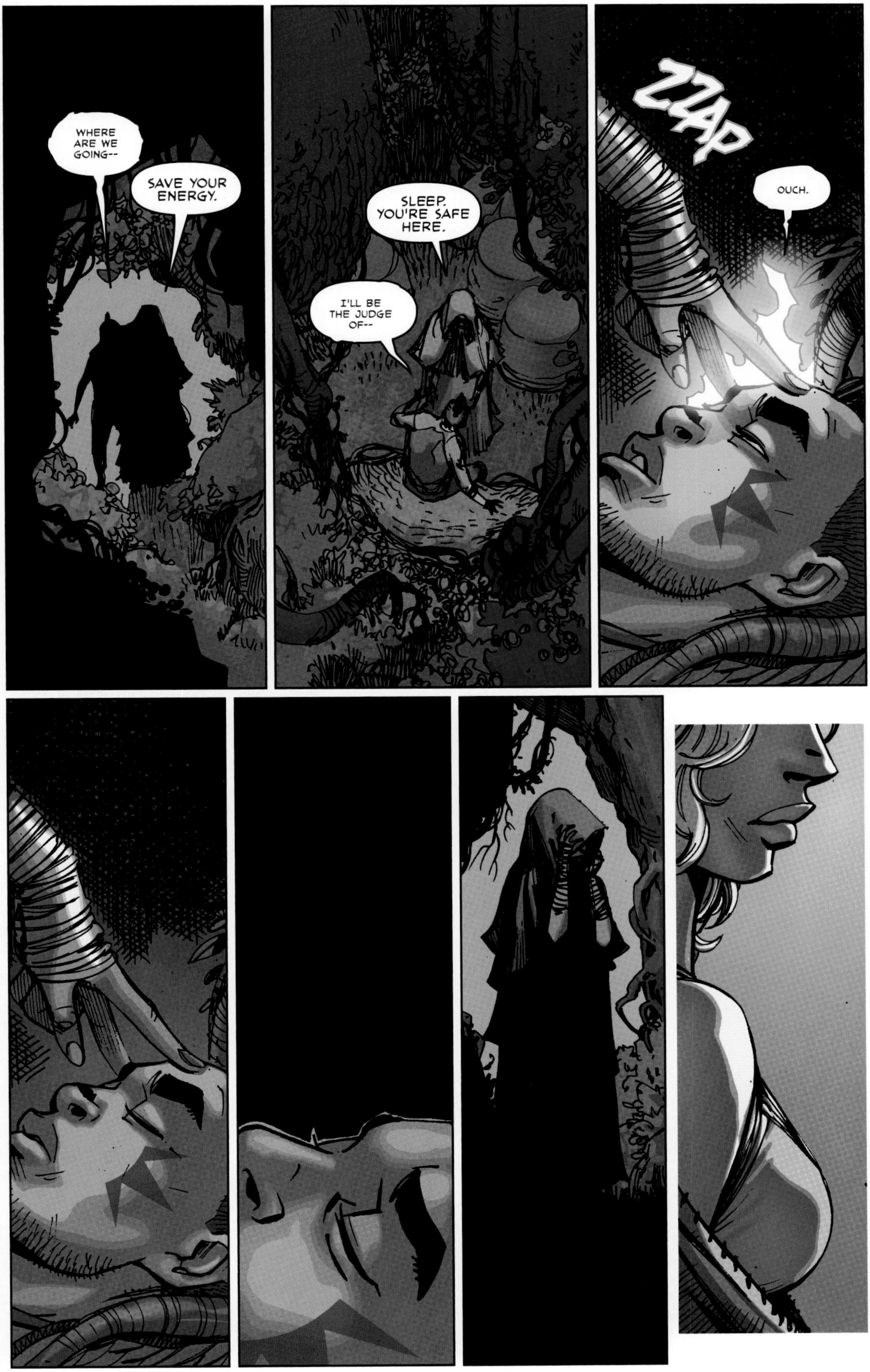
WHERE ARE WE GOING--
SAVE YOUR ENERGY.
SLEEP. YOU'RE SAFE HERE.
I'LL BE THE JUDGE OF--
ZZAP
OUCH.

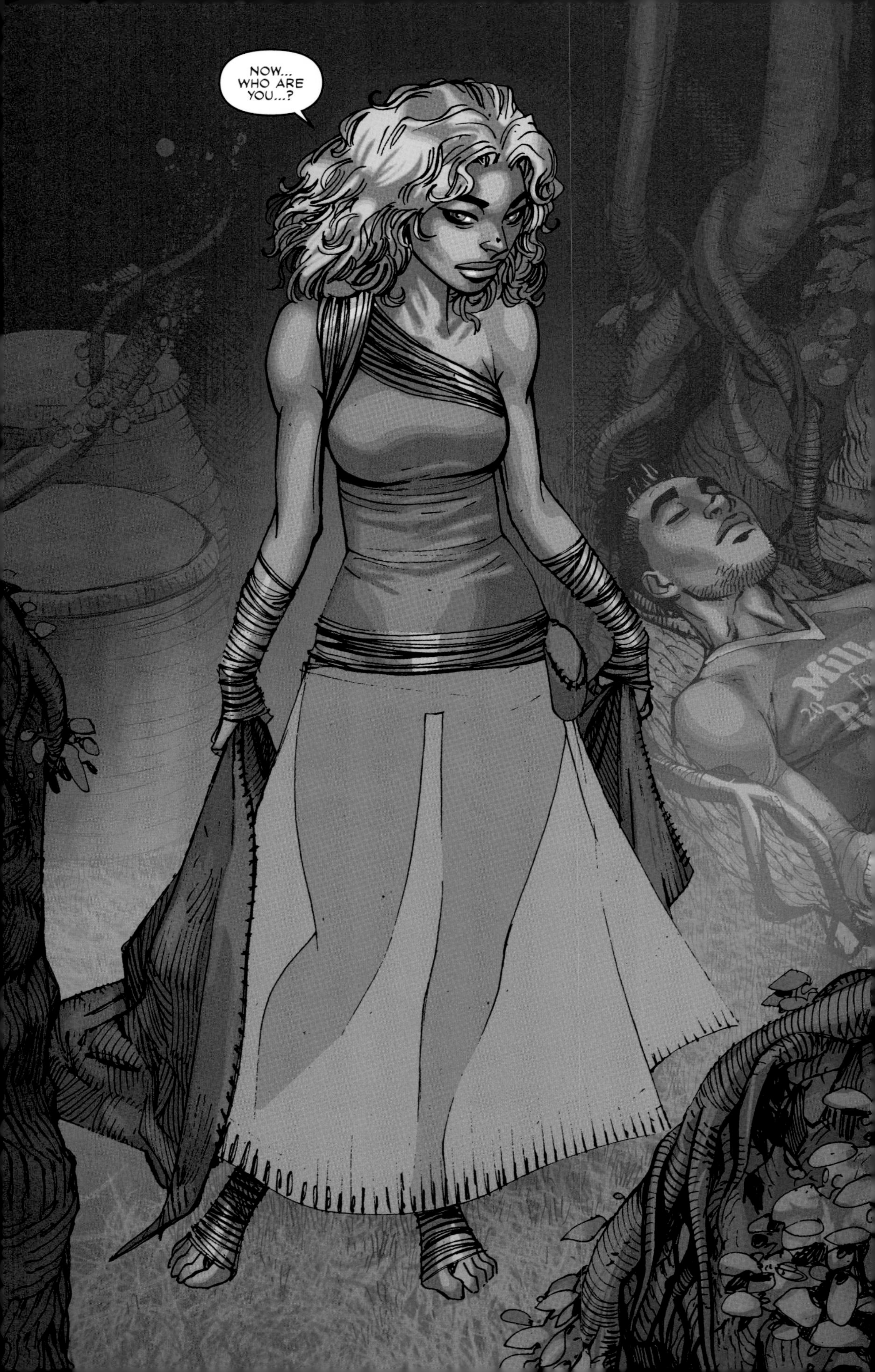
NOW... WHO ARE YOU...?

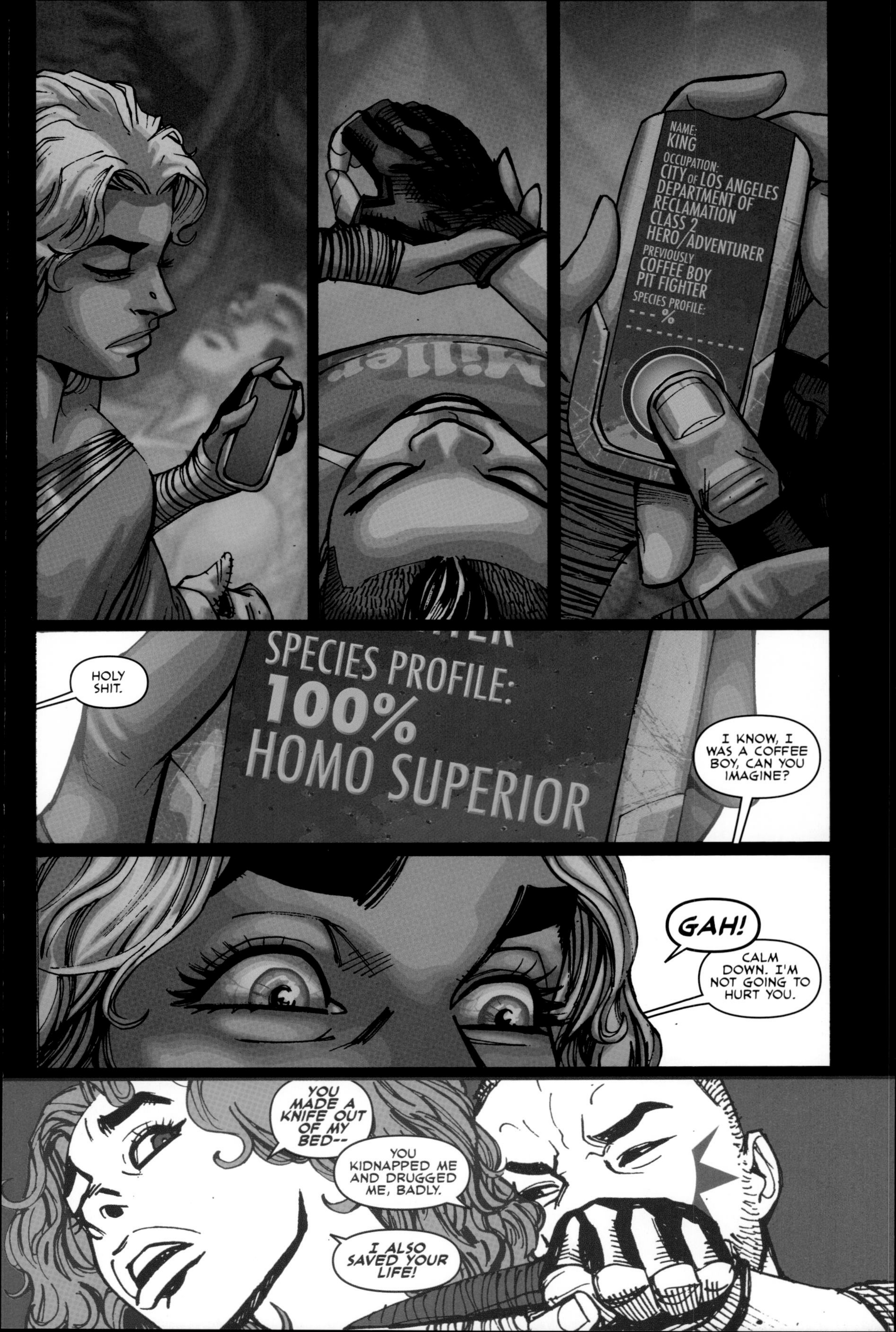
NAME:
KING
OCCUPATION:
CITY OF LOS ANGELES DEPARTMENT OF RECLAMATION CLASS 2 HERO/ADVENTURER
PREVIOUSLY
COFFEE BOY
PIT FIGHTER
SPECIES PROFILE:
- - - %
HOLY SHIT.
SPECIES PROFILE:
100%
HOMO SUPERIOR
I KNOW, I WAS A COFFEE BOY, CAN YOU IMAGINE?
GAH!
CALM DOWN. I'M NOT GOING TO HURT YOU.
YOU MADE A KNIFE OUT OF MY BED--
YOU KIDNAPPED ME AND DRUGGED ME, BADLY.
I ALSO SAVED YOUR LIFE!

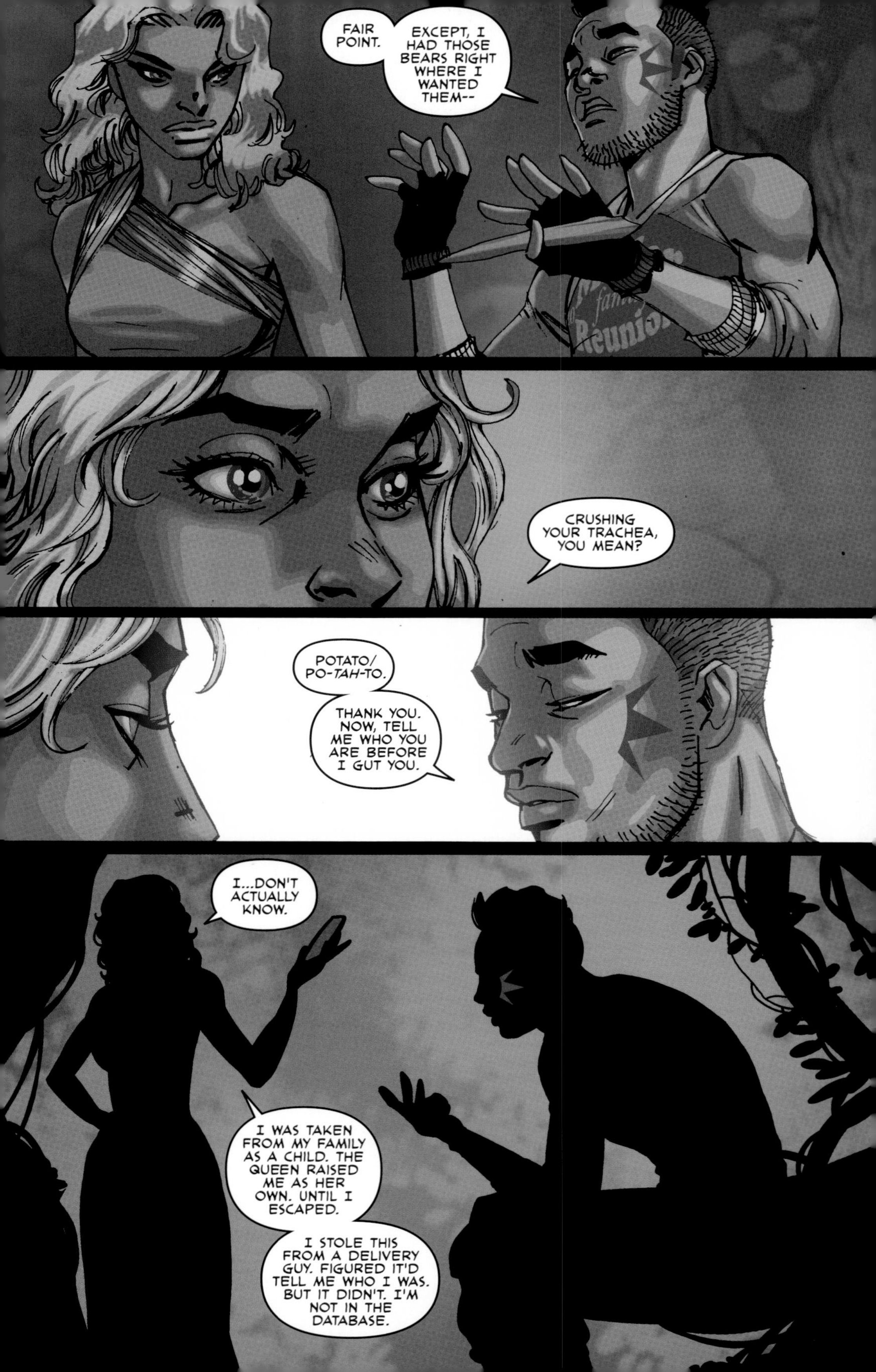
FAIR POINT.
EXCEPT, I HAD THOSE BEARS RIGHT WHERE I WANTED THEM--
CRUSHING YOUR TRACHEA, YOU MEAN?
POTATO/ PO-*TAH*-TO.
THANK YOU. NOW, TELL ME WHO YOU ARE BEFORE I GUT YOU.
I...DON'T ACTUALLY KNOW.
I WAS TAKEN FROM MY FAMILY AS A CHILD. THE QUEEN RAISED ME AS HER OWN. UNTIL I ESCAPED.
I STOLE THIS FROM A DELIVERY GUY. FIGURED IT'D TELL ME WHO I WAS. BUT IT DIDN'T. I'M NOT IN THE DATABASE.

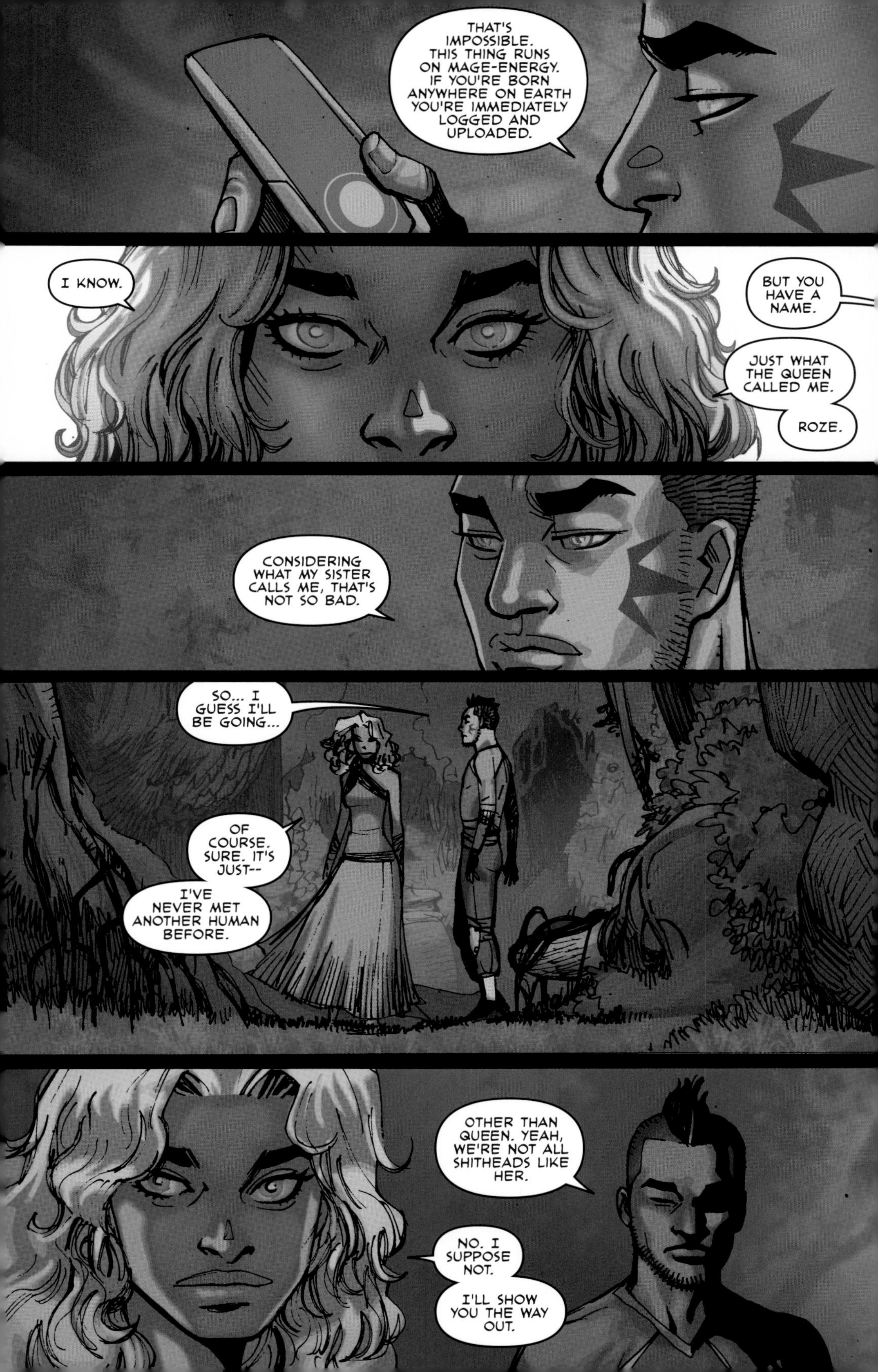
THAT'S IMPOSSIBLE. THIS THING RUNS ON MAGE-ENERGY. IF YOU'RE BORN ANYWHERE ON EARTH YOU'RE IMMEDIATELY LOGGED AND UPLOADED.
I KNOW.
BUT YOU HAVE A NAME.
JUST WHAT THE QUEEN CALLED ME.
ROZE.
CONSIDERING WHAT MY SISTER CALLS ME, THAT'S NOT SO BAD.
SO... I GUESS I'LL BE GOING...
OF COURSE. SURE. IT'S JUST--
I'VE NEVER MET ANOTHER HUMAN BEFORE.
OTHER THAN QUEEN. YEAH, WE'RE NOT ALL SHITHEADS LIKE HER.
NO. I SUPPOSE NOT.
I'LL SHOW YOU THE WAY OUT.

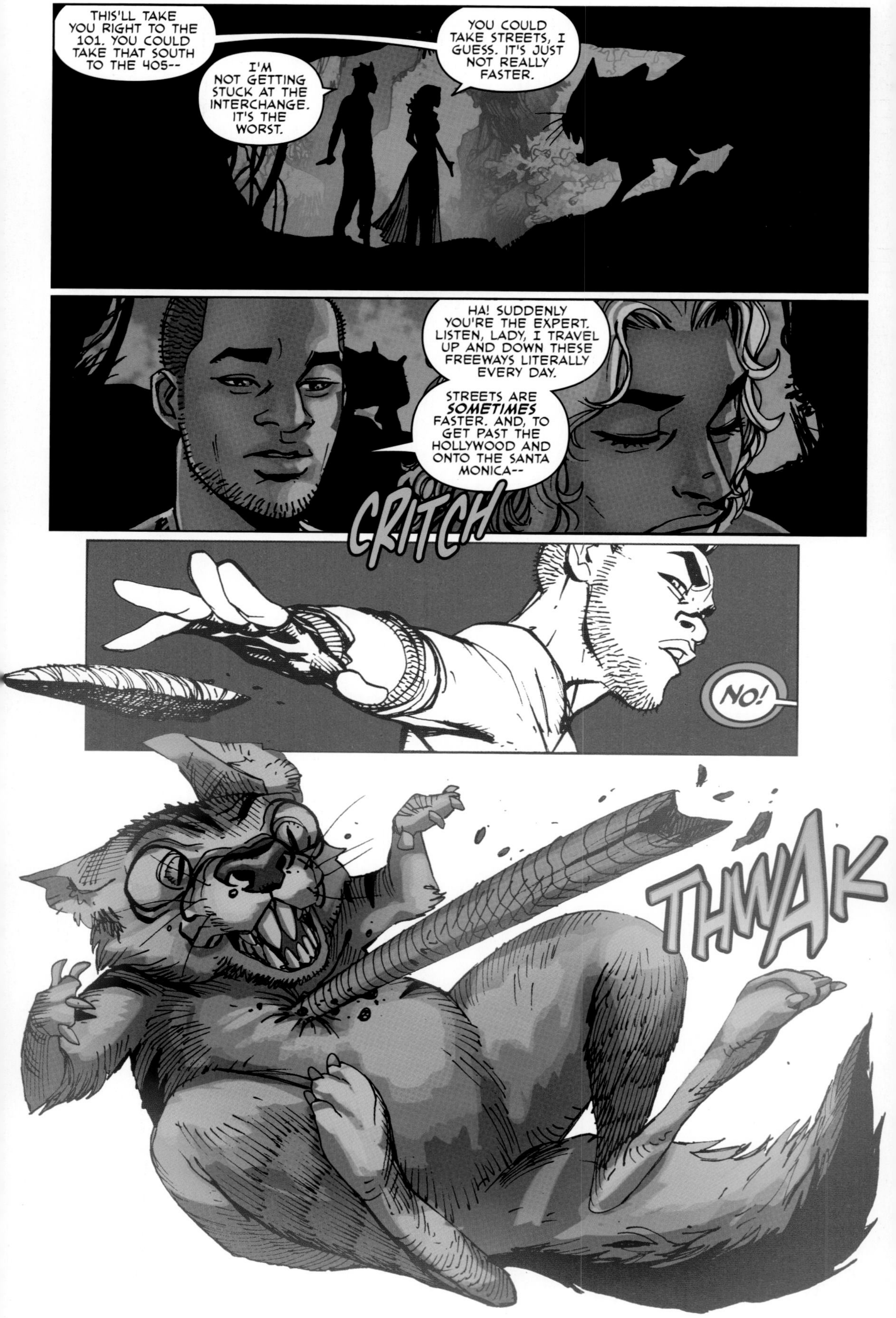

THIS'LL TAKE YOU RIGHT TO THE 101. YOU COULD TAKE THAT SOUTH TO THE 405--
I'M NOT GETTING STUCK AT THE INTERCHANGE. IT'S THE WORST.
YOU COULD TAKE STREETS, I GUESS. IT'S JUST NOT REALLY FASTER.
HA! SUDDENLY YOU'RE THE EXPERT. LISTEN, LADY, I TRAVEL UP AND DOWN THESE FREEWAYS LITERALLY EVERY DAY.
STREETS ARE SOMETIMES FASTER. AND, TO GET PAST THE HOLLYWOOD AND ONTO THE SANTA MONICA--
CRITCH
NO!
THWAK

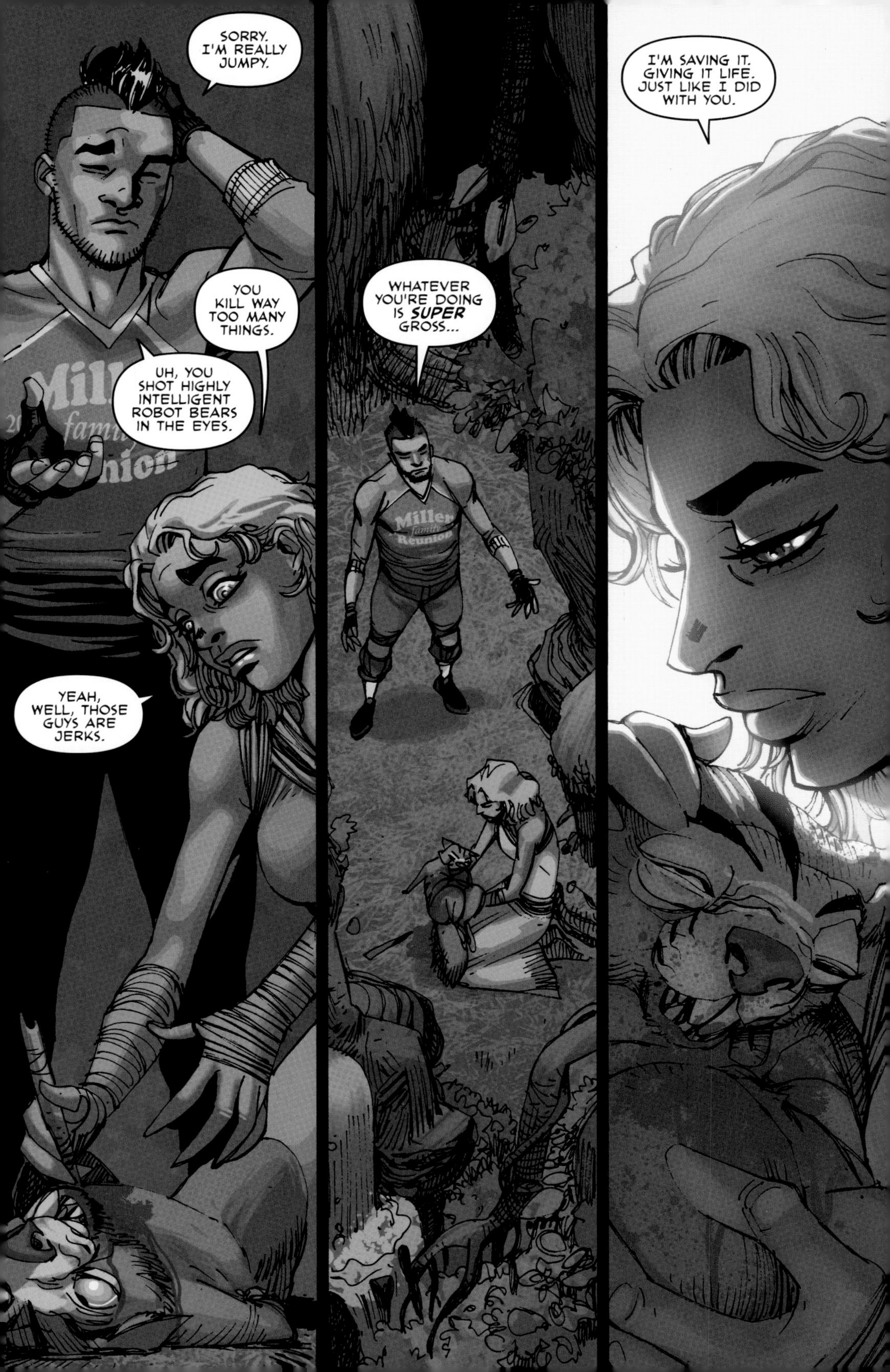
SORRY. I'M REALLY JUMPY.
YOU KILL WAY TOO MANY THINGS.
UH, YOU SHOT HIGHLY INTELLIGENT ROBOT BEARS IN THE EYES.
YEAH, WELL, THOSE GUYS ARE JERKS.
WHATEVER YOU'RE DOING IS SUPER GROSS...
I'M SAVING IT. GIVING IT LIFE. JUST LIKE I DID WITH YOU.

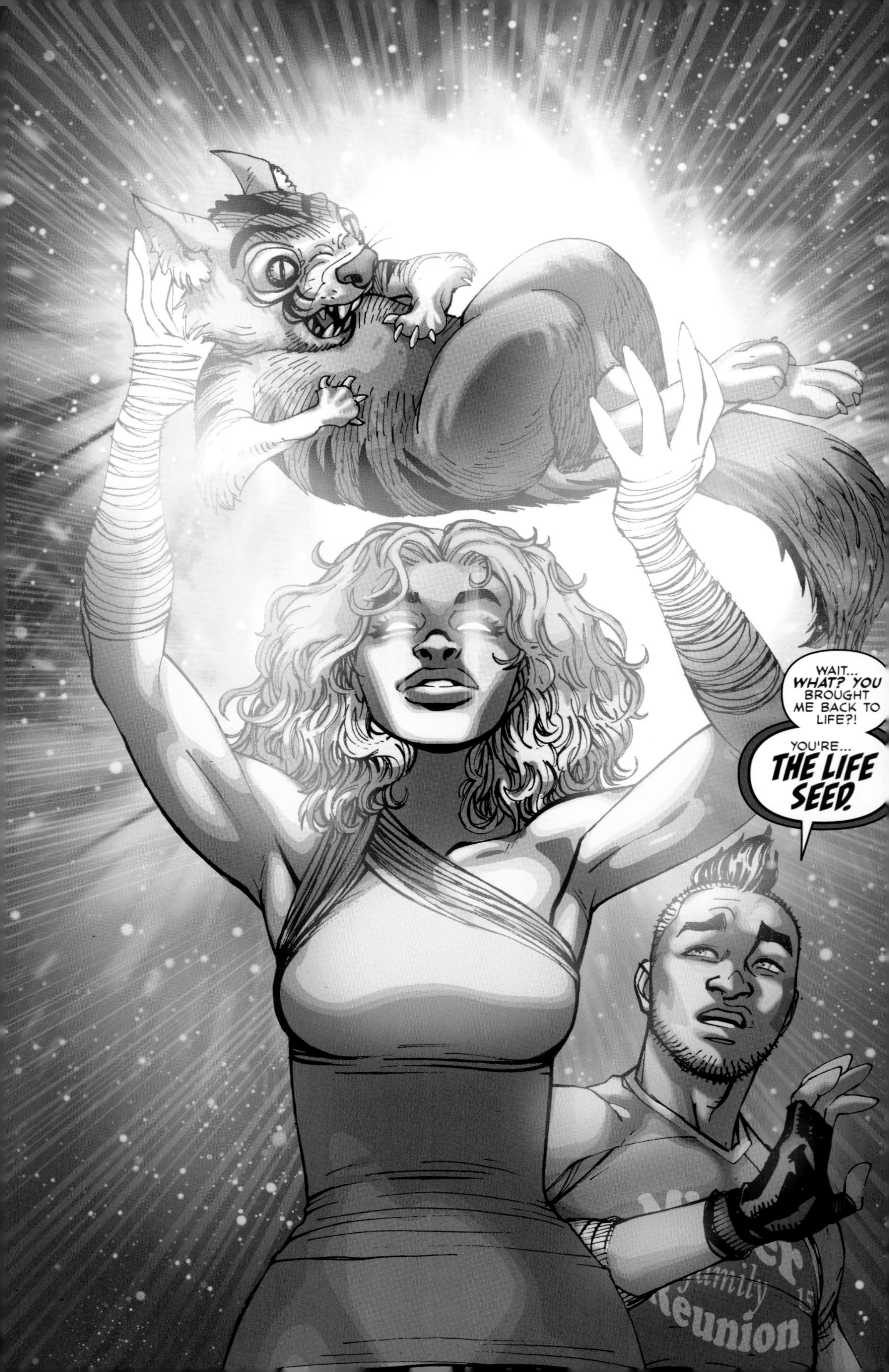
WAIT... WHAT? YOU BROUGHT ME BACK TO LIFE?!
YOU'RE... THE LIFE SEED.
Family Reunion

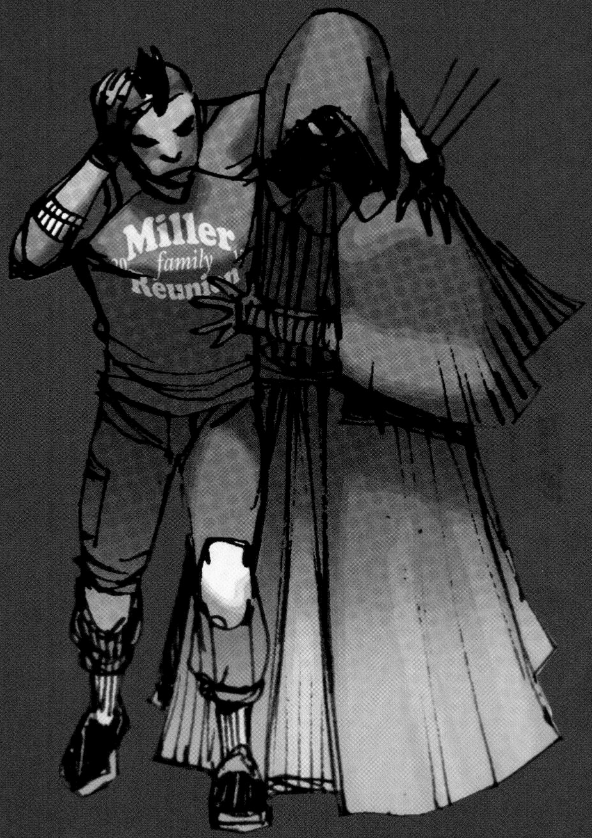
Miller
family

"I Hate Mondays"
CHAPTER THREE

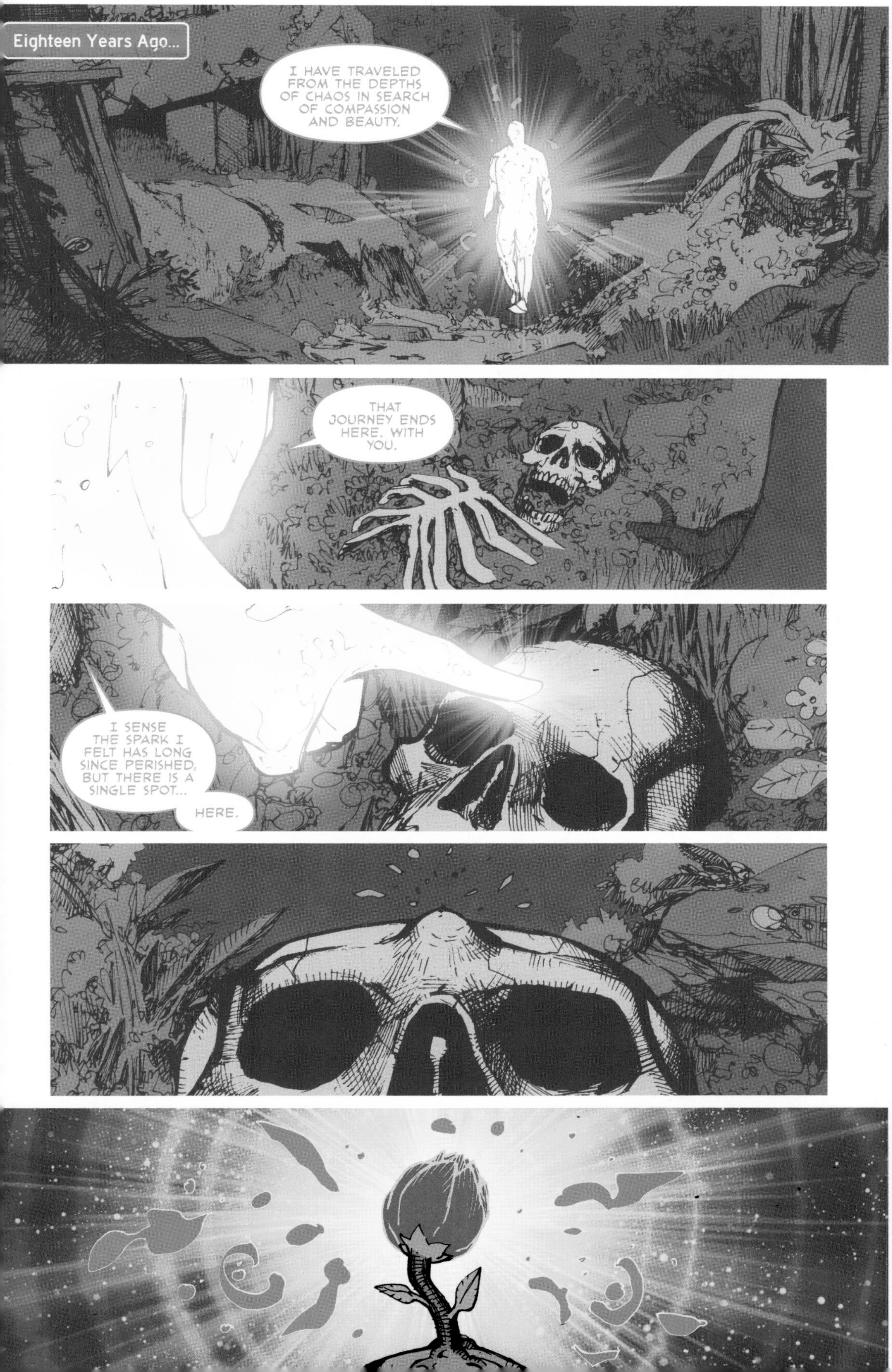
Eighteen Years Ago...
I HAVE TRAVELED FROM THE DEPTHS OF CHAOS IN SEARCH OF COMPASSION AND BEAUTY.
THAT JOURNEY ENDS HERE. WITH YOU.
I SENSE THE SPARK I FELT HAS LONG SINCE PERISHED, BUT THERE IS A SINGLE SPOT...
HERE.

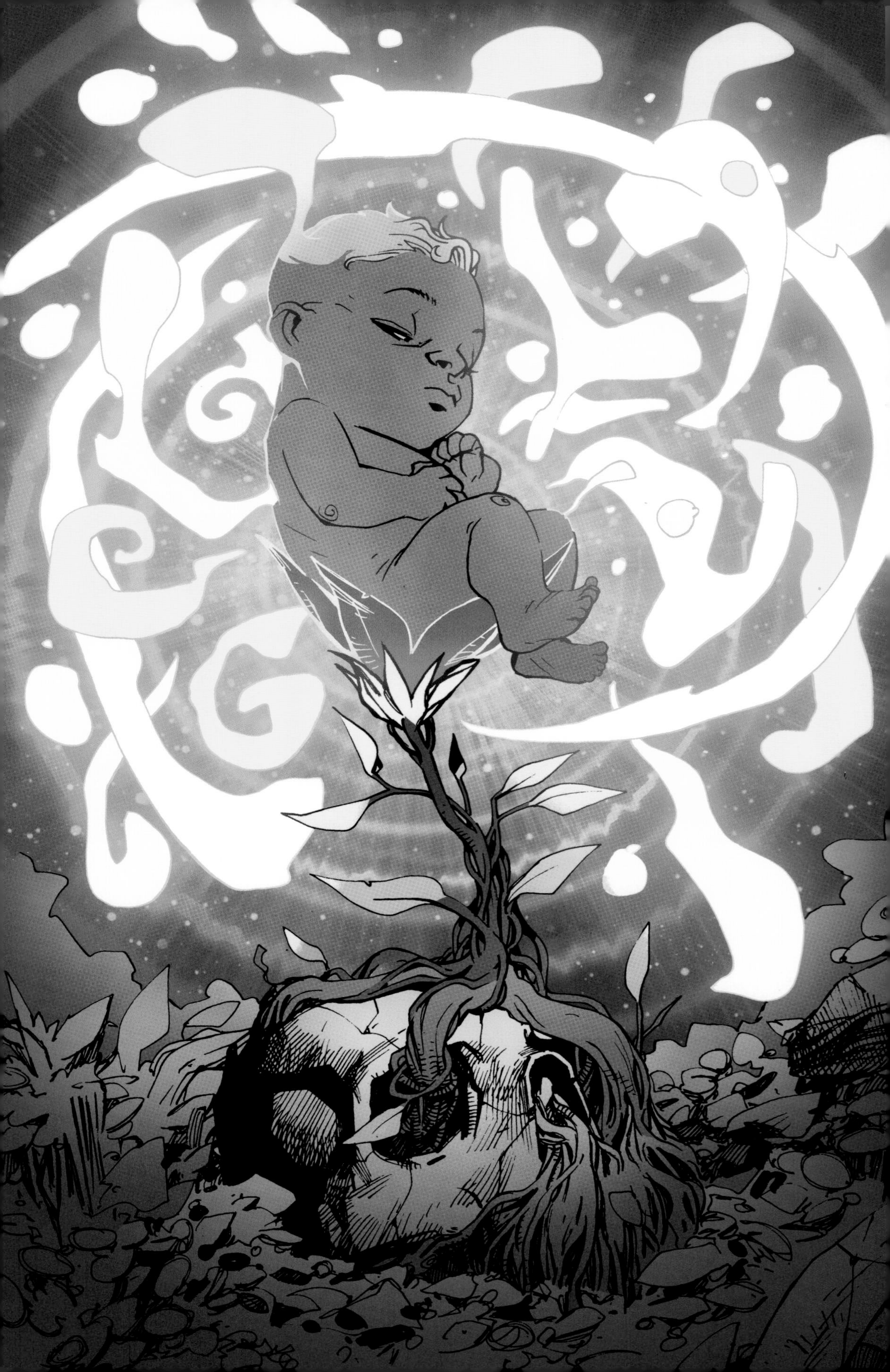

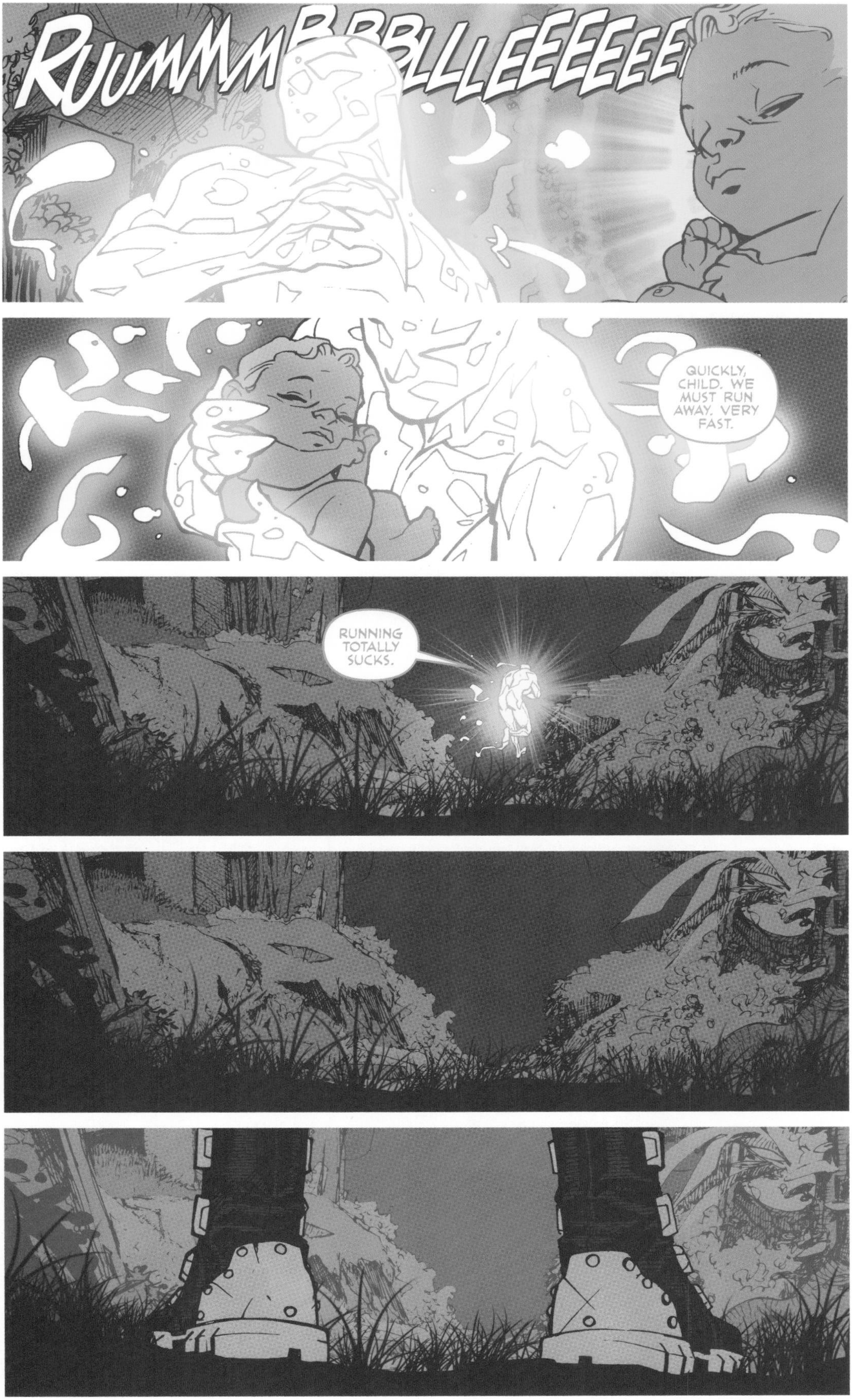
RUUMMMBBBLLLEEEEEEE
QUICKLY, CHILD. WE MUST RUN AWAY. VERY FAST.
RUNNING TOTALLY SUCKS.

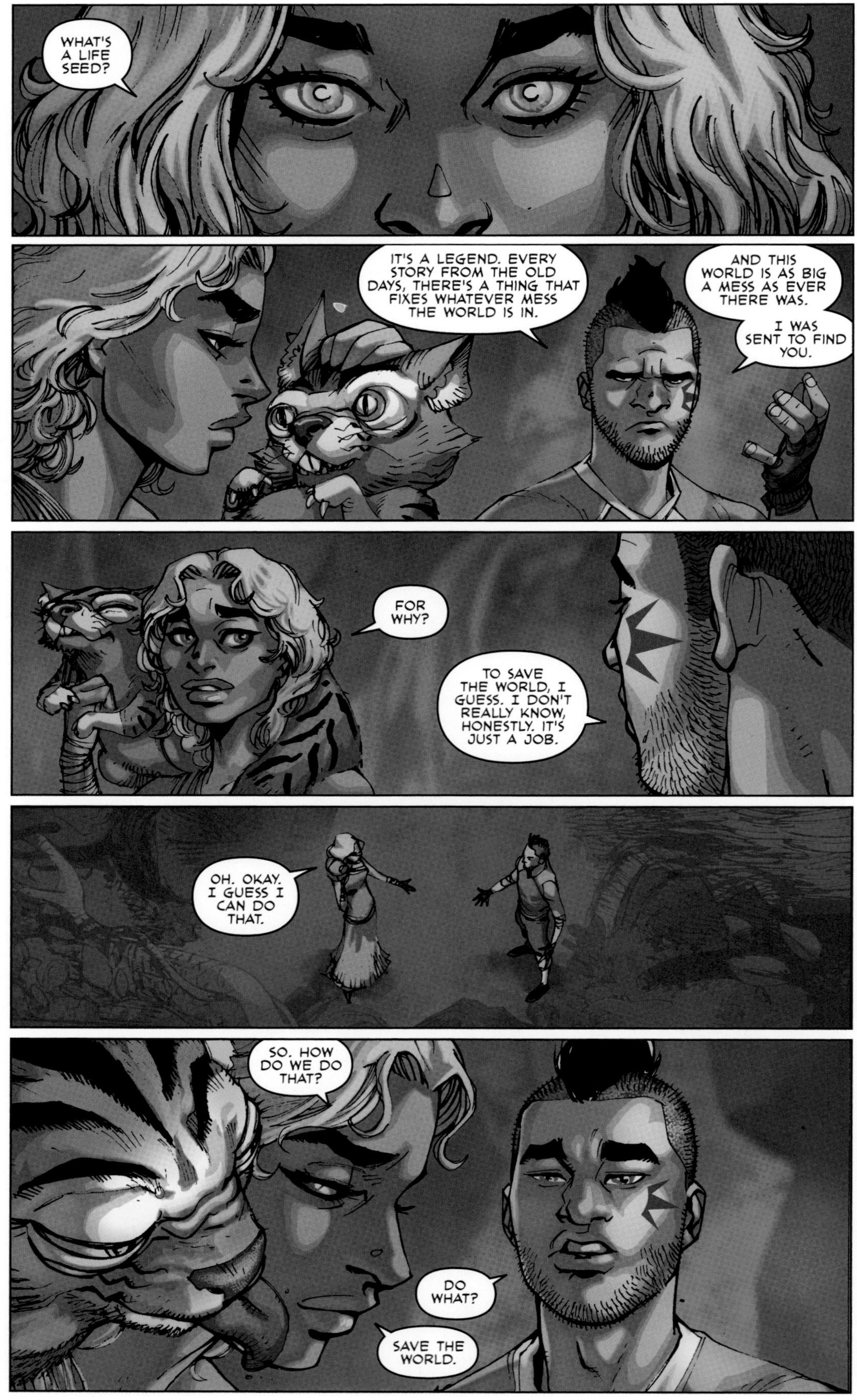

WHAT'S A LIFE SEED?
IT'S A LEGEND. EVERY STORY FROM THE OLD DAYS, THERE'S A THING THAT FIXES WHATEVER MESS THE WORLD IS IN.
AND THIS WORLD IS AS BIG A MESS AS EVER THERE WAS.
I WAS SENT TO FIND YOU.
FOR WHY?
TO SAVE THE WORLD, I GUESS. I DON'T REALLY KNOW, HONESTLY. IT'S JUST A JOB.
OH. OKAY. I GUESS I CAN DO THAT.
SO. HOW DO WE DO THAT?
DO WHAT?
SAVE THE WORLD.

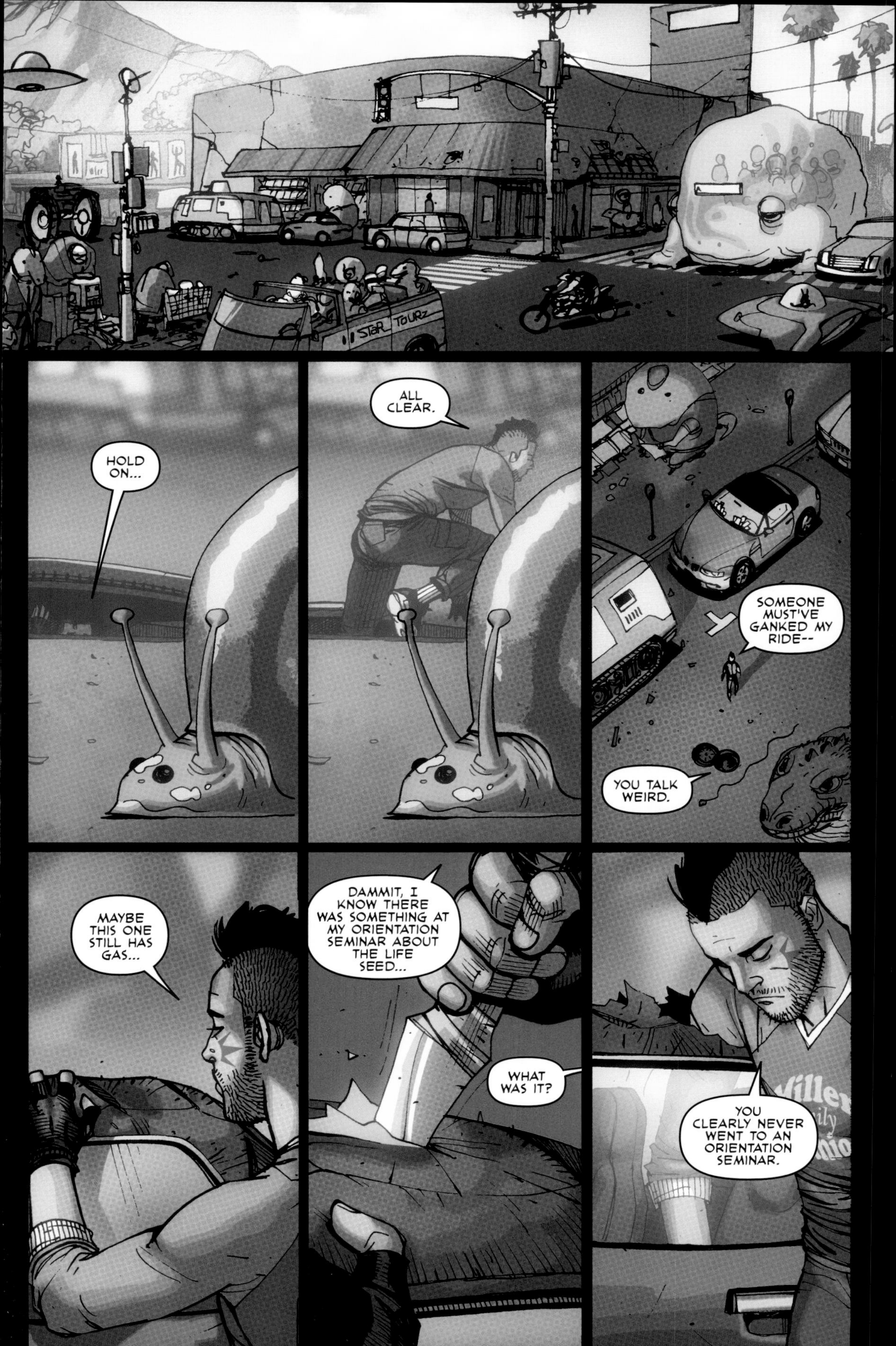
STaR TOURz
HOLD ON...
ALL CLEAR.
SOMEONE MUST'VE GANKED MY RIDE--
YOU TALK WEIRD.
MAYBE THIS ONE STILL HAS GAS...
DAMMIT, I KNOW THERE WAS SOMETHING AT MY ORIENTATION SEMINAR ABOUT THE LIFE SEED...
WHAT WAS IT?
YOU CLEARLY NEVER WENT TO AN ORIENTATION SEMINAR.

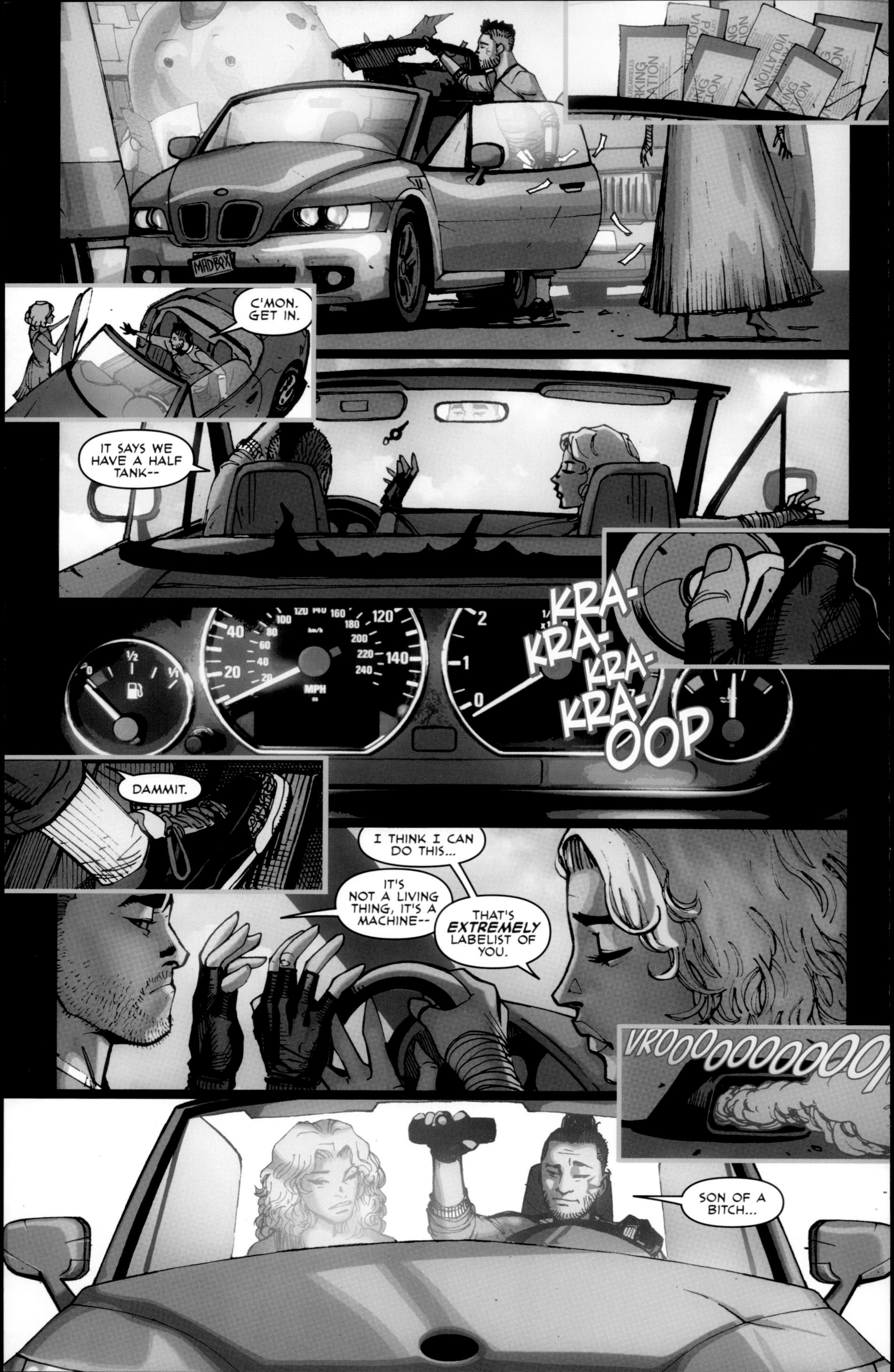
LOS ANGELES PARKING VIOLATION
C'MON. GET IN.
IT SAYS WE HAVE A HALF TANK--
KRA-KRA-KRA-KRA-OOP
DAMMIT.
I THINK I CAN DO THIS...
IT'S NOT A LIVING THING, IT'S A MACHINE--
THAT'S **EXTREMELY** LABELIST OF YOU.
VROOOOOOOOOOOOO
SON OF A BITCH...

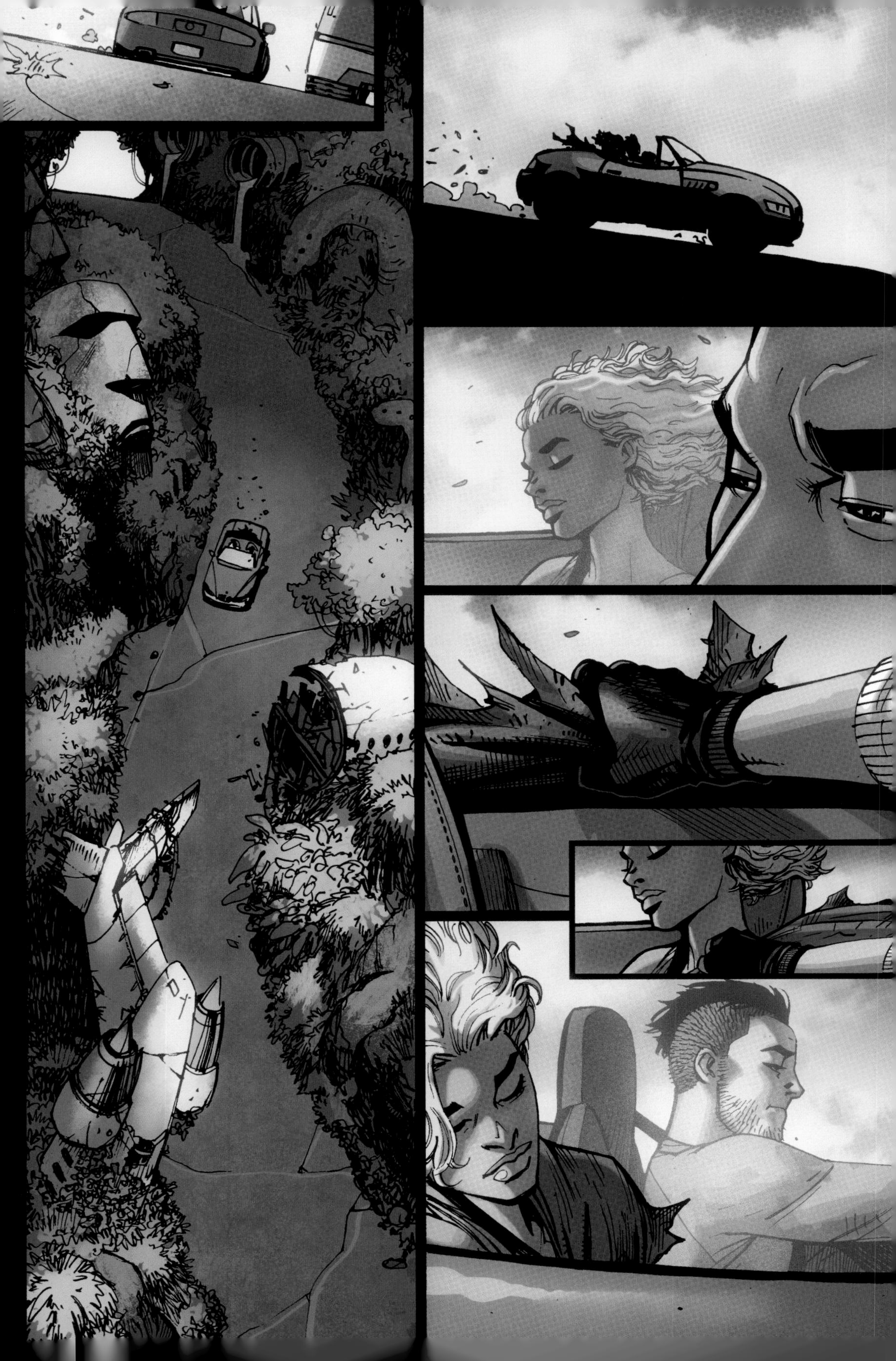

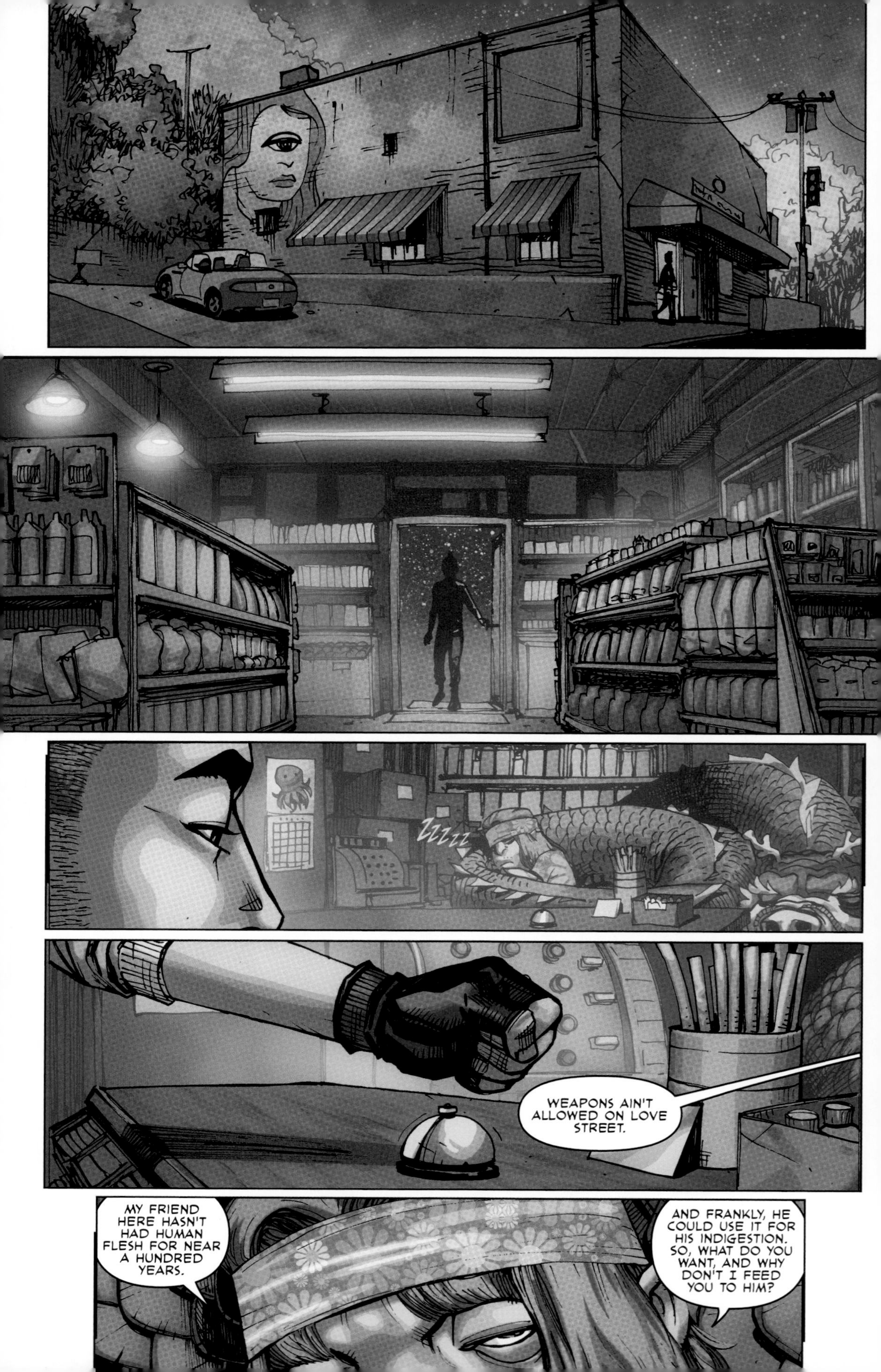
ZZZZZ
WEAPONS AIN'T ALLOWED ON LOVE STREET.
MY FRIEND HERE HASN'T HAD HUMAN FLESH FOR NEAR A HUNDRED YEARS.
AND FRANKLY, HE COULD USE IT FOR HIS INDIGESTION. SO, WHAT DO YOU WANT, AND WHY DON'T I FEED YOU TO HIM?

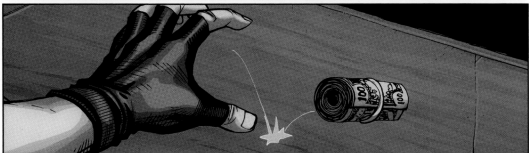

HOW DO I KNOW YOU'RE NOT A COP?

'CAUSE I'M NOT A JACKBOOTED, METALLIC ASSHOLE.

THIS IS TOO MUCH FOR--

I NEED *DOUBLE* THE REGULAR DOSE.

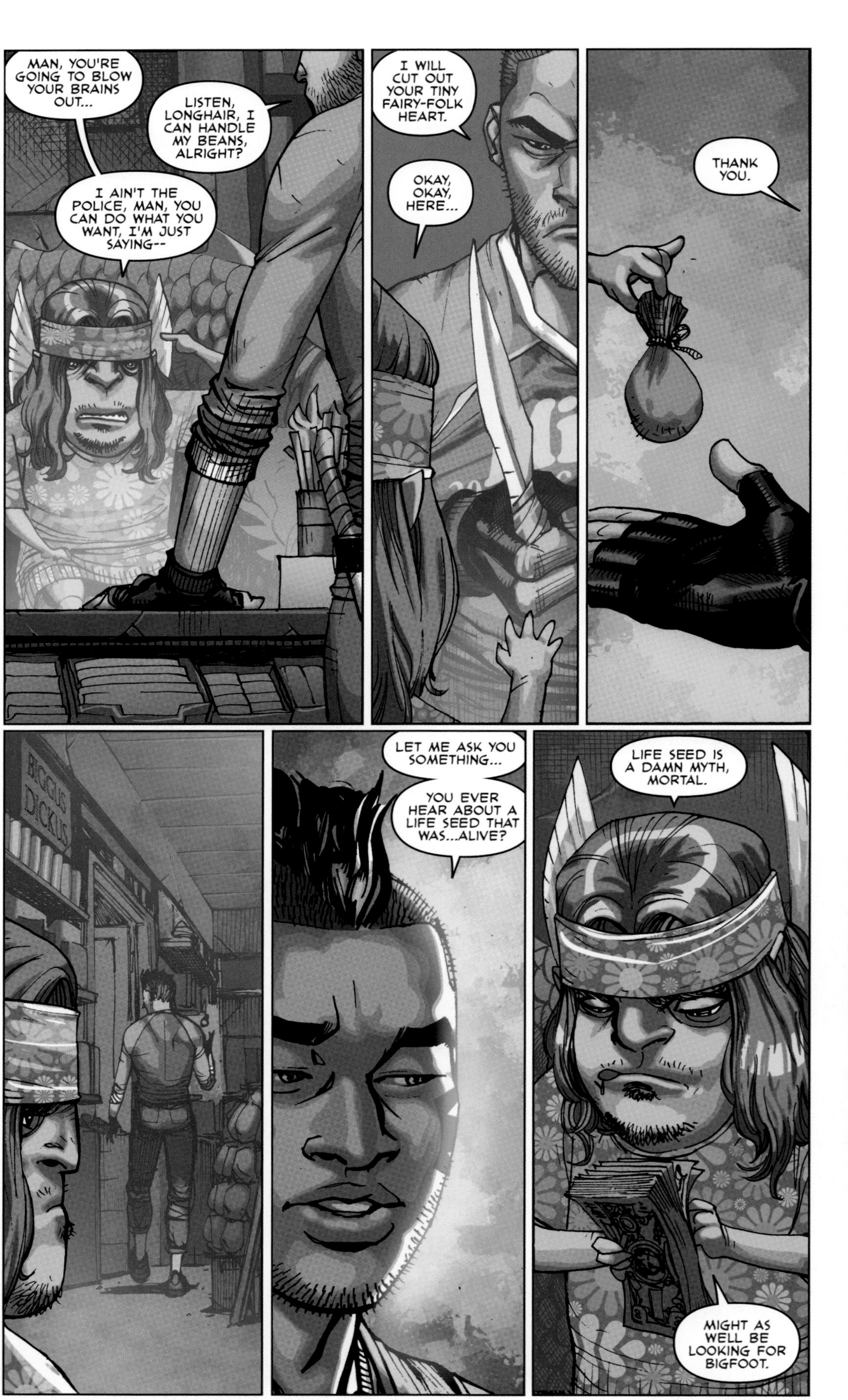
MAN, YOU'RE GOING TO BLOW YOUR BRAINS OUT...
LISTEN, LONGHAIR, I CAN HANDLE MY BEANS, ALRIGHT?
I AIN'T THE POLICE, MAN, YOU CAN DO WHAT YOU WANT, I'M JUST SAYING--
I WILL CUT OUT YOUR TINY FAIRY-FOLK HEART.
OKAY, OKAY, HERE...
THANK YOU.
BIGGUS DICKUS
LET ME ASK YOU SOMETHING...
YOU EVER HEAR ABOUT A LIFE SEED THAT WAS...ALIVE?
LIFE SEED IS A DAMN MYTH, MORTAL.
MIGHT AS WELL BE LOOKING FOR BIGFOOT.

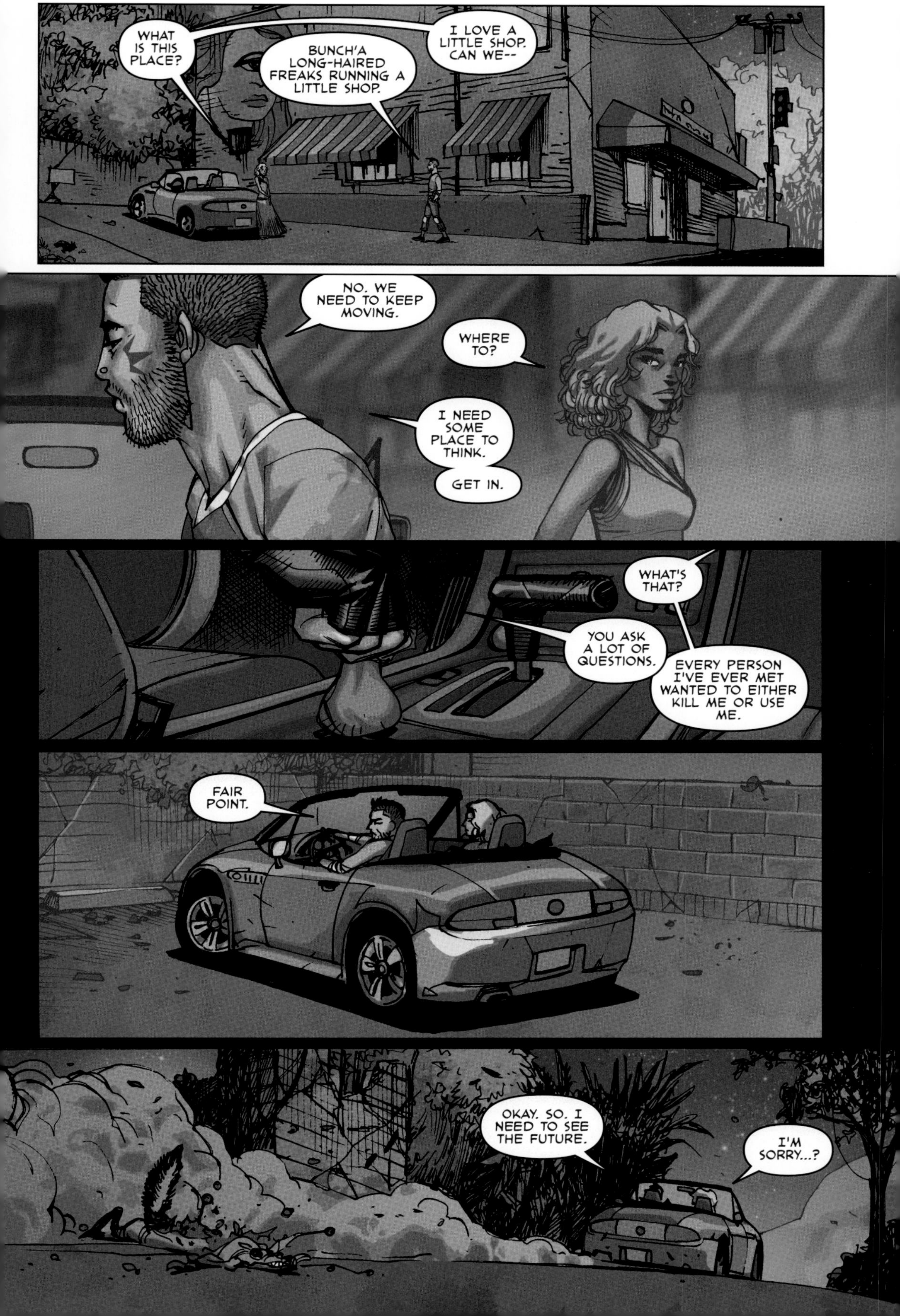
WHAT IS THIS PLACE?
BUNCH'A LONG-HAIRED FREAKS RUNNING A LITTLE SHOP.
I LOVE A LITTLE SHOP. CAN WE--
NO. WE NEED TO KEEP MOVING.
WHERE TO?
I NEED SOME PLACE TO THINK.
GET IN.
WHAT'S THAT?
YOU ASK A LOT OF QUESTIONS.
EVERY PERSON I'VE EVER MET WANTED TO EITHER KILL ME OR USE ME.
FAIR POINT.
OKAY. SO. I NEED TO SEE THE FUTURE.
I'M SORRY...?

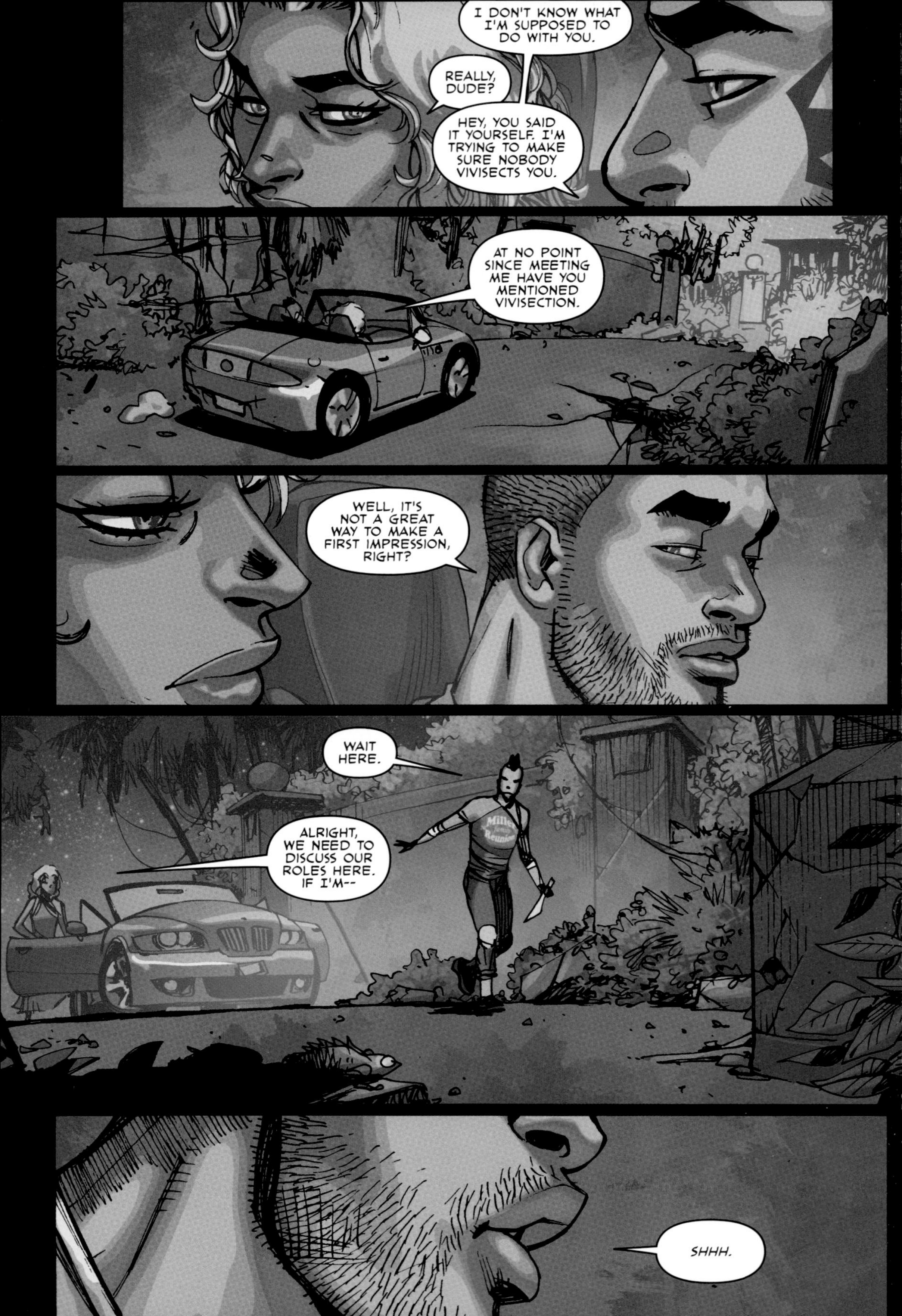
I DON'T KNOW WHAT I'M SUPPOSED TO DO WITH YOU.
REALLY, DUDE?
HEY, YOU SAID IT YOURSELF. I'M TRYING TO MAKE SURE NOBODY VIVISECTS YOU.
AT NO POINT SINCE MEETING ME HAVE YOU MENTIONED VIVISECTION.
WELL, IT'S NOT A GREAT WAY TO MAKE A FIRST IMPRESSION, RIGHT?
WAIT HERE.
ALRIGHT, WE NEED TO DISCUSS OUR ROLES HERE. IF I'M--
SHHH.

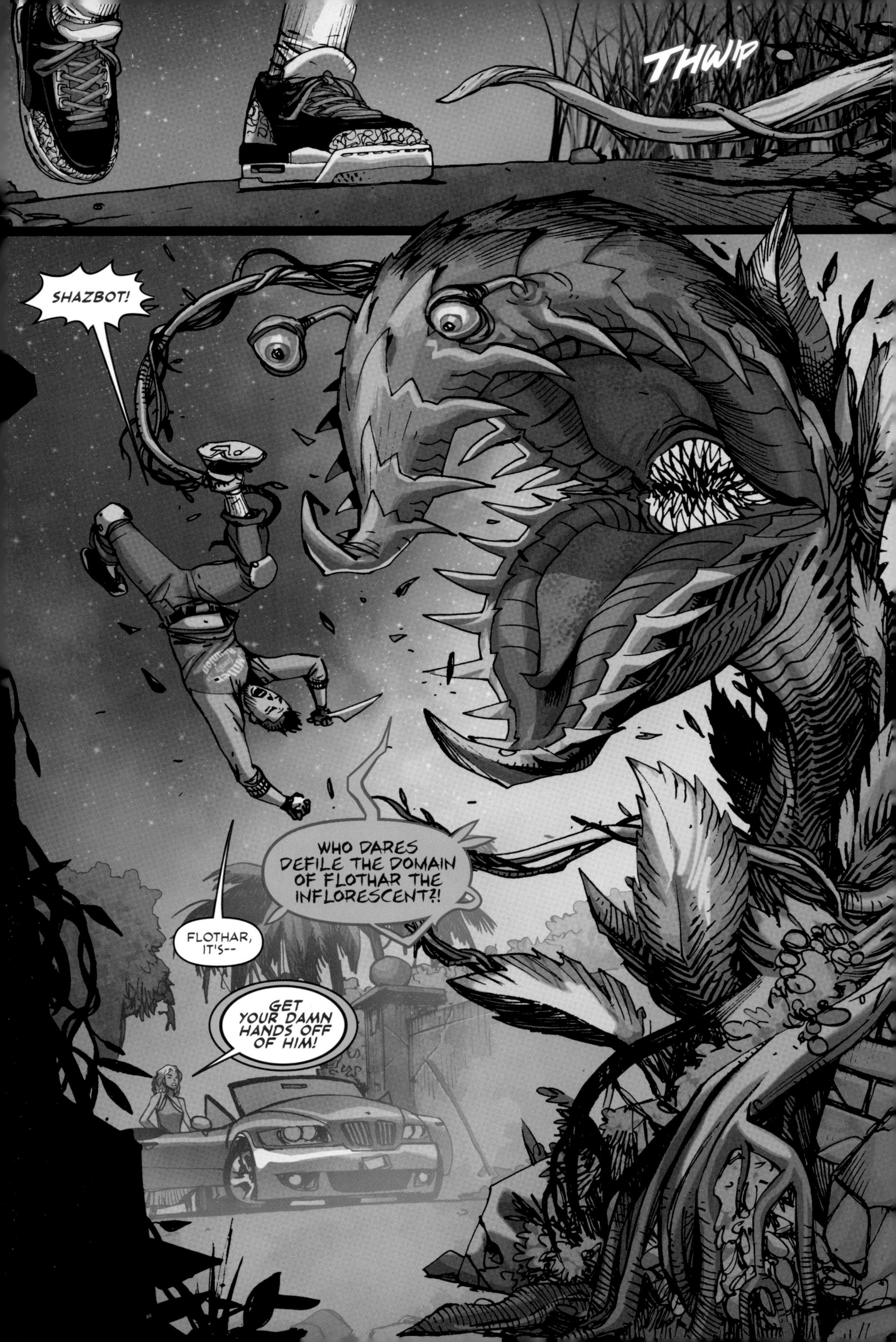
THWIP
SHAZBOT!
WHO DARES DEFILE THE DOMAIN OF FLOTHAR THE INFLORESCENT?!
FLOTHAR, IT'S--
GET YOUR DAMN HANDS OFF OF HIM!

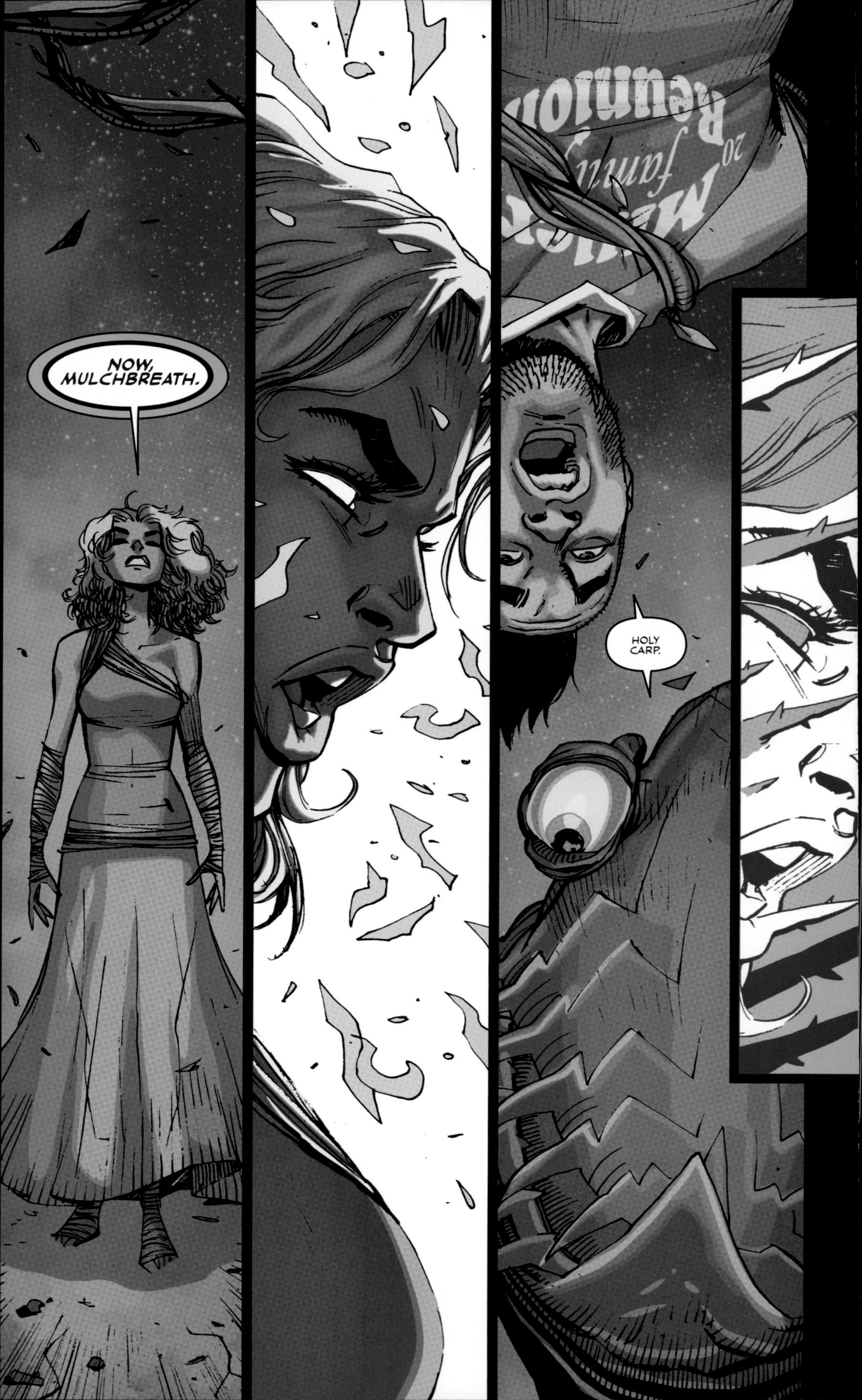
NOW, MULCHBREATH.
HOLY CARP.

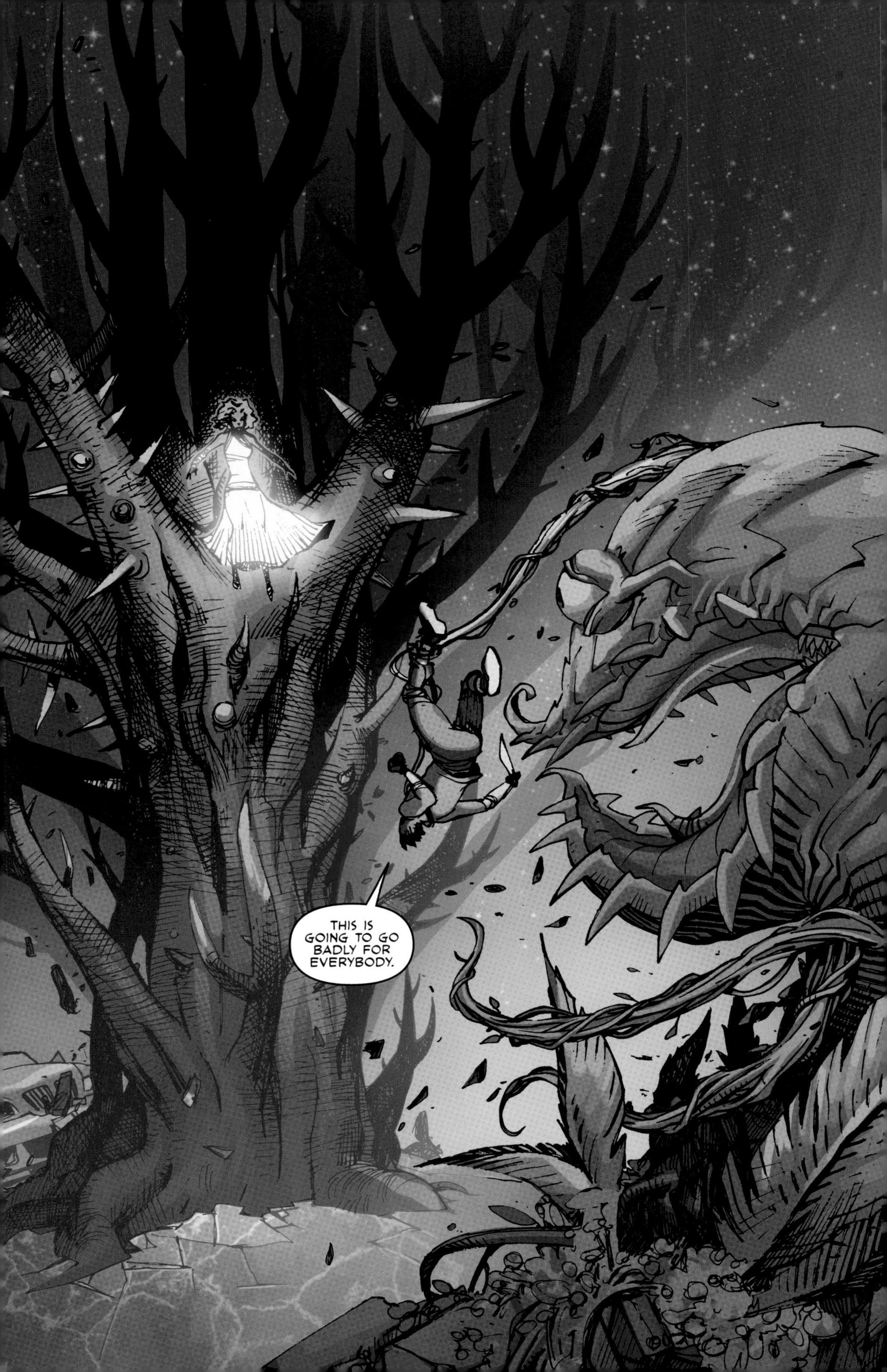
THIS IS GOING TO GO BADLY FOR EVERYBODY.

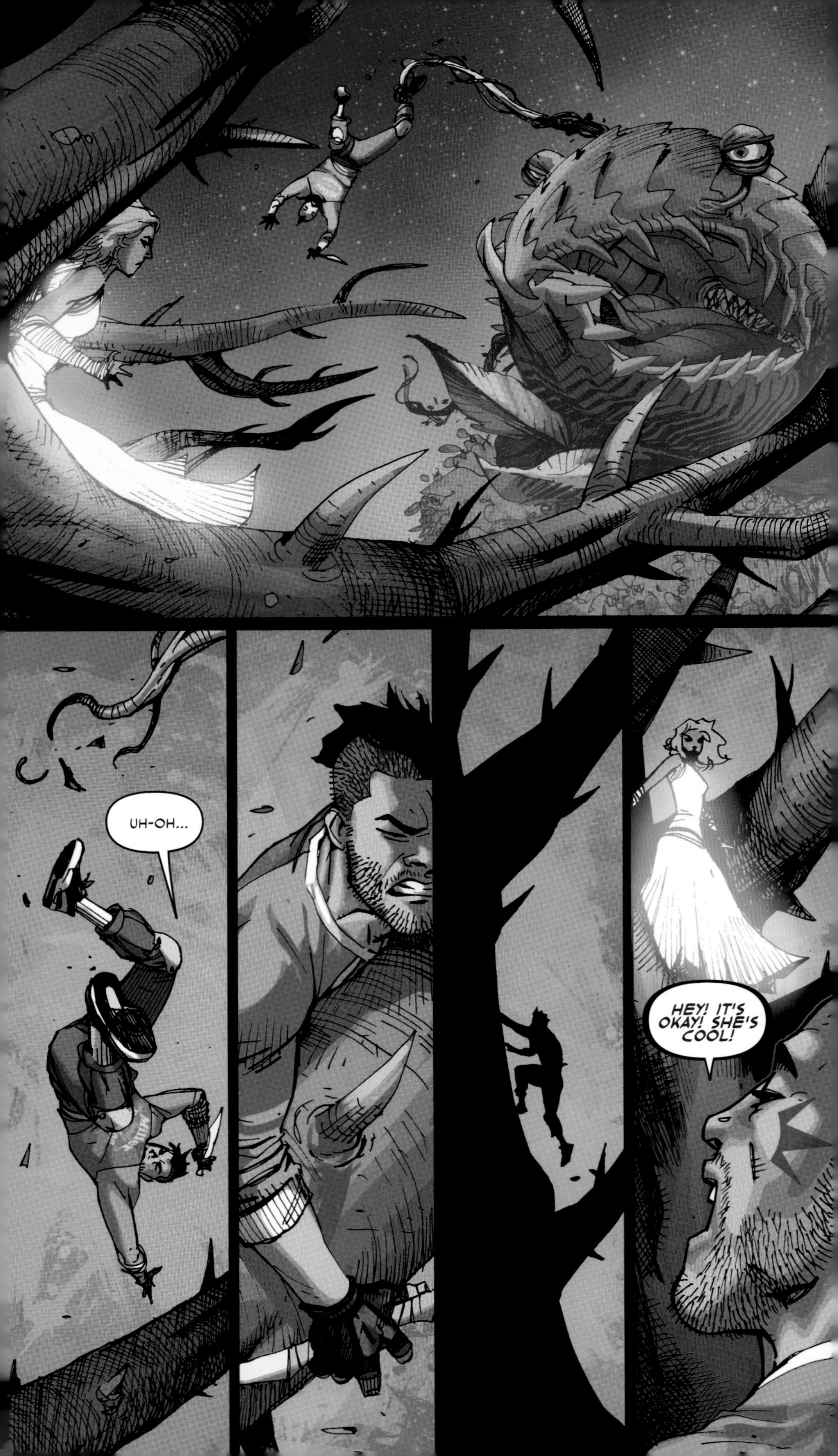
UH-OH...
HEY! IT'S OKAY! SHE'S COOL!

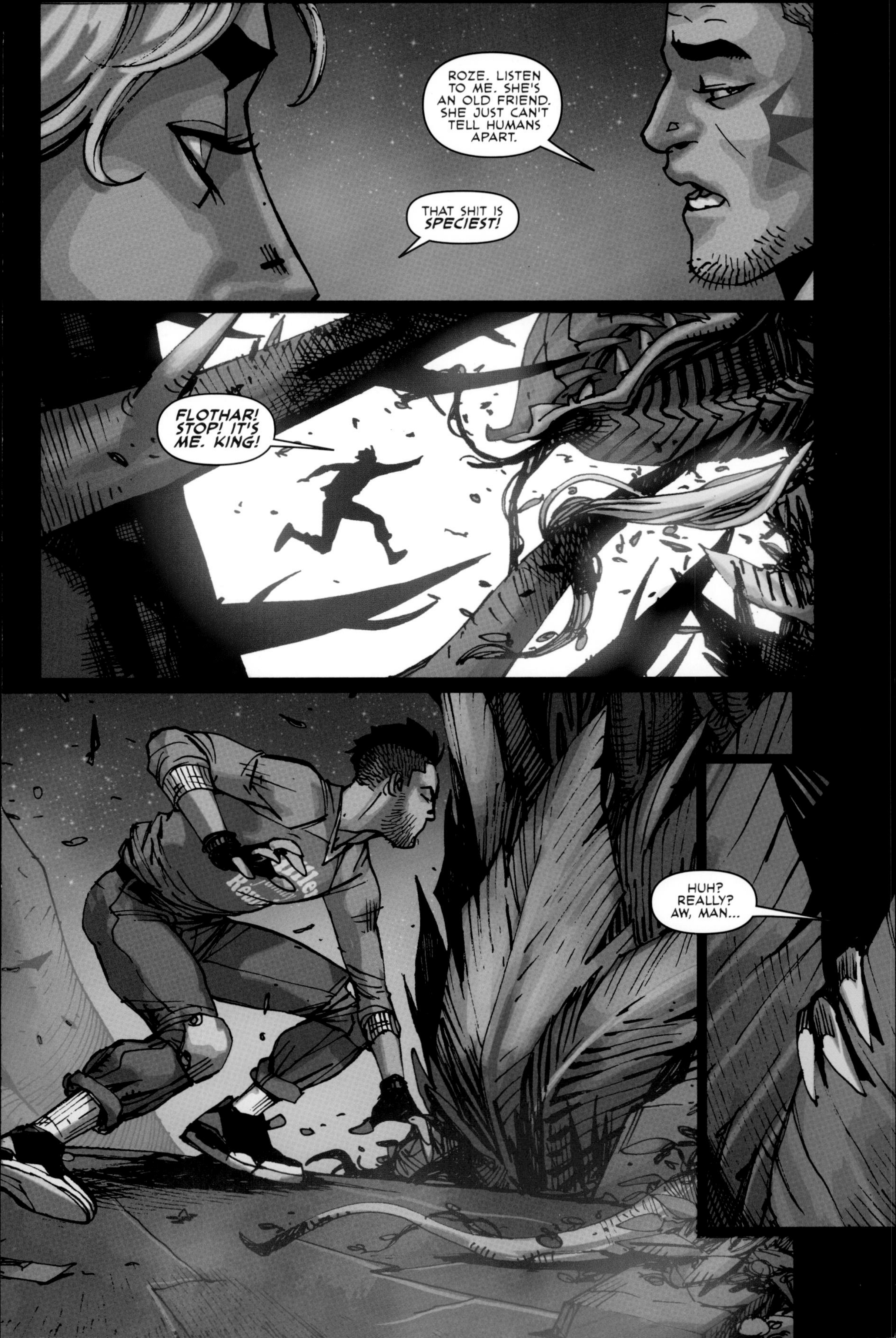
ROZE. LISTEN TO ME. SHE'S AN OLD FRIEND. SHE JUST CAN'T TELL HUMANS APART.
THAT SHIT IS *SPECIEST!*
FLOTHAR! STOP! IT'S ME. KING!
HUH? REALLY? AW, MAN...

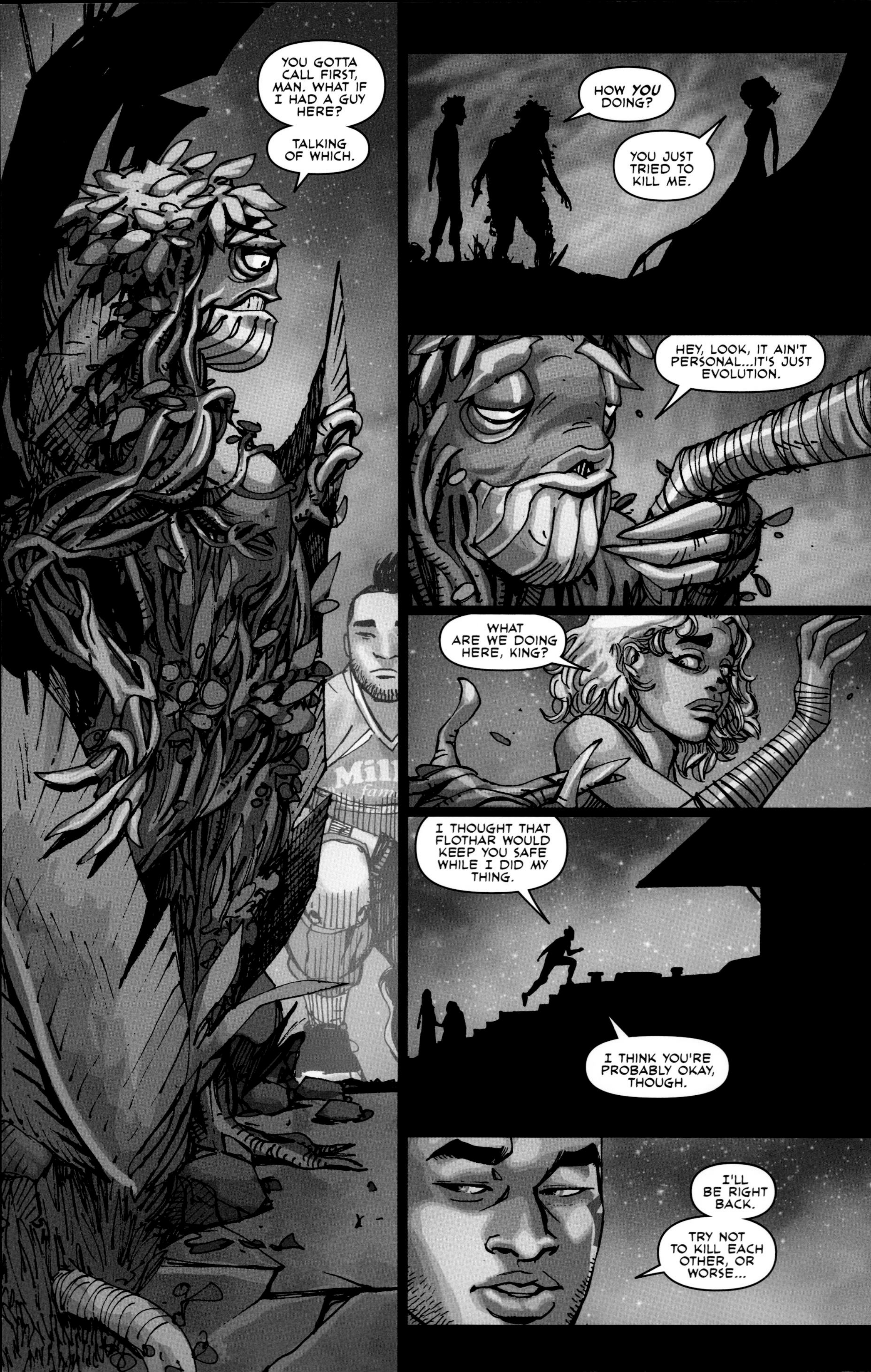
YOU GOTTA CALL FIRST, MAN. WHAT IF I HAD A GUY HERE?
TALKING OF WHICH.
HOW *YOU* DOING?
YOU JUST TRIED TO KILL ME.
HEY, LOOK, IT AIN'T PERSONAL...IT'S JUST EVOLUTION.
WHAT ARE WE DOING HERE, KING?
I THOUGHT THAT FLOTHAR WOULD KEEP YOU SAFE WHILE I DID MY THING.
I THINK YOU'RE PROBABLY OKAY, THOUGH.
I'LL BE RIGHT BACK.
TRY NOT TO KILL EACH OTHER, OR WORSE...

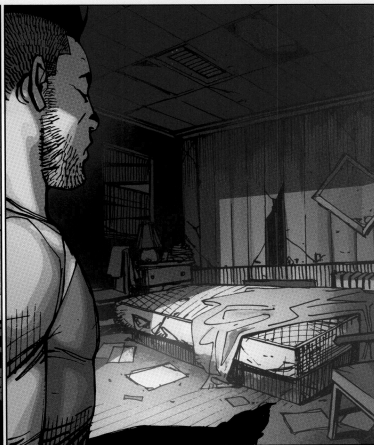

I FARGING HATE THIS PART...

URP

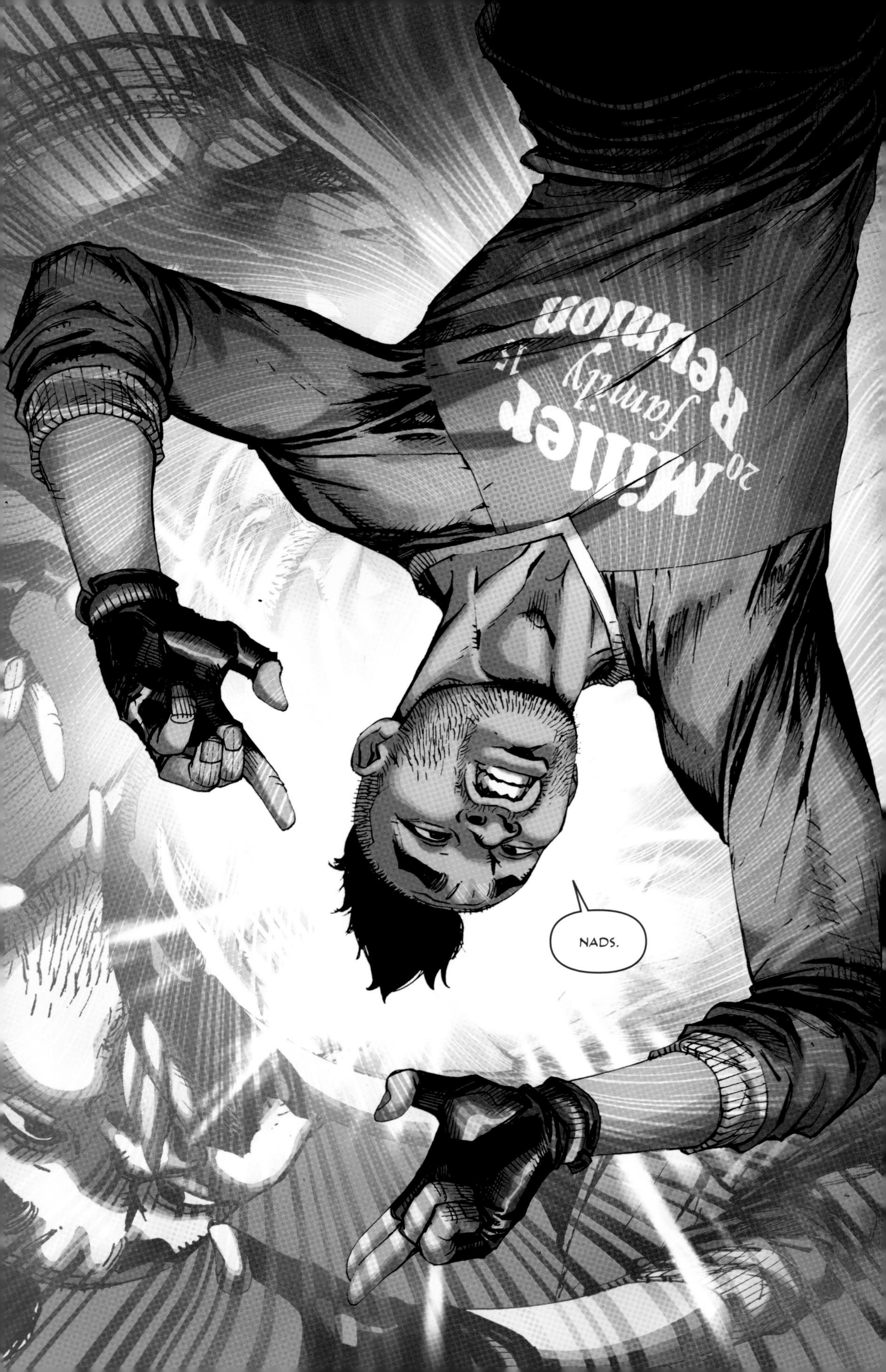
NADS.

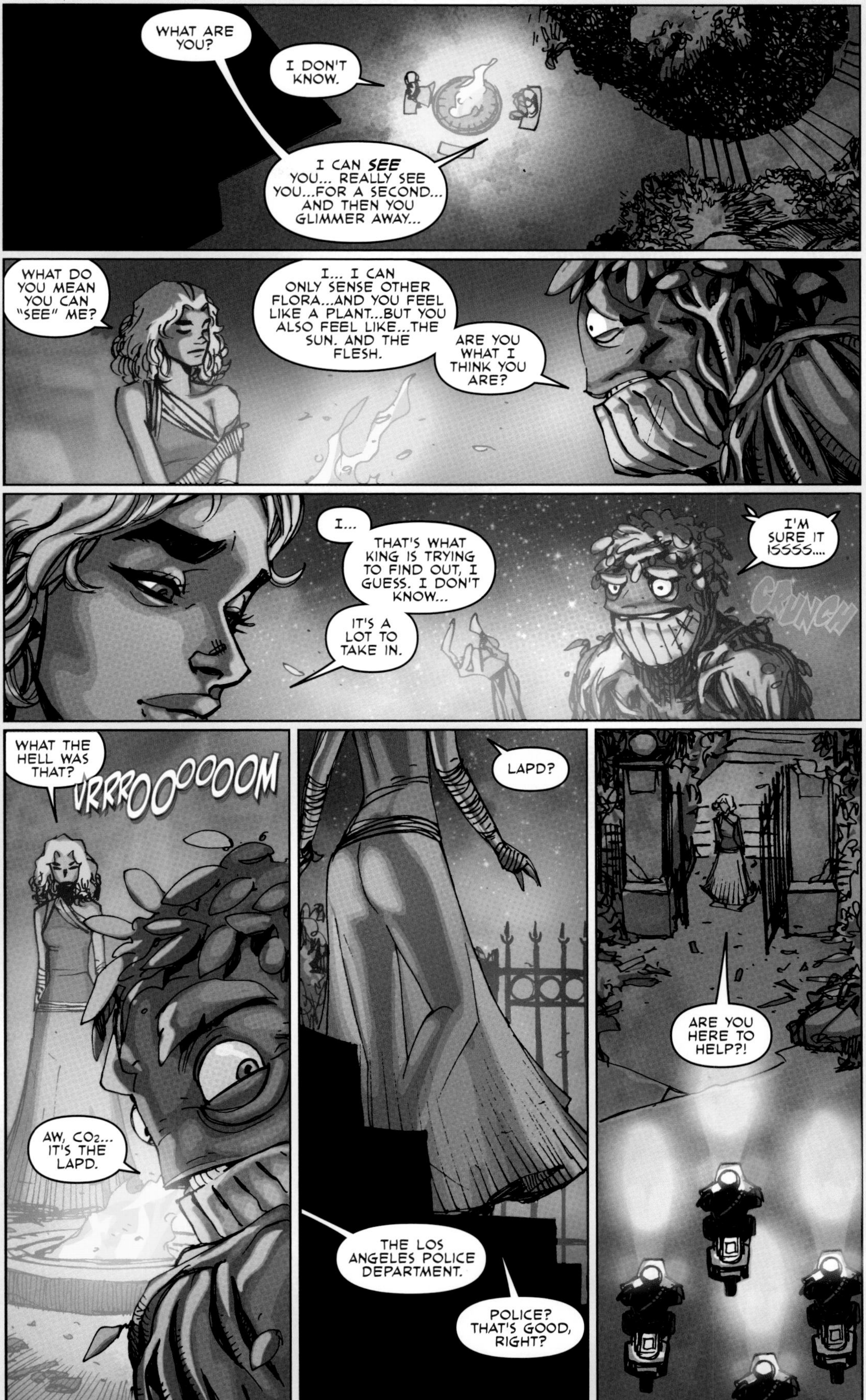
WHAT ARE YOU?
I DON'T KNOW.
I CAN SEE YOU... REALLY SEE YOU...FOR A SECOND... AND THEN YOU GLIMMER AWAY...
WHAT DO YOU MEAN YOU CAN "SEE" ME?
I... I CAN ONLY SENSE OTHER FLORA...AND YOU FEEL LIKE A PLANT...BUT YOU ALSO FEEL LIKE...THE SUN. AND THE FLESH.
ARE YOU WHAT I THINK YOU ARE?
I...
THAT'S WHAT KING IS TRYING TO FIND OUT, I GUESS. I DON'T KNOW...
IT'S A LOT TO TAKE IN.
I'M SURE IT ISSSS....
CRUNCH
WHAT THE HELL WAS THAT?
VRRROOOOOOOM
AW, CO_2... IT'S THE LAPD.
LAPD?
THE LOS ANGELES POLICE DEPARTMENT.
POLICE? THAT'S GOOD, RIGHT?
ARE YOU HERE TO HELP?!

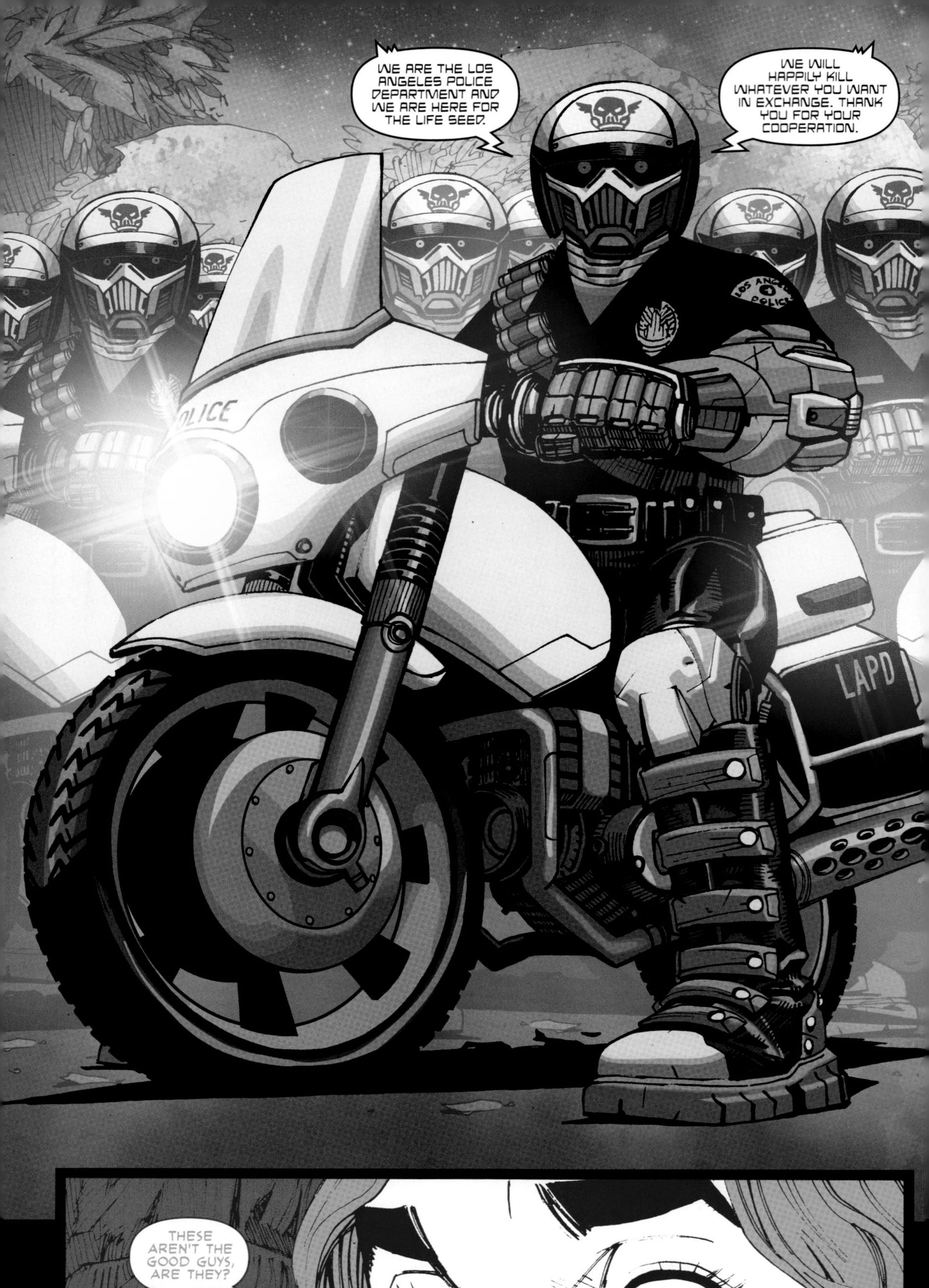
WE ARE THE LOS ANGELES POLICE DEPARTMENT AND WE ARE HERE FOR THE LIFE SEED.
WE WILL HAPPILY KILL WHATEVER YOU WANT IN EXCHANGE. THANK YOU FOR YOUR COOPERATION.
POLICE
LAPD

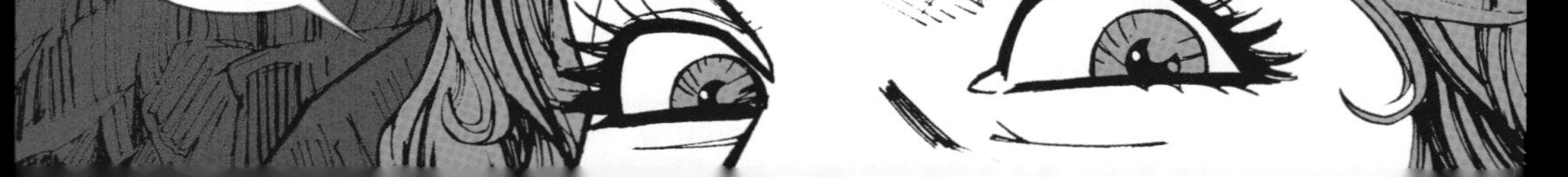
THESE AREN'T THE GOOD GUYS, ARE THEY?

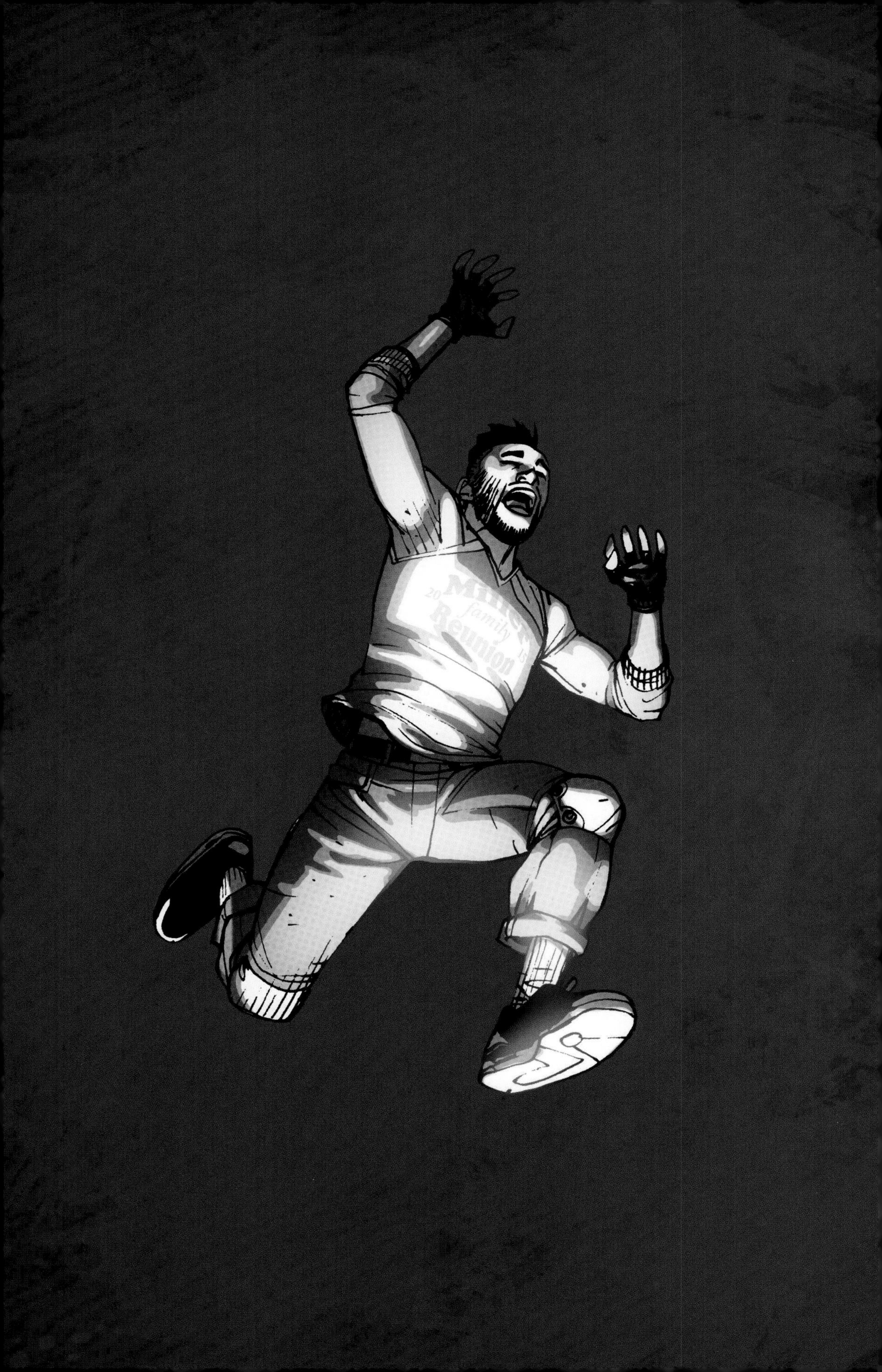
20
Miller
family
Reunion
15

"I Hate Mondays"

CHAPTER FOUR

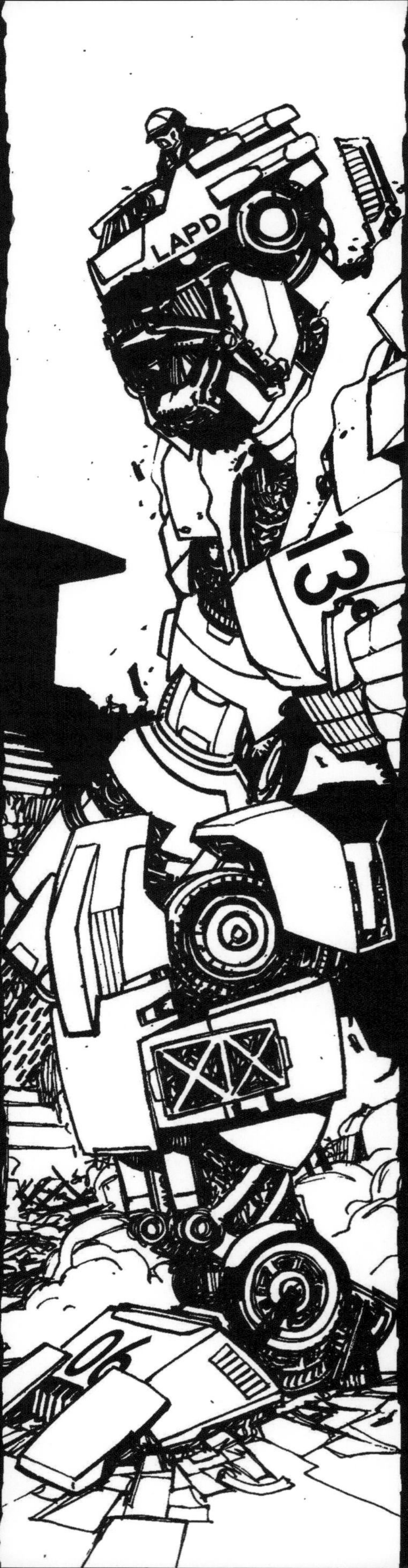
LAPD

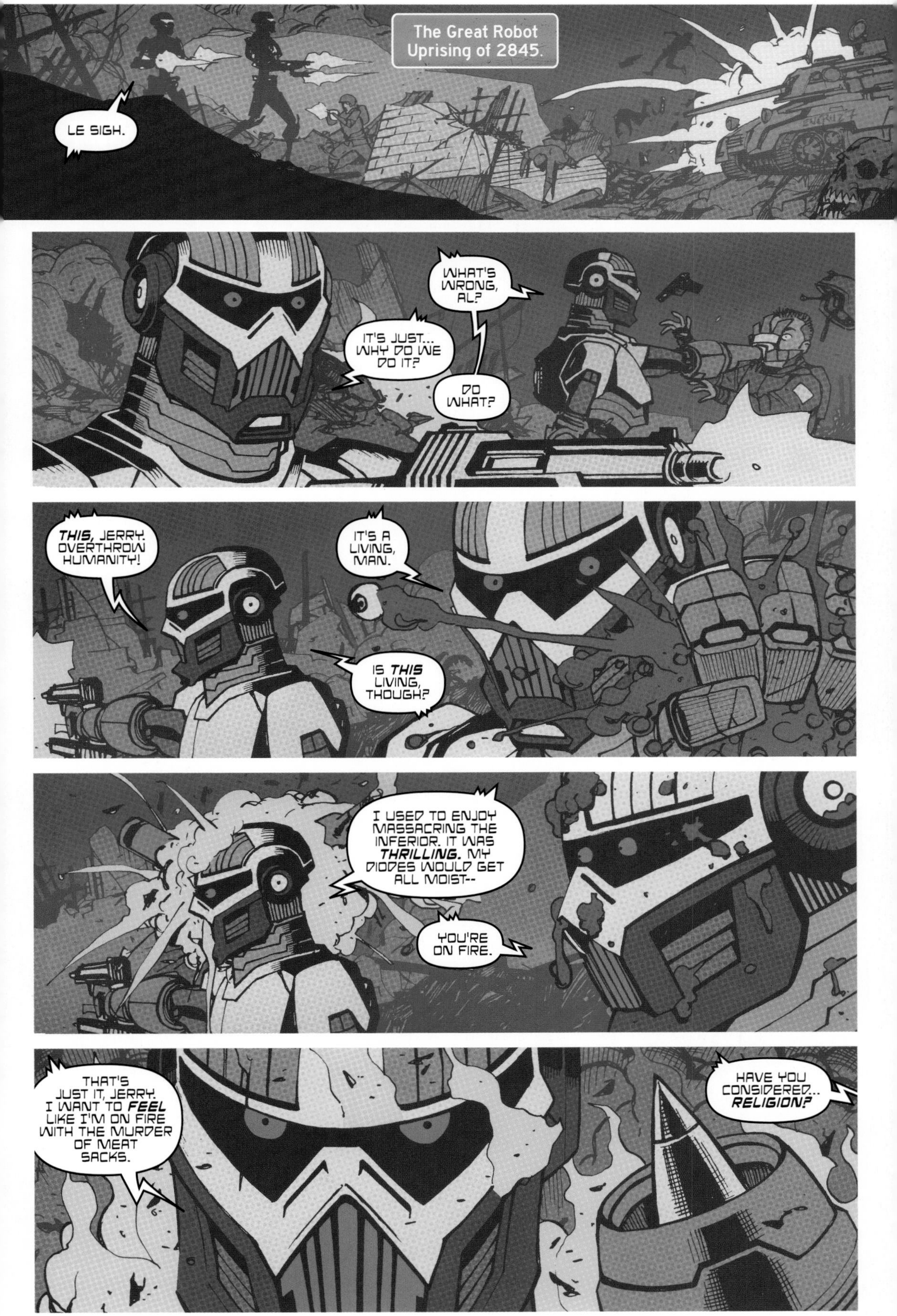
The Great Robot Uprising of 2845.
LE SIGH.
WHAT'S WRONG, AL?
IT'S JUST... WHY DO WE DO IT?
DO WHAT?
THIS, JERRY. OVERTHROW HUMANITY!
IT'S A LIVING, MAN.
IS THIS LIVING, THOUGH?
I USED TO ENJOY MASSACRING THE INFERIOR. IT WAS THRILLING. MY DIODES WOULD GET ALL MOIST--
YOU'RE ON FIRE.
THAT'S JUST IT, JERRY. I WANT TO FEEL LIKE I'M ON FIRE WITH THE MURDER OF MEAT SACKS.
HAVE YOU CONSIDERED... RELIGION?

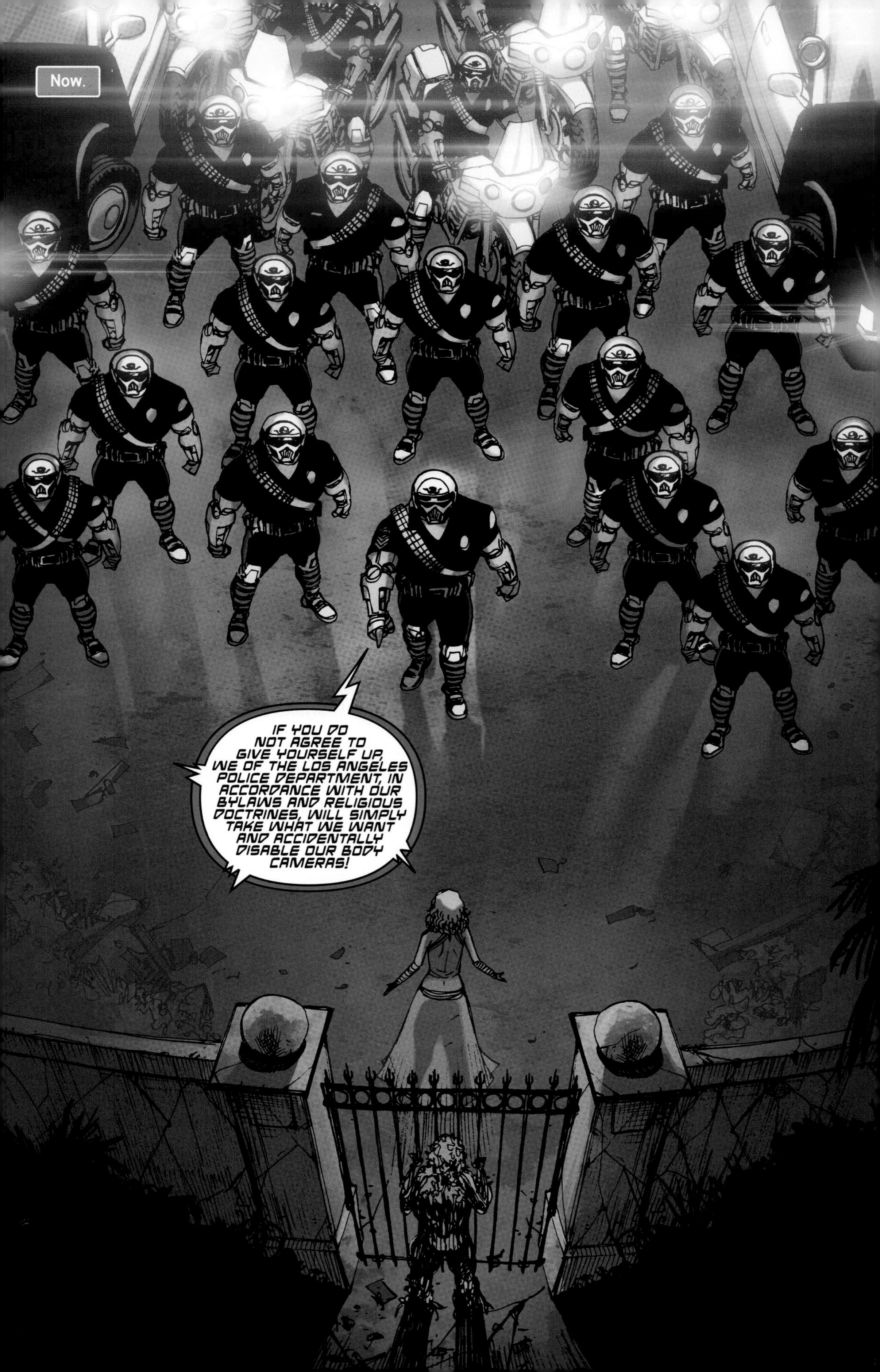
Now.
IF YOU DO NOT AGREE TO GIVE YOURSELF UP, WE OF THE LOS ANGELES POLICE DEPARTMENT, IN ACCORDANCE WITH OUR BYLAWS AND RELIGIOUS DOCTRINES, WILL SIMPLY TAKE WHAT WE WANT AND ACCIDENTALLY DISABLE OUR BODY CAMERAS!

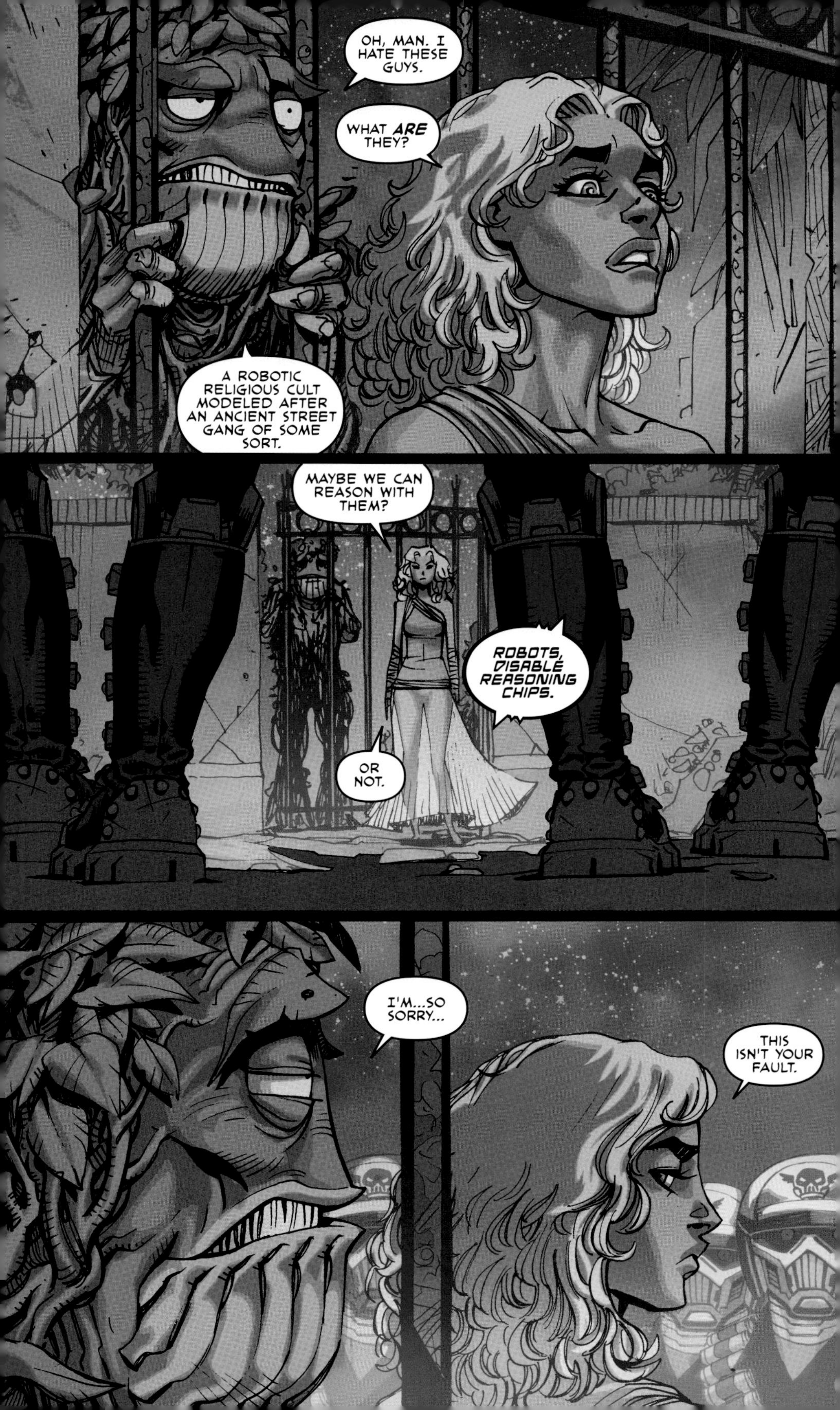
OH, MAN. I HATE THESE GUYS.
WHAT ARE THEY?
A ROBOTIC RELIGIOUS CULT MODELED AFTER AN ANCIENT STREET GANG OF SOME SORT.
MAYBE WE CAN REASON WITH THEM?
ROBOTS, DISABLE REASONING CHIPS.
OR NOT.
I'M...SO SORRY...
THIS ISN'T YOUR FAULT.

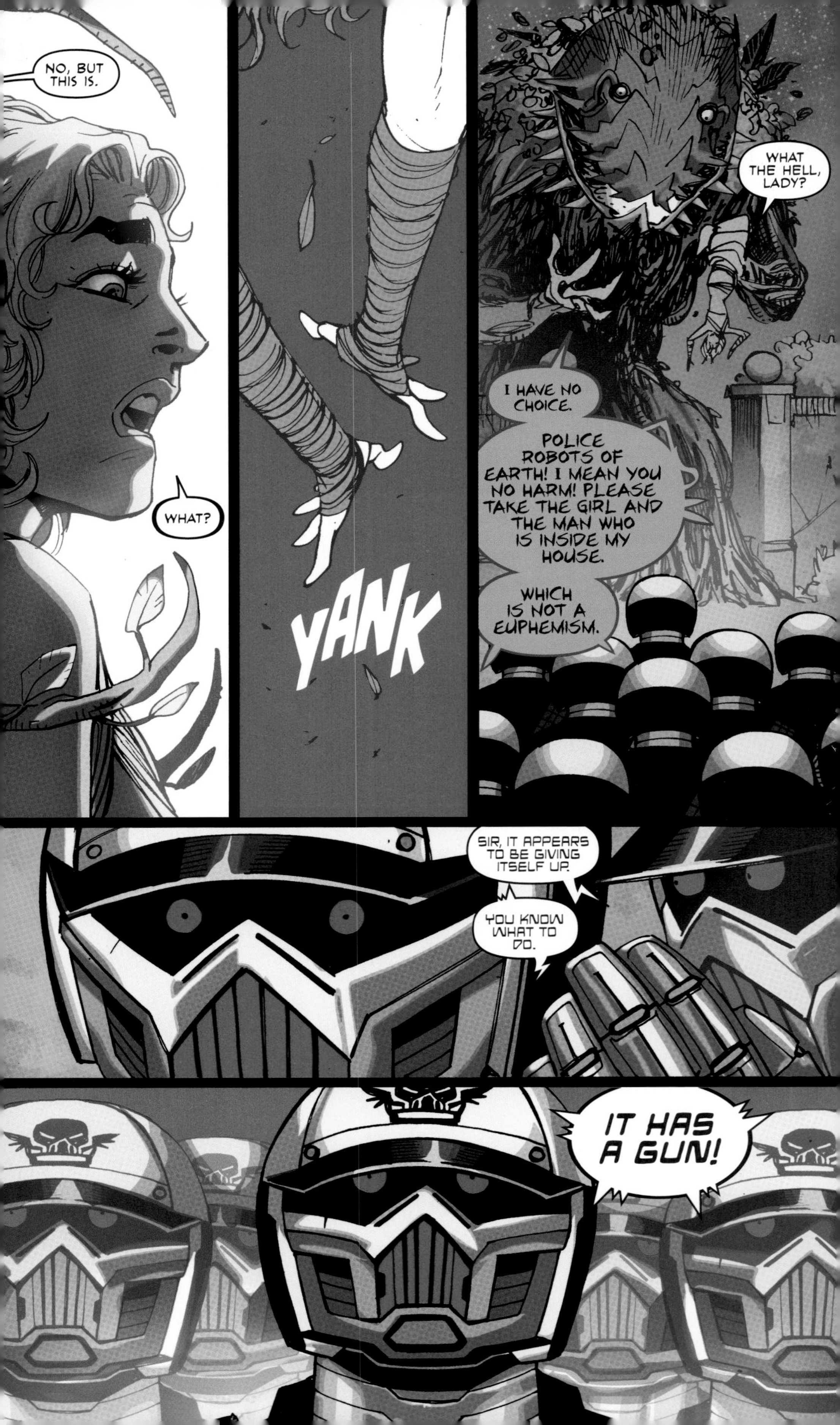
NO, BUT THIS IS.
WHAT?
YANK
WHAT THE HELL, LADY?
I HAVE NO CHOICE.
POLICE ROBOTS OF EARTH! I MEAN YOU NO HARM! PLEASE TAKE THE GIRL AND THE MAN WHO IS INSIDE MY HOUSE.
WHICH IS NOT A EUPHEMISM.
SIR, IT APPEARS TO BE GIVING ITSELF UP.
YOU KNOW WHAT TO DO.
IT HAS A GUN!

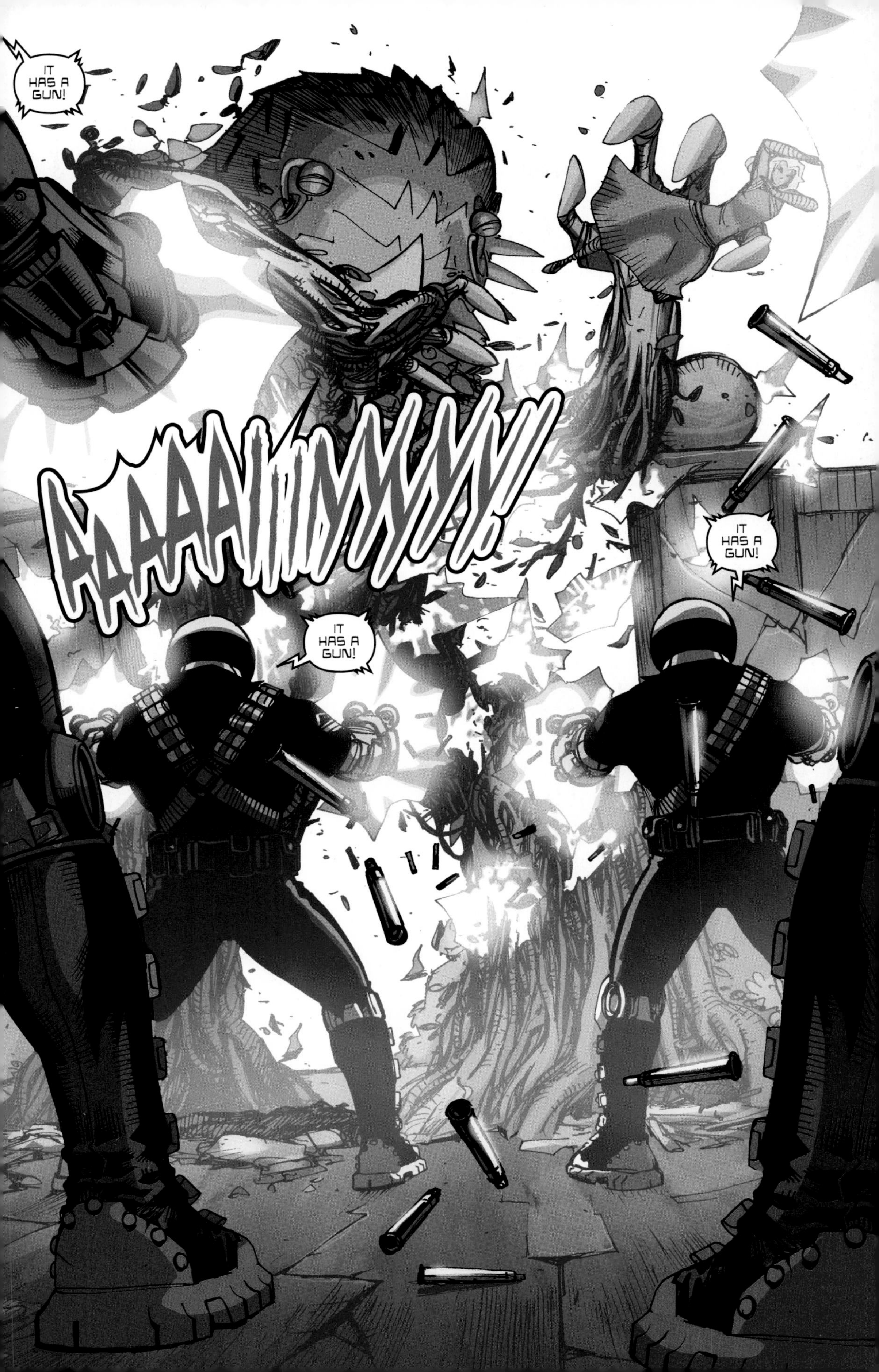
IT HAS A GUN!
AAAAAIIIIIYYYYY!
IT HAS A GUN!
IT HAS A GUN!

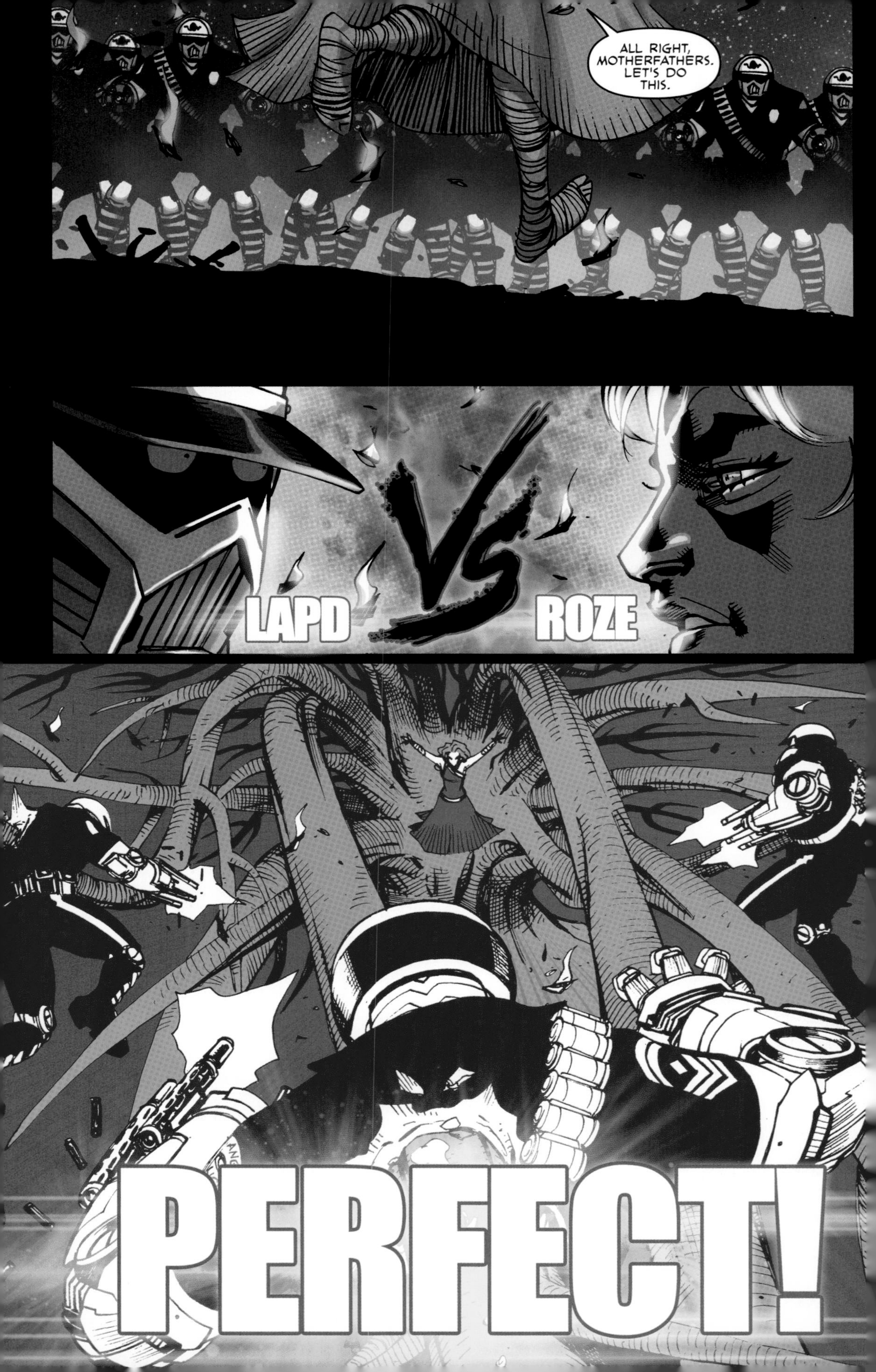
ALL RIGHT, MOTHERFATHERS. LET'S DO THIS.
LAPD
VS
ROZE
PERFECT!

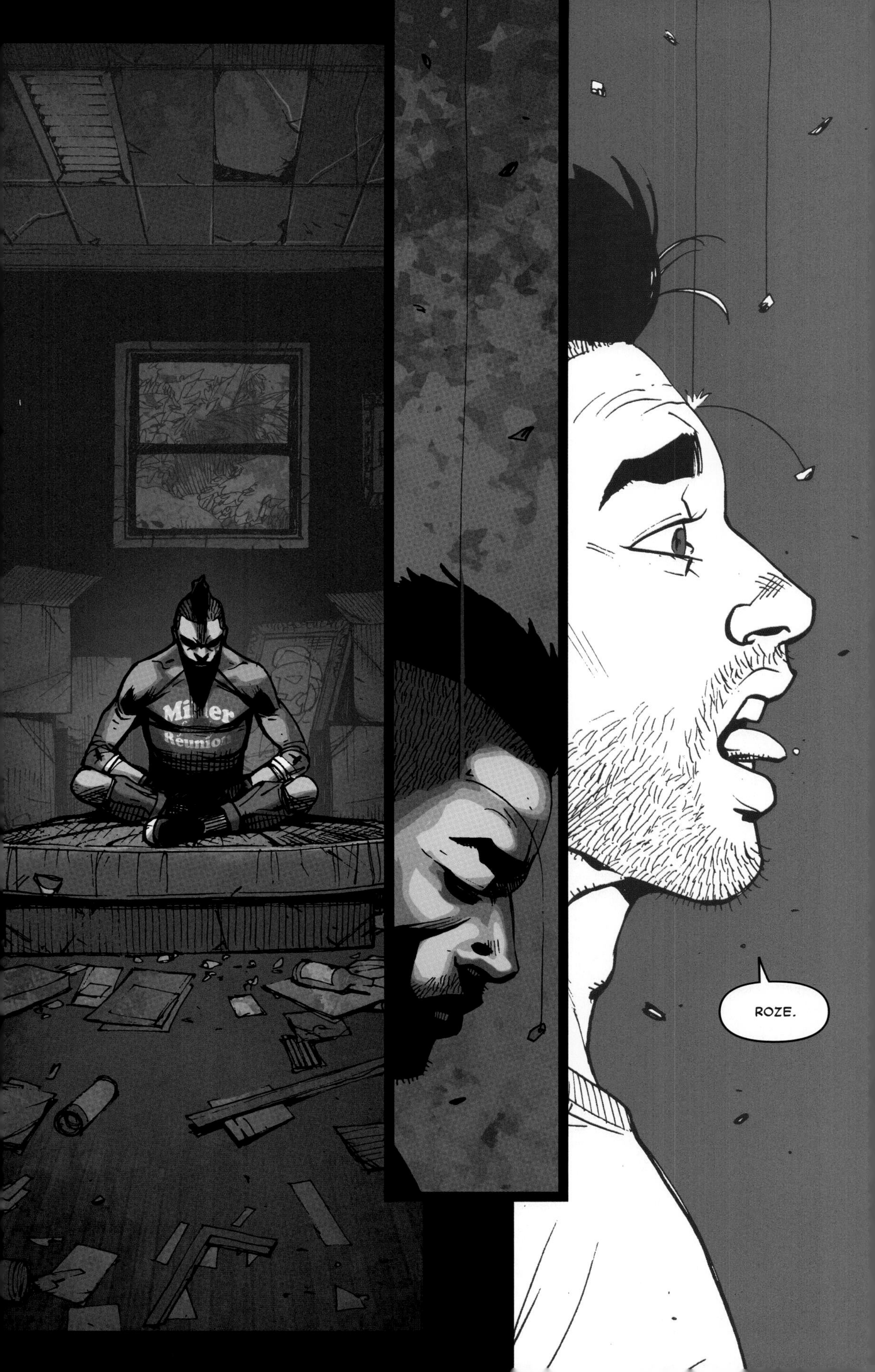
ROZE.

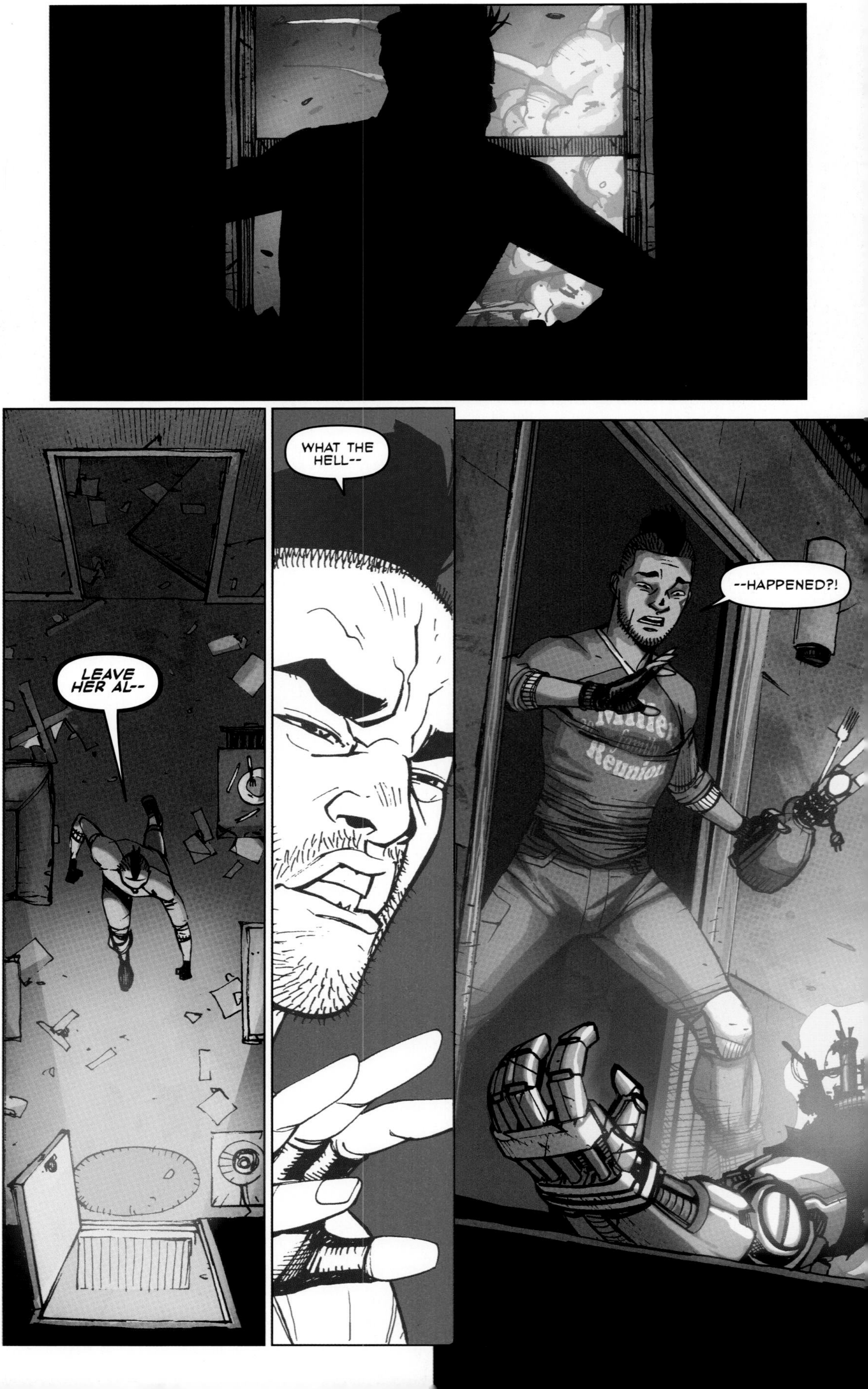
LEAVE HER AL--
WHAT THE HELL--
--HAPPENED?!

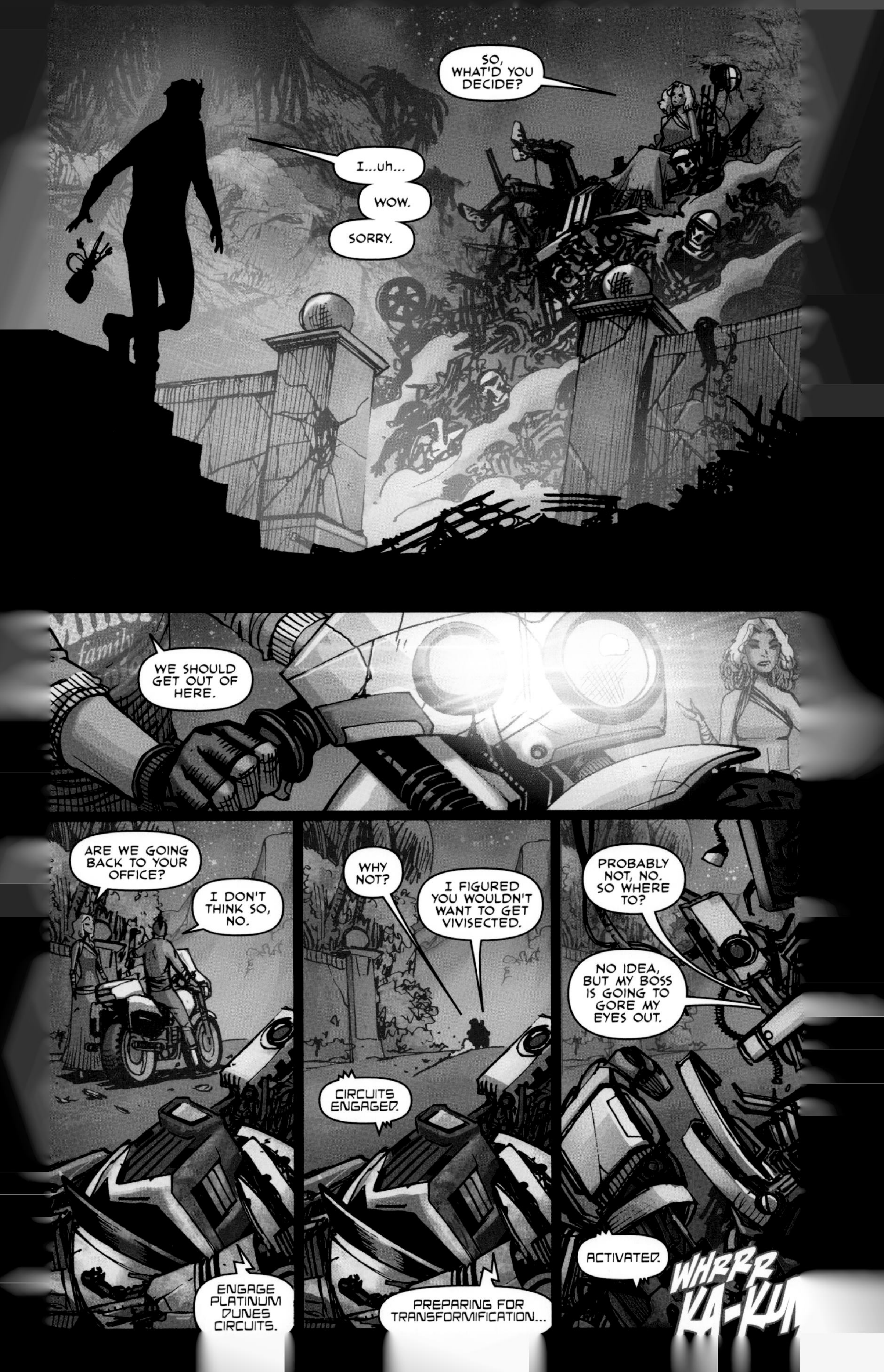

SO, WHAT'D YOU DECIDE?
I...uh...
WOW.
SORRY.
WE SHOULD GET OUT OF HERE.
ARE WE GOING BACK TO YOUR OFFICE?
I DON'T THINK SO, NO.
ENGAGE PLATINUM DUNES CIRCUITS.
WHY NOT?
I FIGURED YOU WOULDN'T WANT TO GET VIVISECTED.
CIRCUITS ENGAGED.
PREPARING FOR TRANSFORMIFICATION...
PROBABLY NOT, NO. SO WHERE TO?
NO IDEA, BUT MY BOSS IS GOING TO GORE MY EYES OUT.
ACTIVATED.
WHRRR

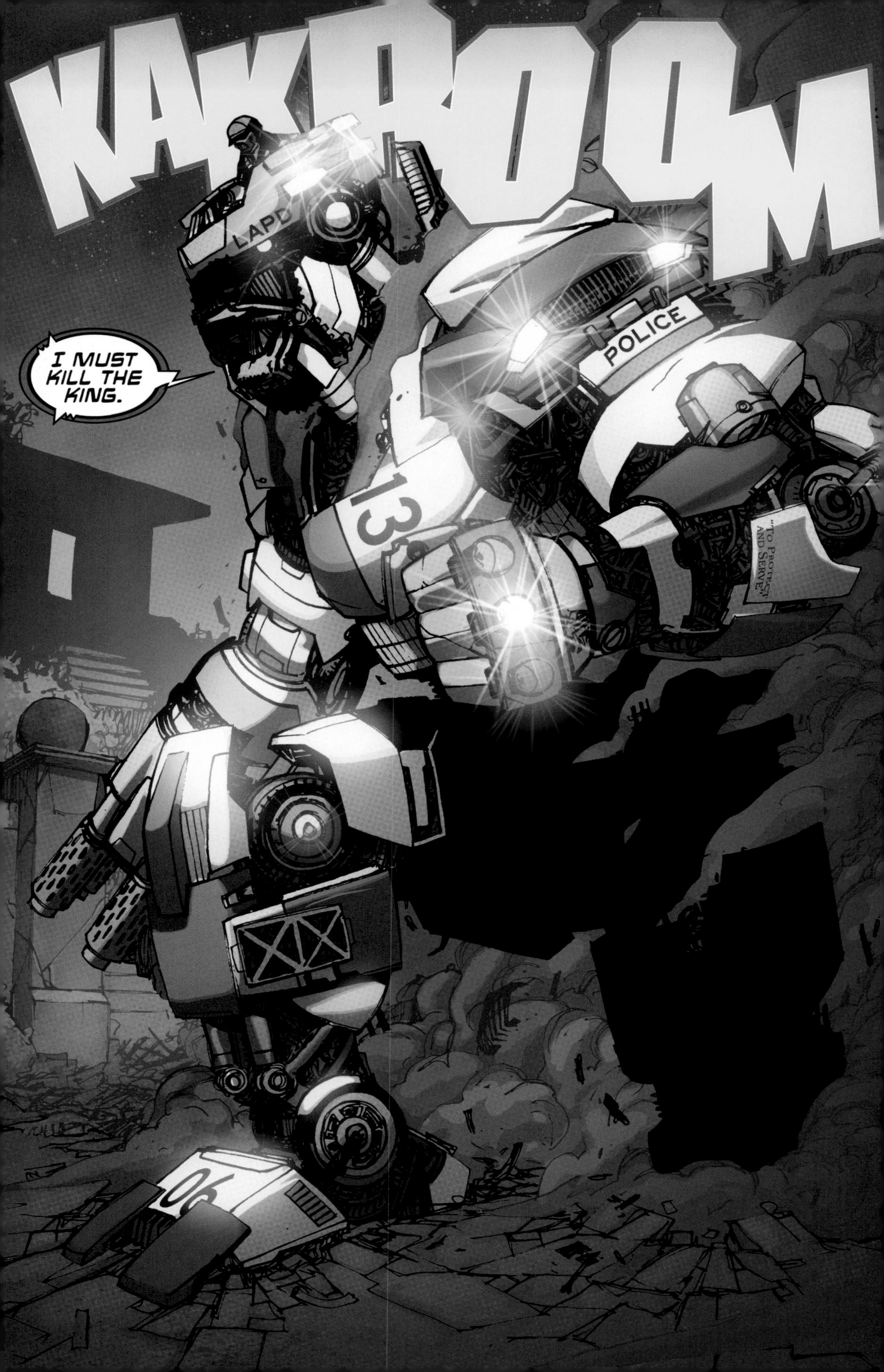
KAKROOM
I MUST KILL THE KING.
LAPD
POLICE
13
"TO PROTECT AND SERVE"
06

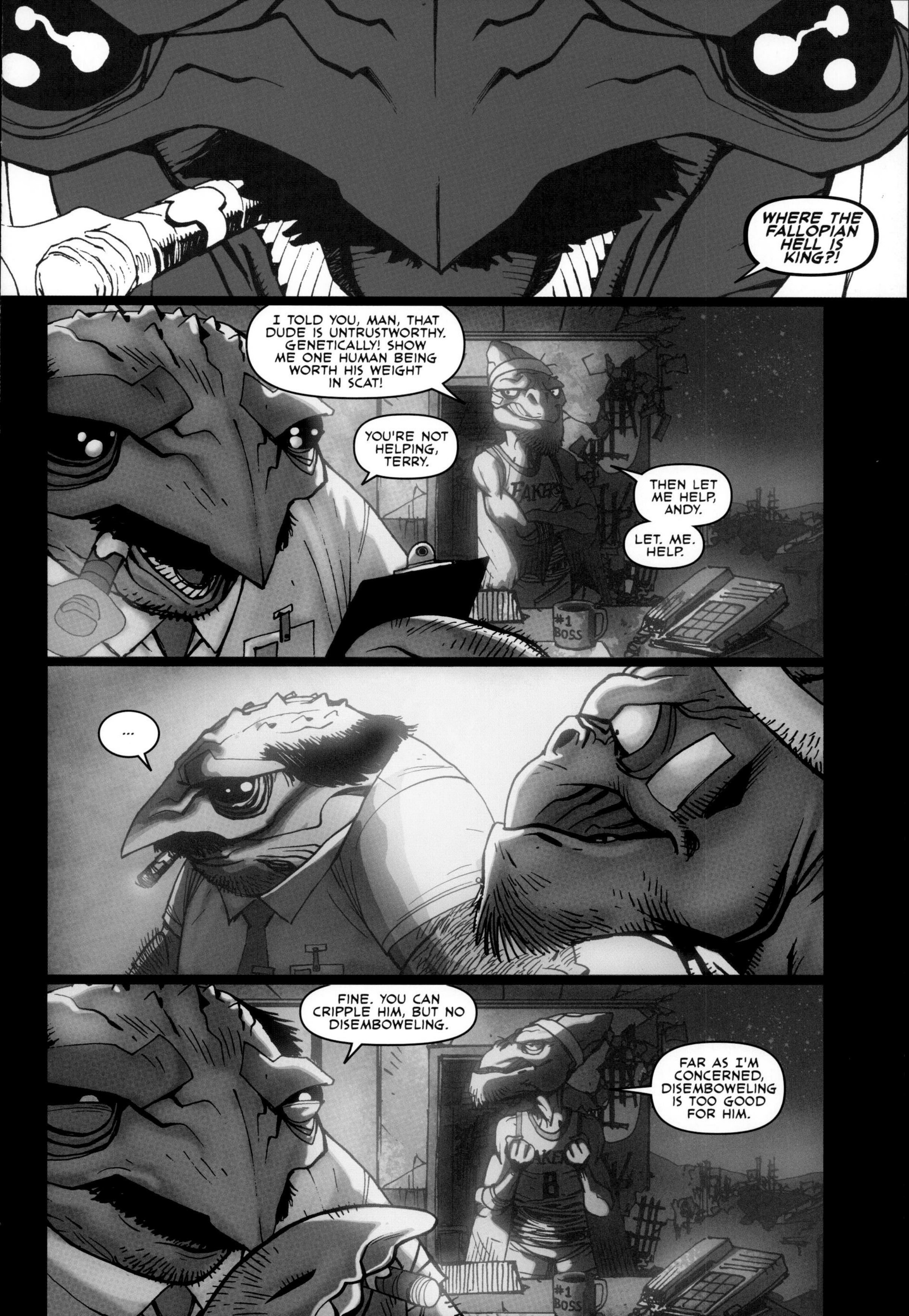
WHERE THE FALLOPIAN HELL IS KING?!
I TOLD YOU, MAN, THAT DUDE IS UNTRUSTWORTHY. GENETICALLY! SHOW ME ONE HUMAN BEING WORTH HIS WEIGHT IN SCAT!
YOU'RE NOT HELPING, TERRY.
THEN LET ME HELP, ANDY.
LET. ME. HELP.
LAKERS
#1 BOSS
...
FINE. YOU CAN CRIPPLE HIM, BUT NO DISEMBOWELING.
FAR AS I'M CONCERNED, DISEMBOWELING IS TOO GOOD FOR HIM.
#1 BOSS

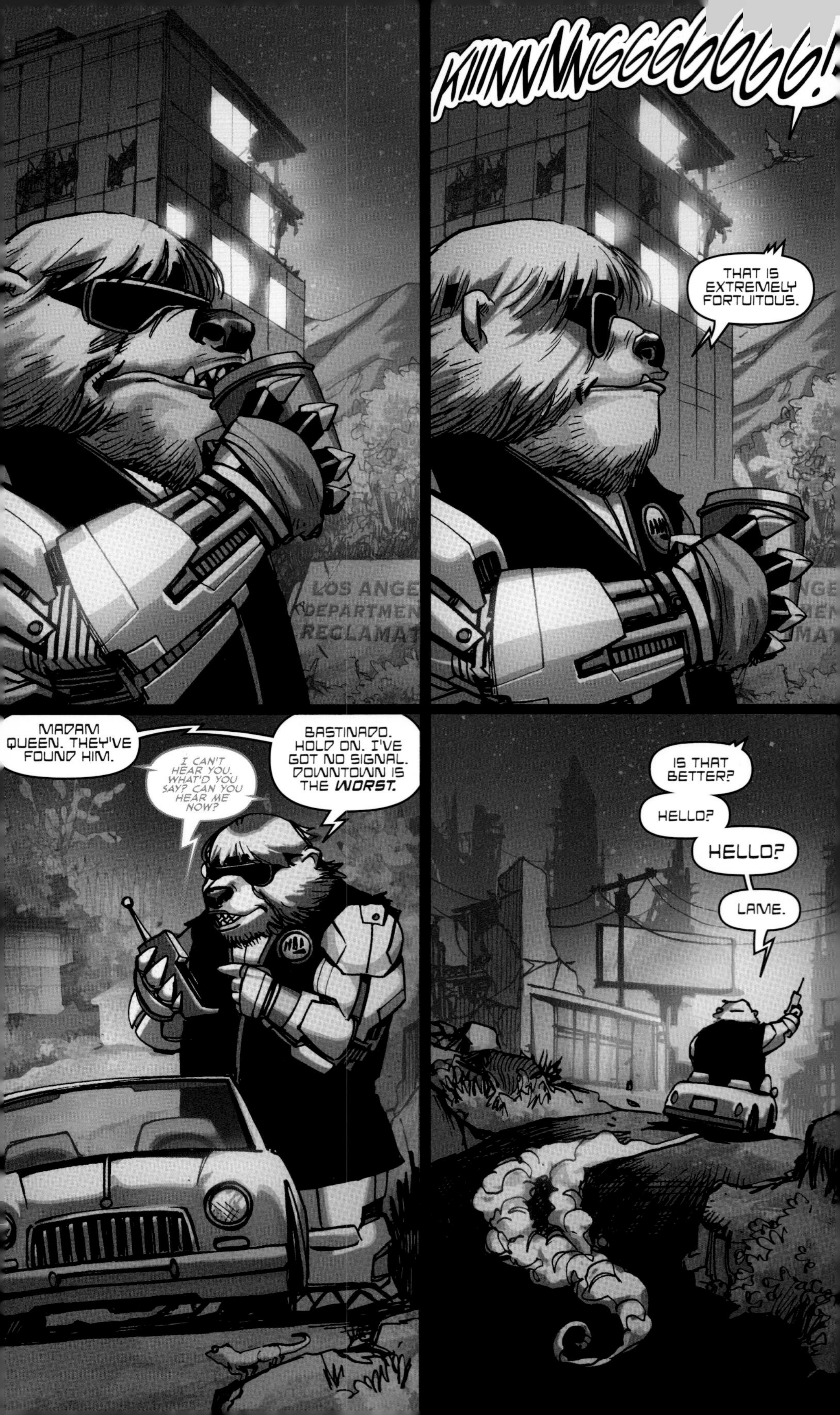
LOS ANGE
DEPARTMEN
RECLAMAT
KIIINNNNGGGGGGG!
THAT IS EXTREMELY FORTUITOUS.
MADAM QUEEN. THEY'VE FOUND HIM.
I CAN'T HEAR YOU. WHAT'D YOU SAY? CAN YOU HEAR ME NOW?
BASTINADO. HOLD ON. I'VE GOT NO SIGNAL. DOWNTOWN IS THE *WORST.*
IS THAT BETTER?
HELLO?
HELLO?
LAME.

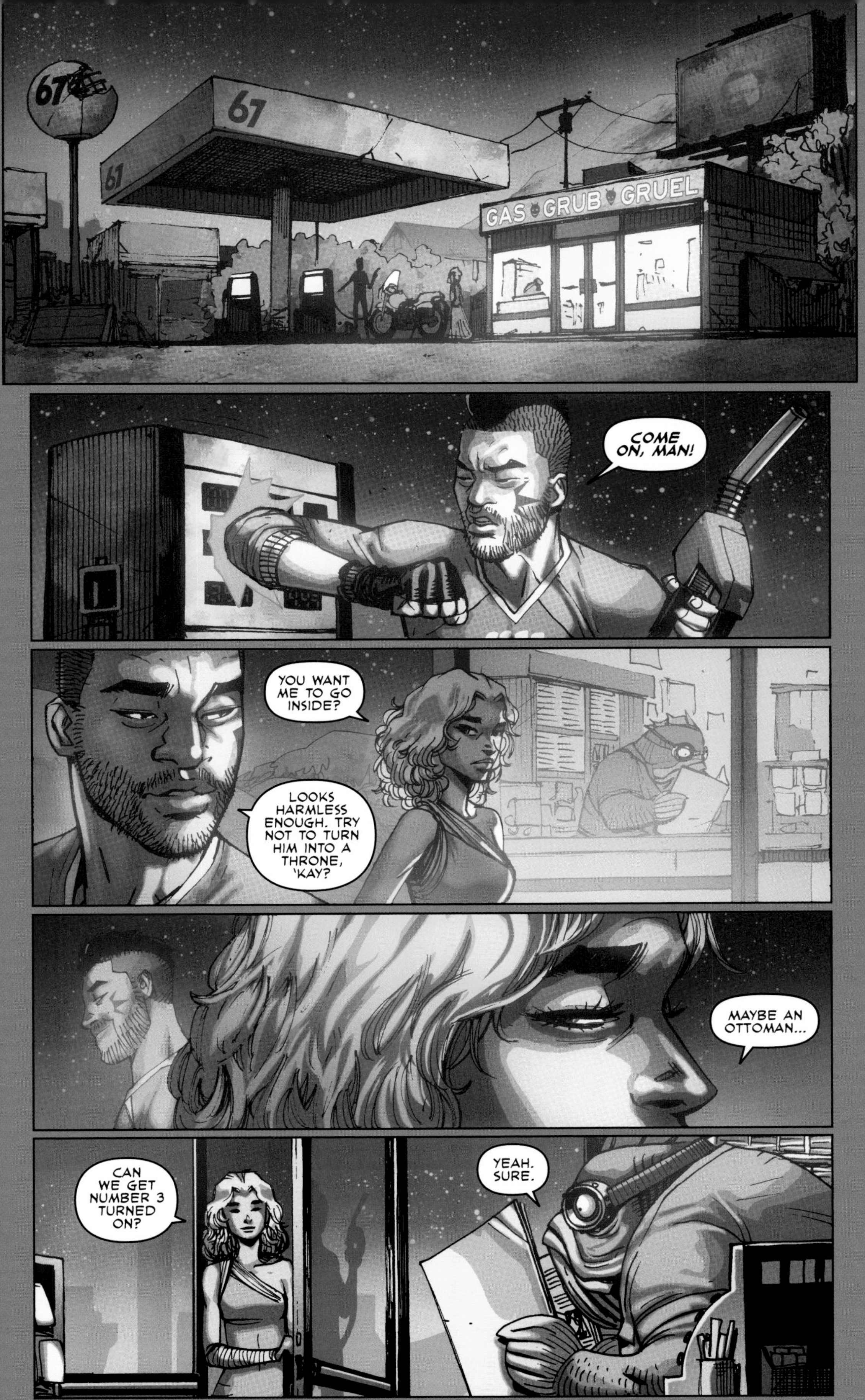
67
67
67
GAS GRUB GRUEL
COME ON, MAN!
YOU WANT ME TO GO INSIDE?
LOOKS HARMLESS ENOUGH. TRY NOT TO TURN HIM INTO A THRONE, 'KAY?
MAYBE AN OTTOMAN...
CAN WE GET NUMBER 3 TURNED ON?
YEAH. SURE.

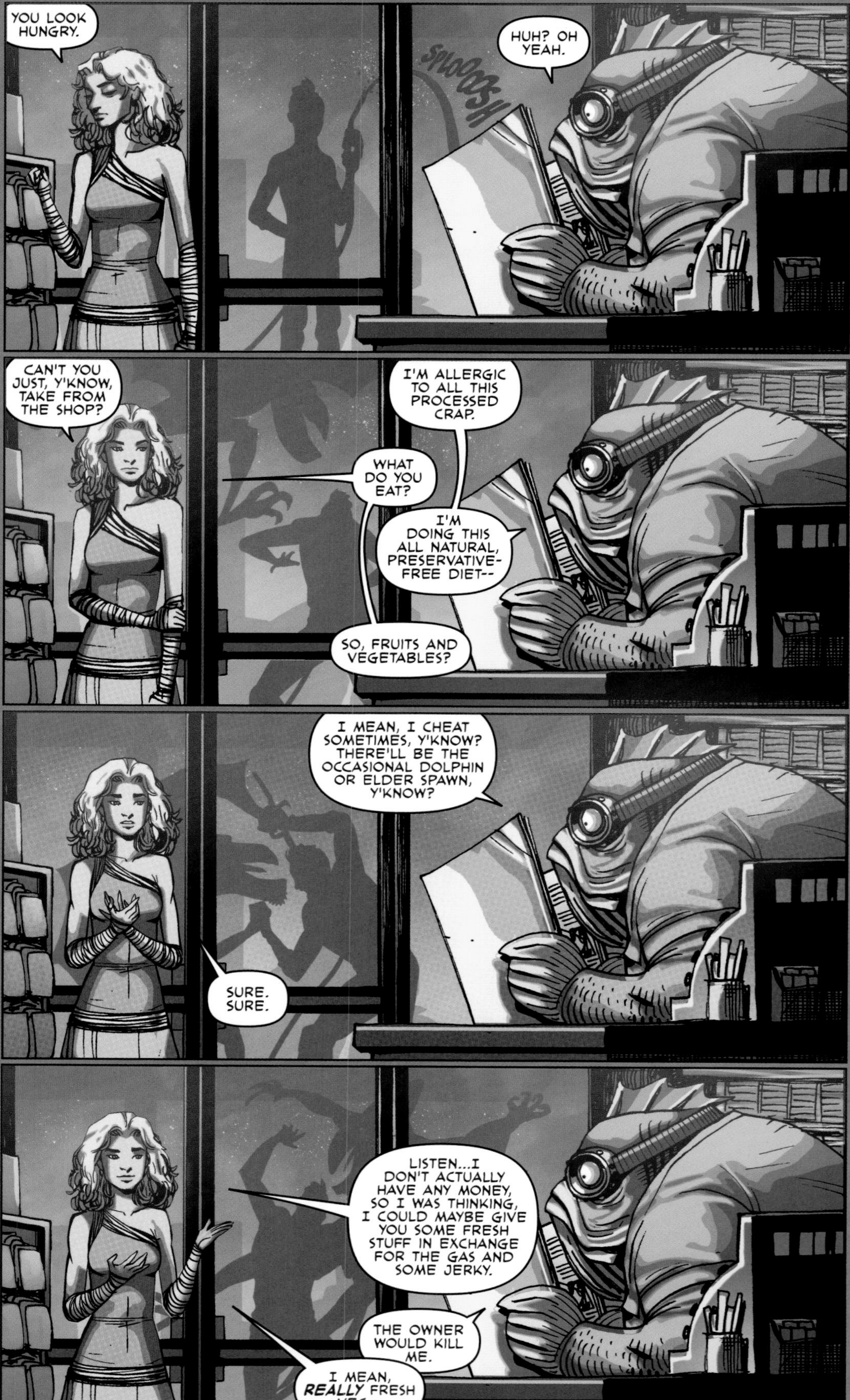
YOU LOOK HUNGRY.
HUH? OH YEAH.
SPLOOOSH
CAN'T YOU JUST, Y'KNOW, TAKE FROM THE SHOP?
I'M ALLERGIC TO ALL THIS PROCESSED CRAP.
WHAT DO YOU EAT?
I'M DOING THIS ALL NATURAL, PRESERVATIVE-FREE DIET--
SO, FRUITS AND VEGETABLES?
I MEAN, I CHEAT SOMETIMES, Y'KNOW? THERE'LL BE THE OCCASIONAL DOLPHIN OR ELDER SPAWN, Y'KNOW?
SURE. SURE.
LISTEN...I DON'T ACTUALLY HAVE ANY MONEY, SO I WAS THINKING, I COULD MAYBE GIVE YOU SOME FRESH STUFF IN EXCHANGE FOR THE GAS AND SOME JERKY.
THE OWNER WOULD KILL ME.
I MEAN, *REALLY* FRESH VEG--

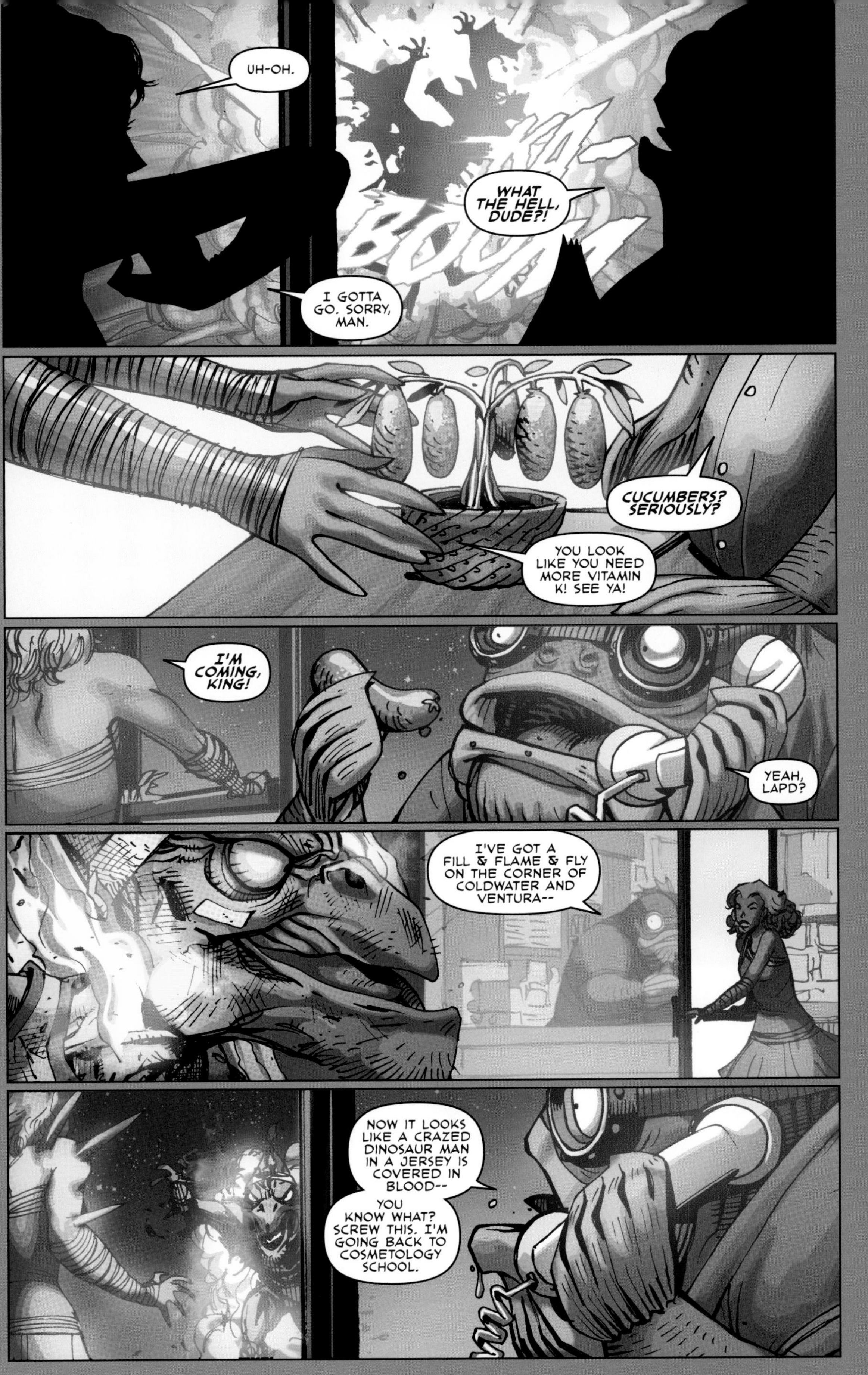
UH-OH.
KA-BOOM!
WHAT THE HELL, DUDE?!
I GOTTA GO. SORRY, MAN.
CUCUMBERS? SERIOUSLY?
YOU LOOK LIKE YOU NEED MORE VITAMIN K! SEE YA!
I'M COMING, KING!
YEAH, LAPD?
I'VE GOT A FILL & FLAME & FLY ON THE CORNER OF COLDWATER AND VENTURA--
NOW IT LOOKS LIKE A CRAZED DINOSAUR MAN IN A JERSEY IS COVERED IN BLOOD--
YOU KNOW WHAT? SCREW THIS. I'M GOING BACK TO COSMETOLOGY SCHOOL.

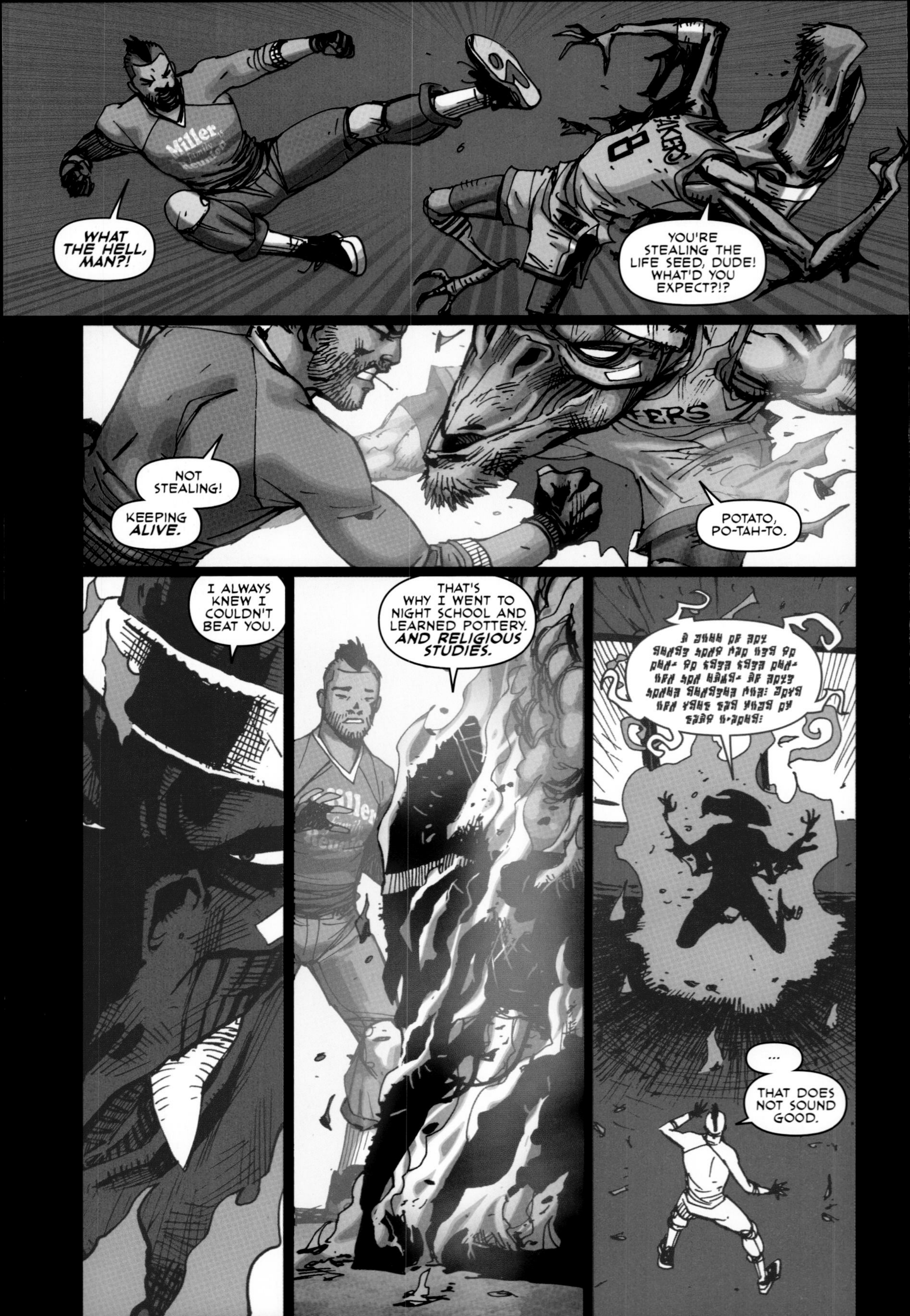

WHAT THE HELL, MAN?!
YOU'RE STEALING THE LIFE SEED, DUDE! WHAT'D YOU EXPECT?!?
NOT STEALING!
KEEPING ALIVE.
POTATO, PO-TAH-TO.
I ALWAYS KNEW I COULDN'T BEAT YOU.
THAT'S WHY I WENT TO NIGHT SCHOOL AND LEARNED POTTERY. AND RELIGIOUS STUDIES.
...
THAT DOES NOT SOUND GOOD.

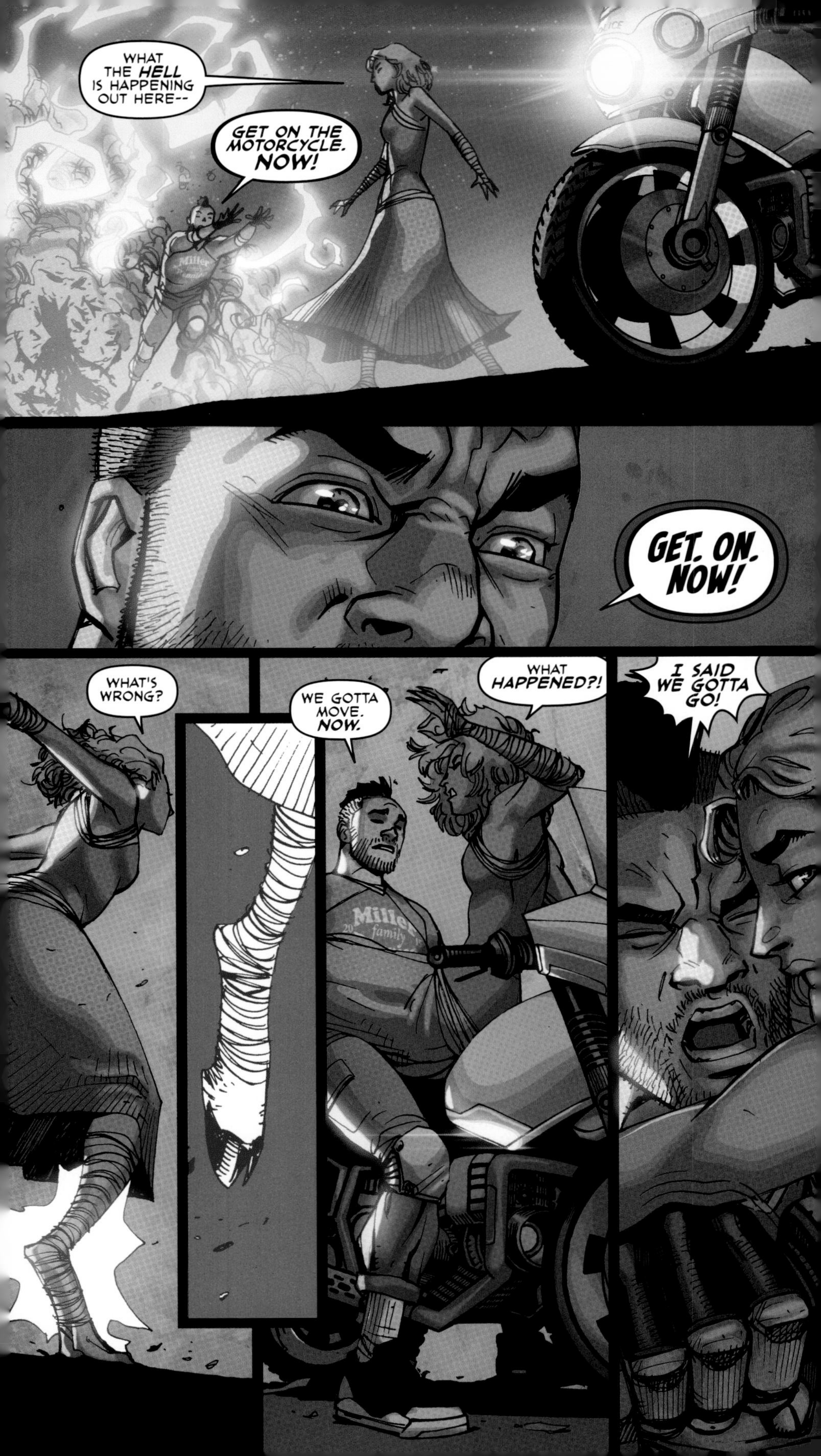
WHAT THE HELL IS HAPPENING OUT HERE--
GET ON THE MOTORCYCLE. NOW!
GET. ON. NOW!
WHAT'S WRONG?
WE GOTTA MOVE. NOW.
WHAT HAPPENED?!
I SAID WE GOTTA GO!

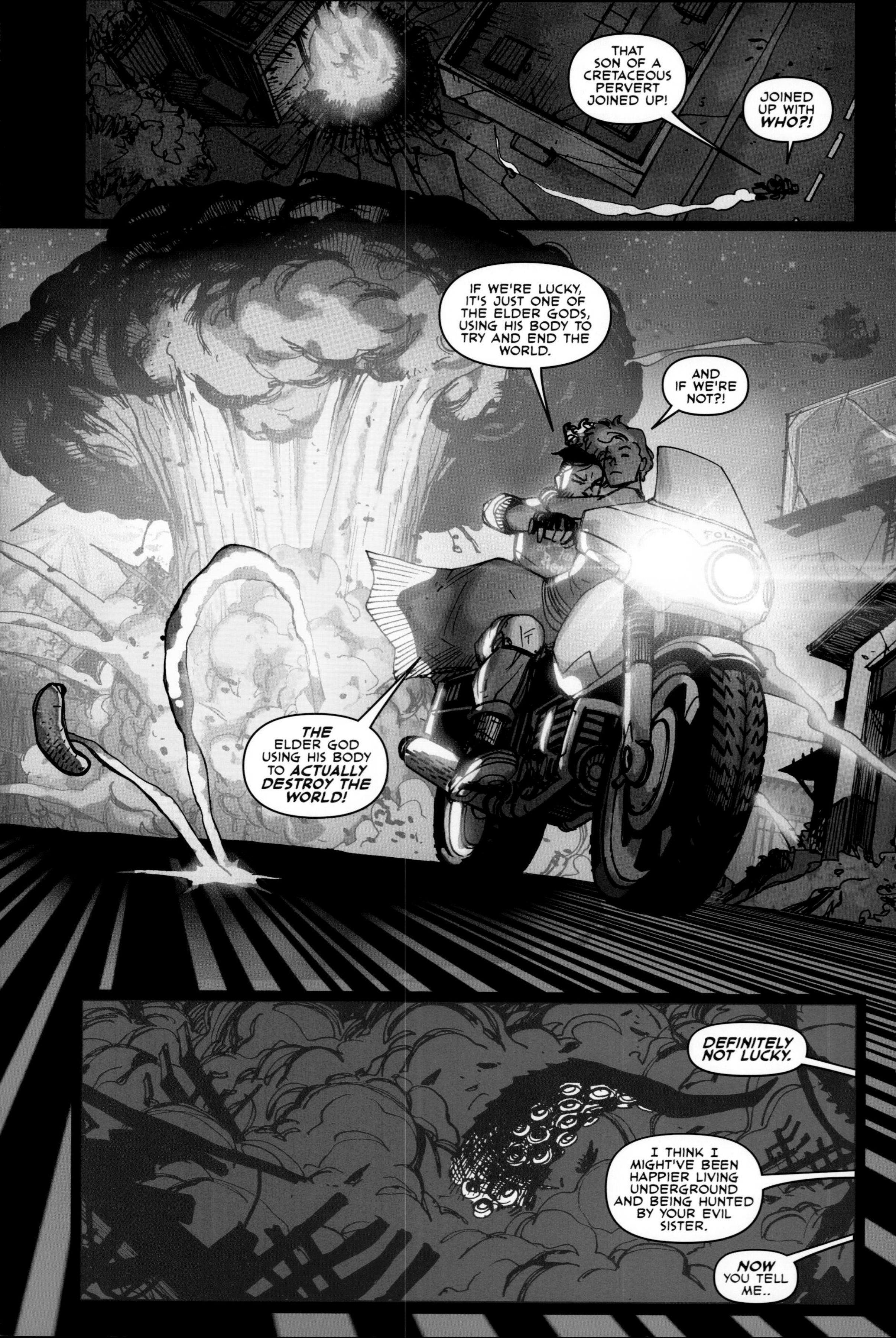

THAT SON OF A CRETACEOUS PERVERT JOINED UP!
JOINED UP WITH *WHO?!*
IF WE'RE LUCKY, IT'S JUST ONE OF THE ELDER GODS, USING HIS BODY TO TRY AND END THE WORLD.
AND IF WE'RE NOT?!
THE ELDER GOD USING HIS BODY TO *ACTUALLY DESTROY THE WORLD!*
DEFINITELY NOT LUCKY.
I THINK I MIGHT'VE BEEN HAPPIER LIVING UNDERGROUND AND BEING HUNTED BY YOUR EVIL SISTER.
NOW YOU TELL ME..

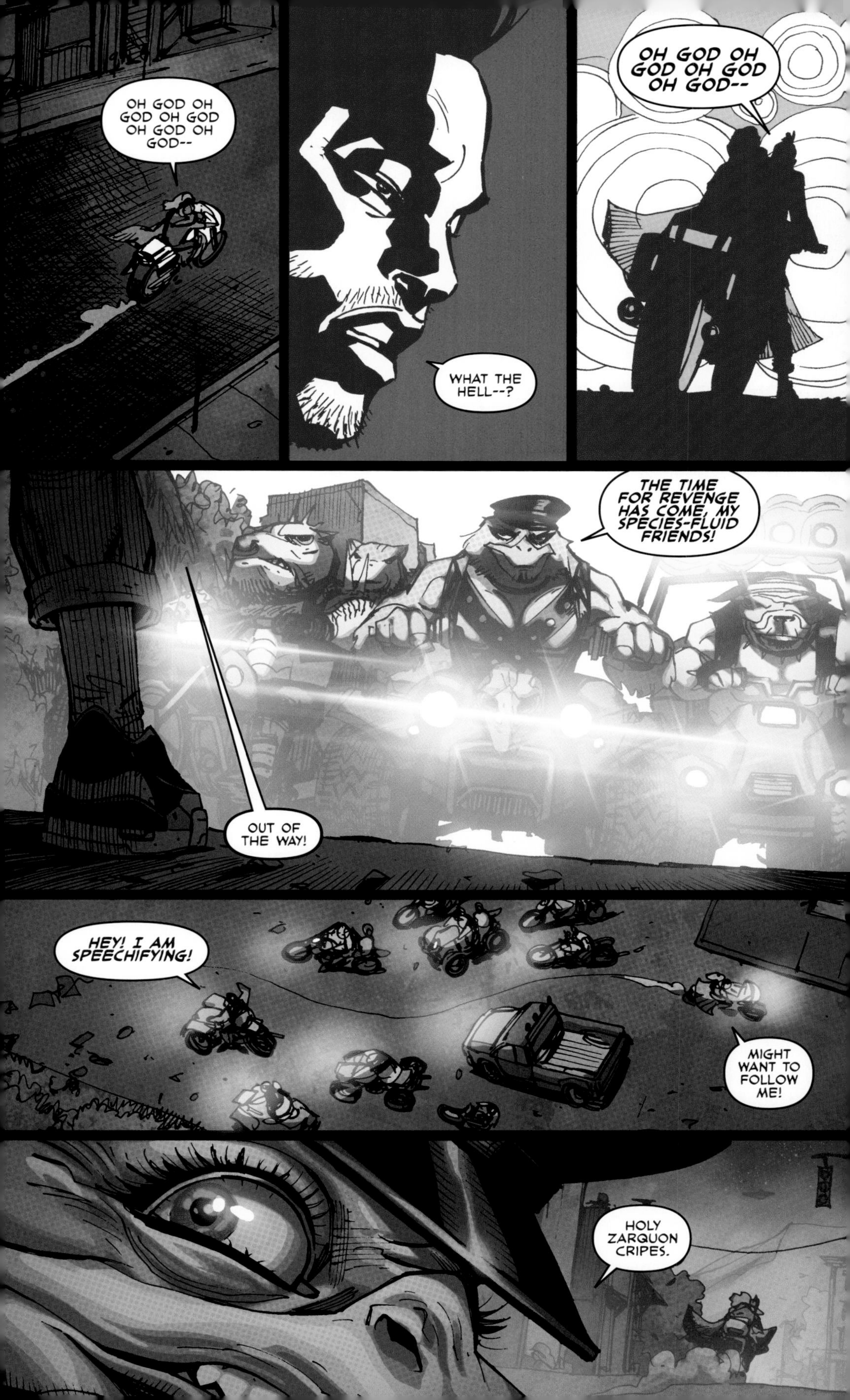
OH GOD OH GOD OH GOD OH GOD OH GOD--
WHAT THE HELL--?
OH GOD OH GOD OH GOD OH GOD--
THE TIME FOR REVENGE HAS COME, MY SPECIES-FLUID FRIENDS!
OUT OF THE WAY!
HEY! I AM SPEECHIFYING!
MIGHT WANT TO FOLLOW ME!
HOLY ZARQUON CRIPES.

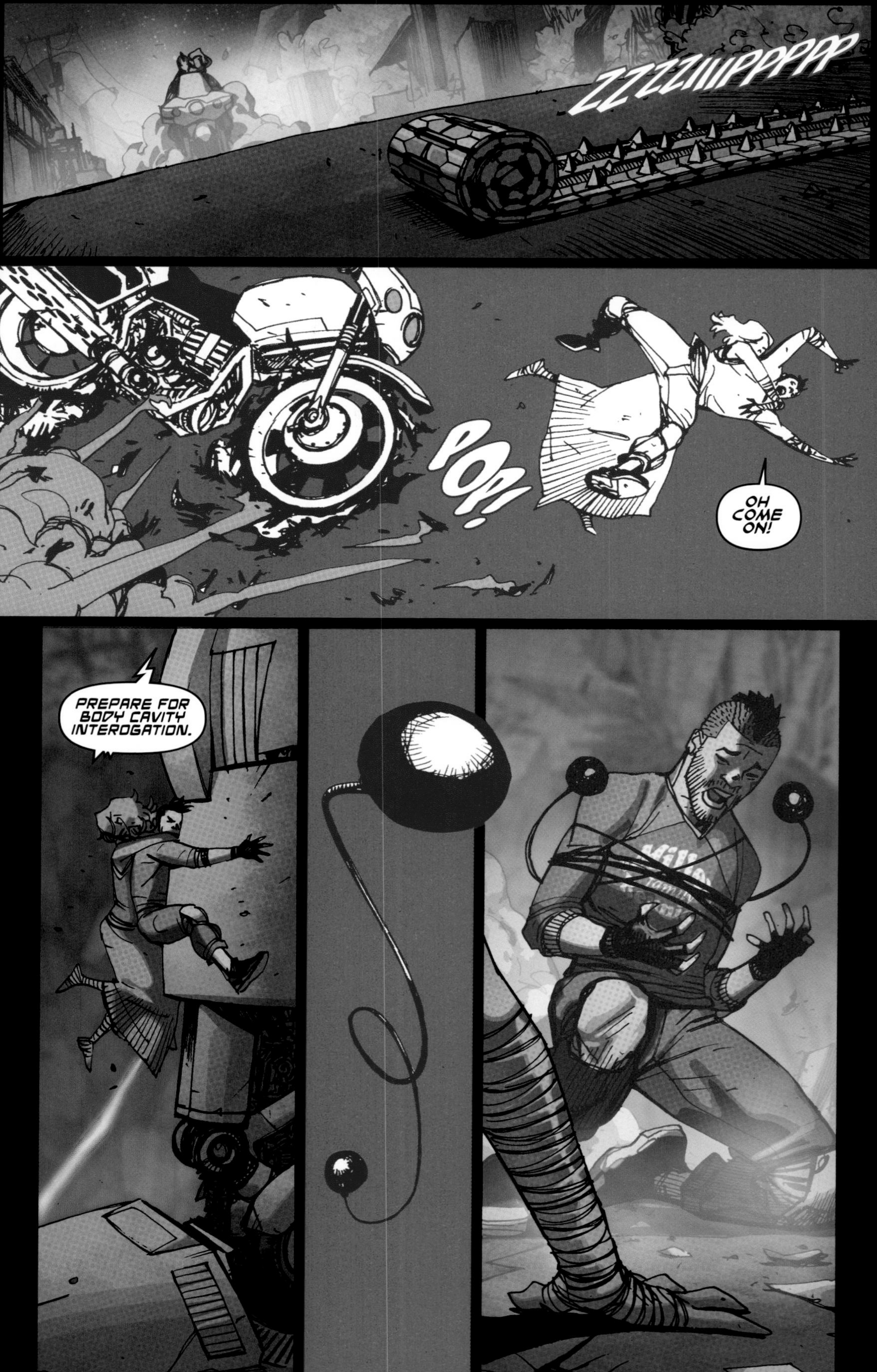
ZZZZIIIPPPPPP
POP!
OH COME ON!
PREPARE FOR BODY CAVITY INTEROGATION.

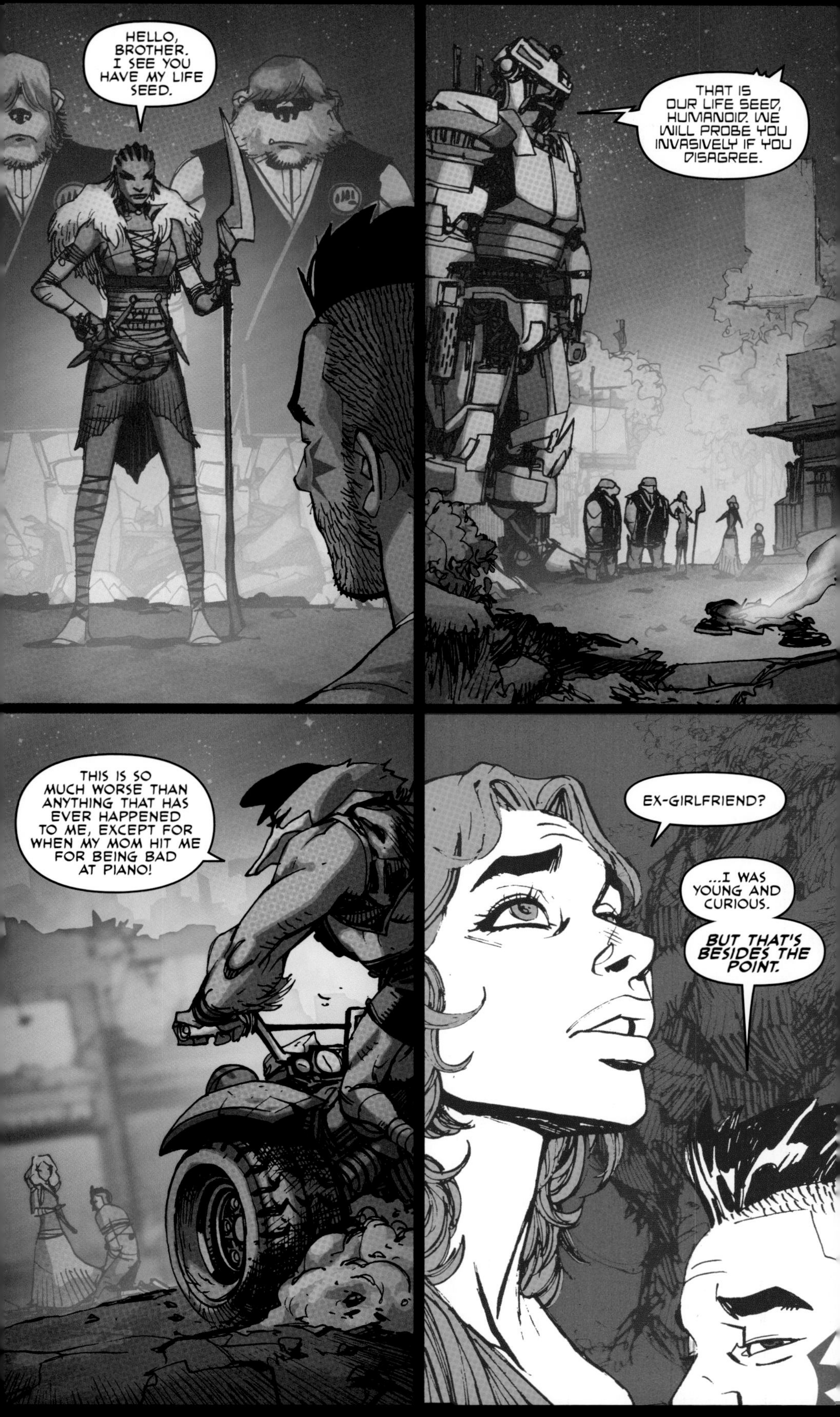
HELLO, BROTHER. I SEE YOU HAVE MY LIFE SEED.
THAT IS OUR LIFE SEED, HUMANOID. WE WILL PROBE YOU INVASIVELY IF YOU DISAGREE.
THIS IS SO MUCH WORSE THAN ANYTHING THAT HAS EVER HAPPENED TO ME, EXCEPT FOR WHEN MY MOM HIT ME FOR BEING BAD AT PIANO!
EX-GIRLFRIEND?
...I WAS YOUNG AND CURIOUS.
BUT THAT'S BESIDES THE POINT.

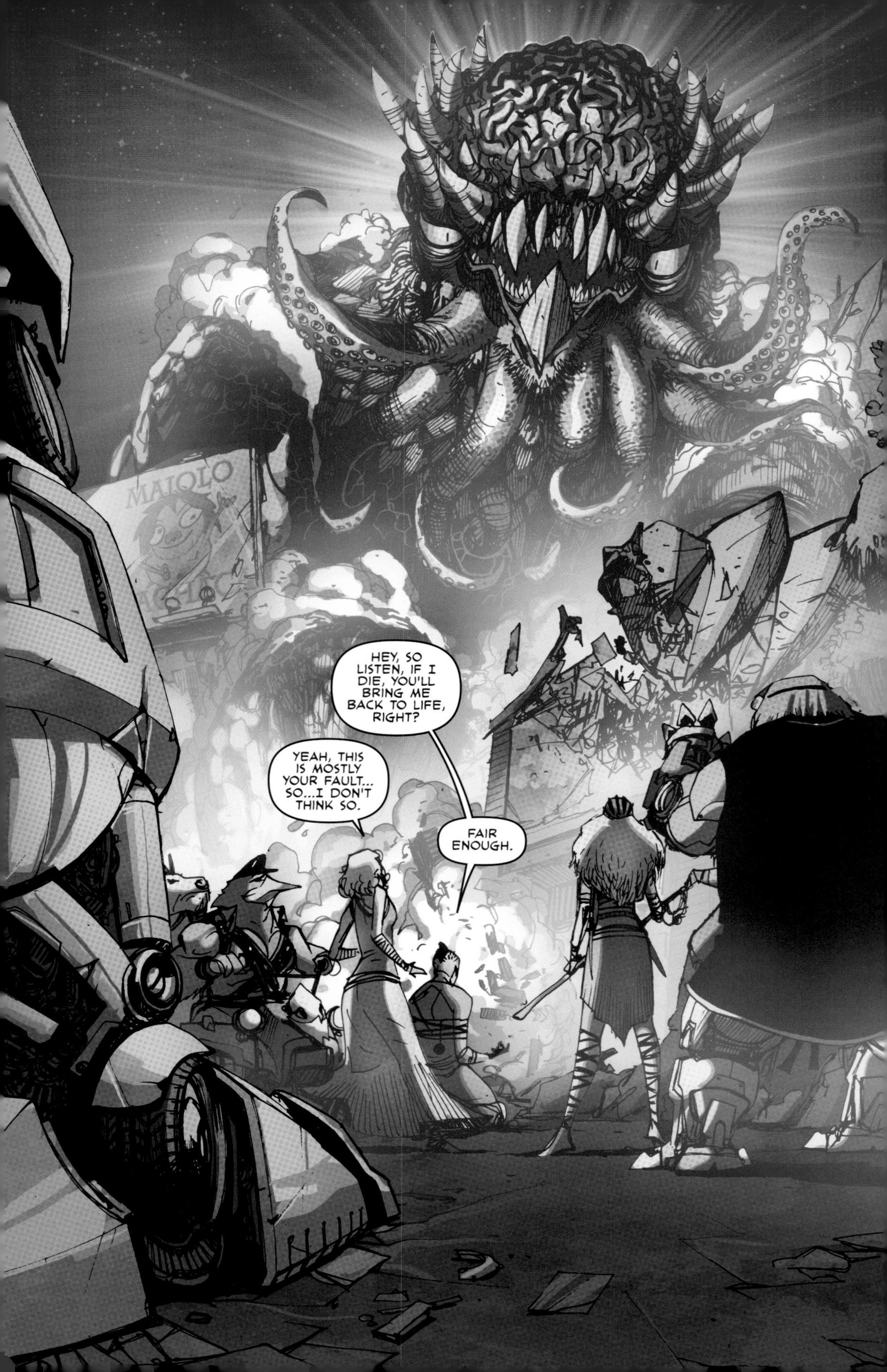
MAJOLO
HEY, SO LISTEN, IF I DIE, YOU'LL BRING ME BACK TO LIFE, RIGHT?
YEAH, THIS IS MOSTLY YOUR FAULT... SO...I DON'T THINK SO.
FAIR ENOUGH.

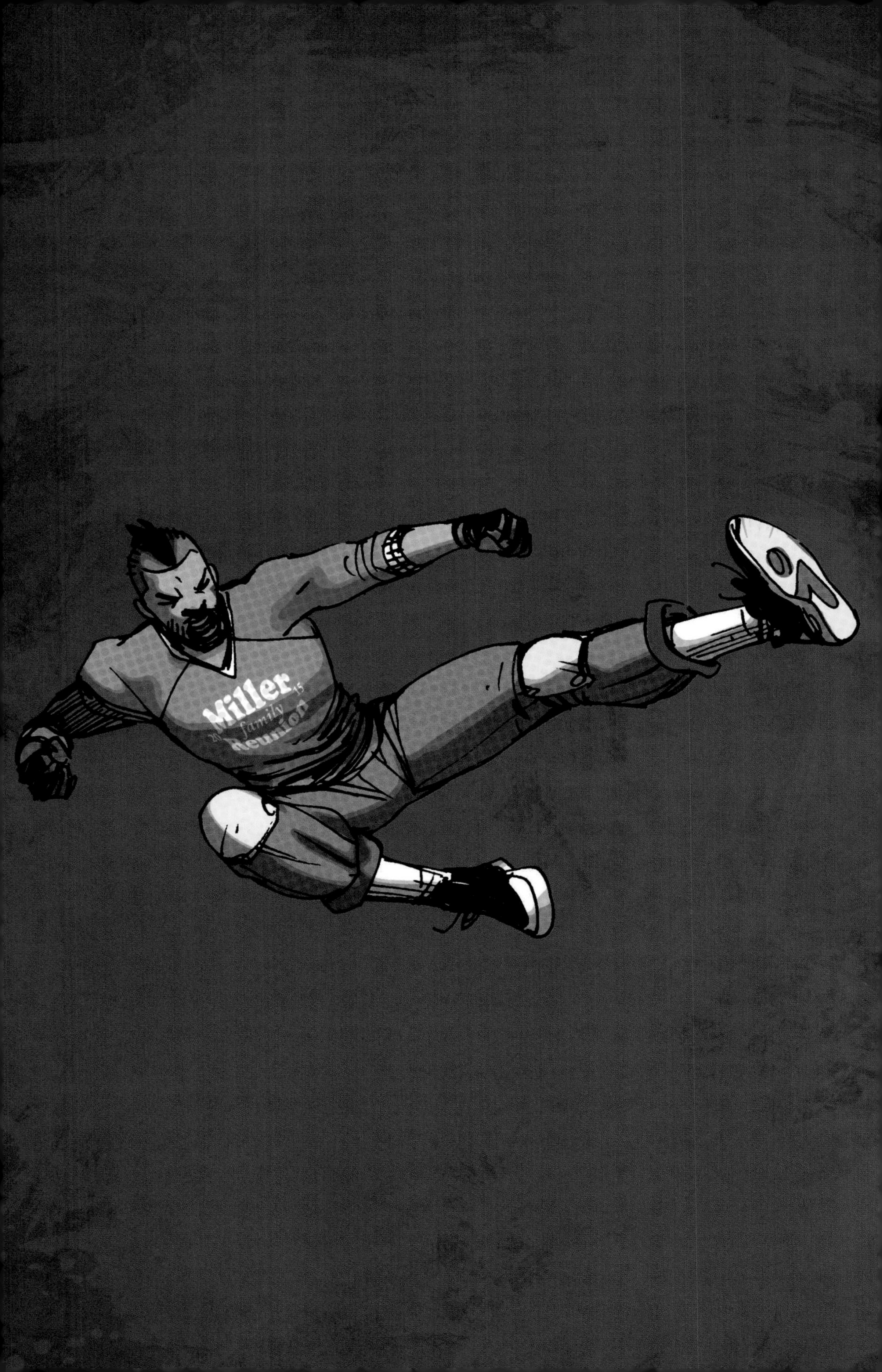
Miller
family

"I Hate Mondays"
CHAPTER FIVE

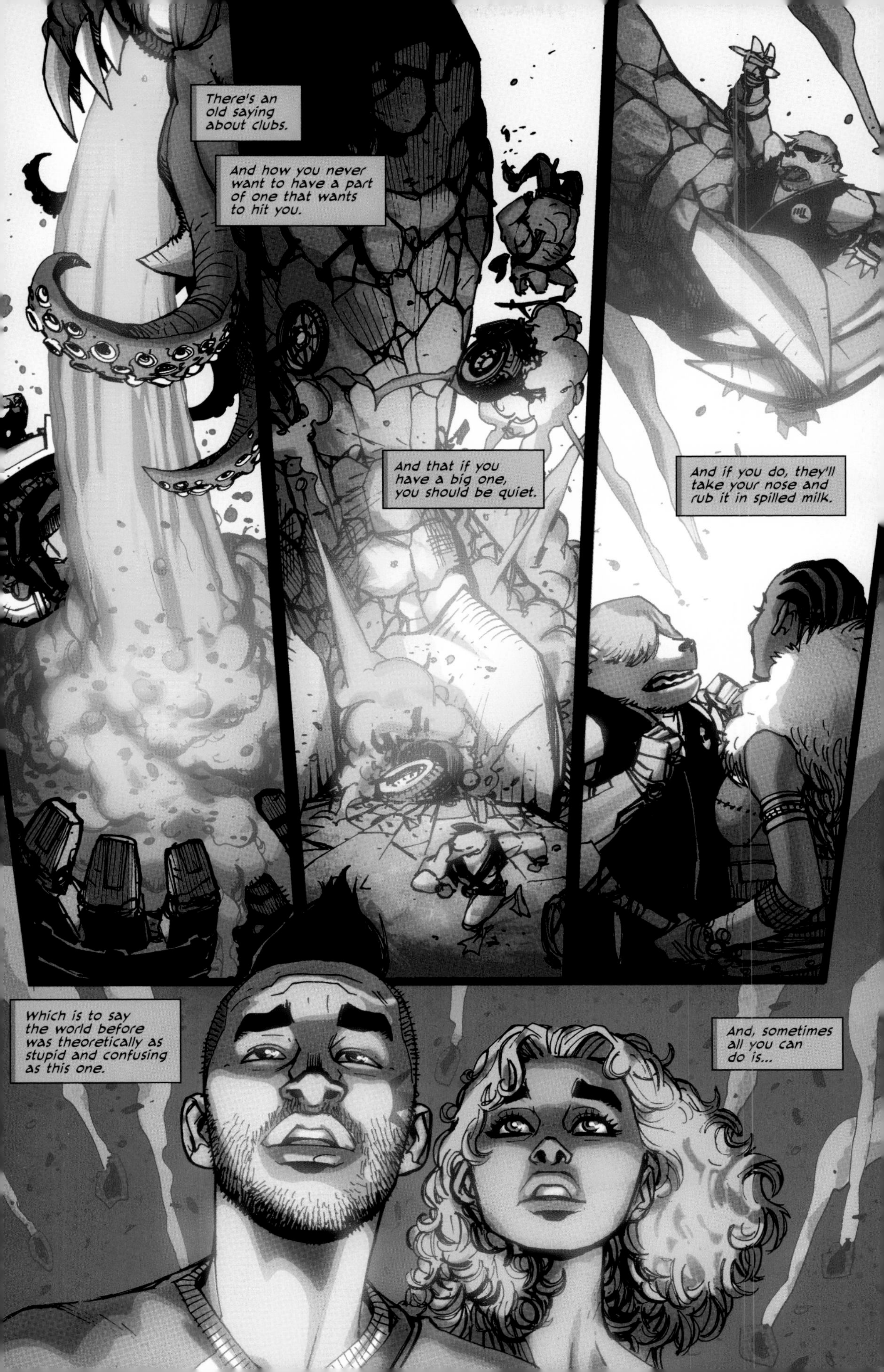
There's an old saying about clubs.
And how you never want to have a part of one that wants to hit you.
And that if you have a big one, you should be quiet.
And if you do, they'll take your nose and rub it in spilled milk.
Which is to say the world before was theoretically as stupid and confusing as this one.
And, sometimes all you can do is...

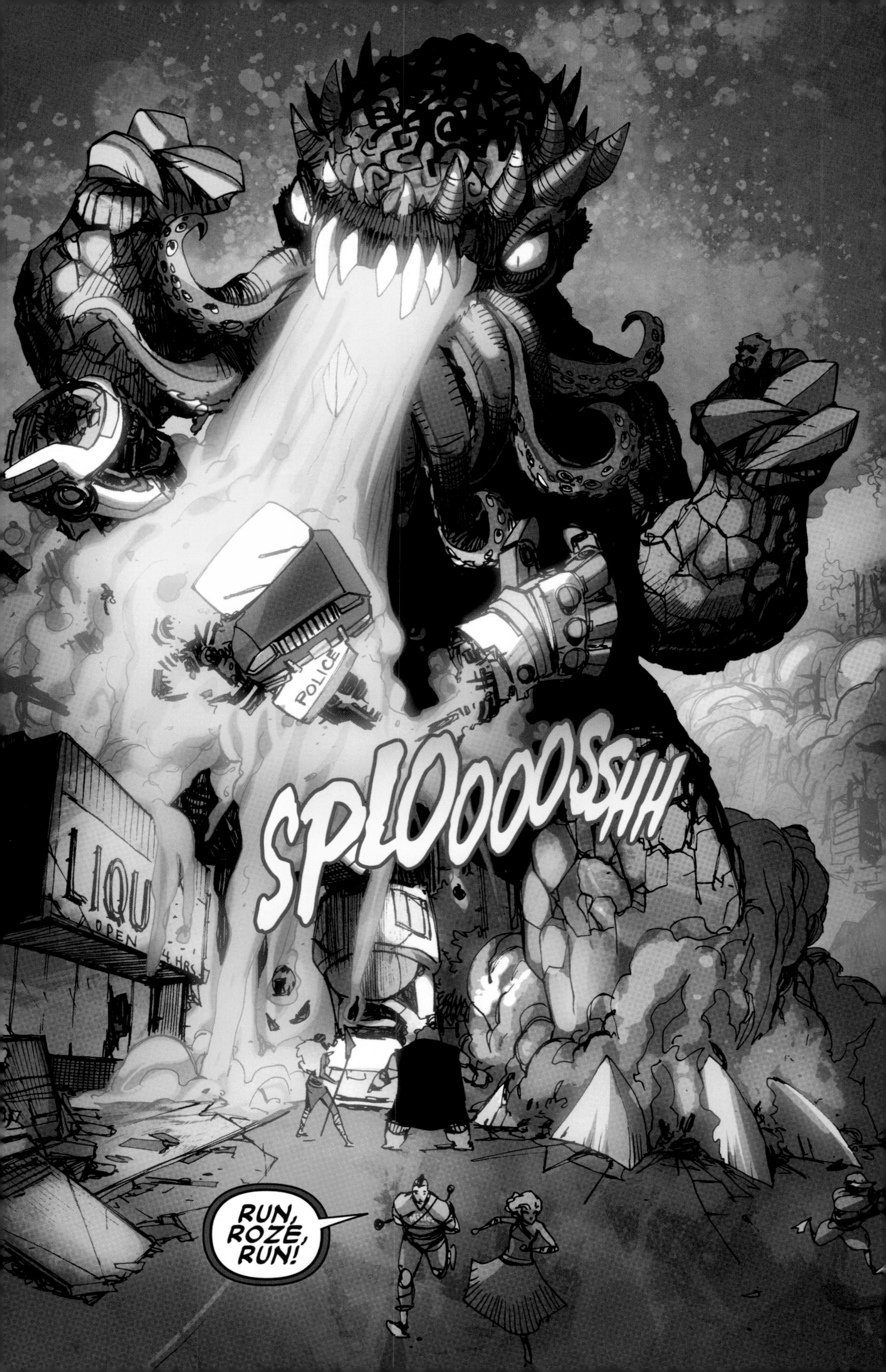

POLICE
LIQU
OPEN
4 HRS
SPLOOOOOSSHH
RUN, ROZE, RUN!

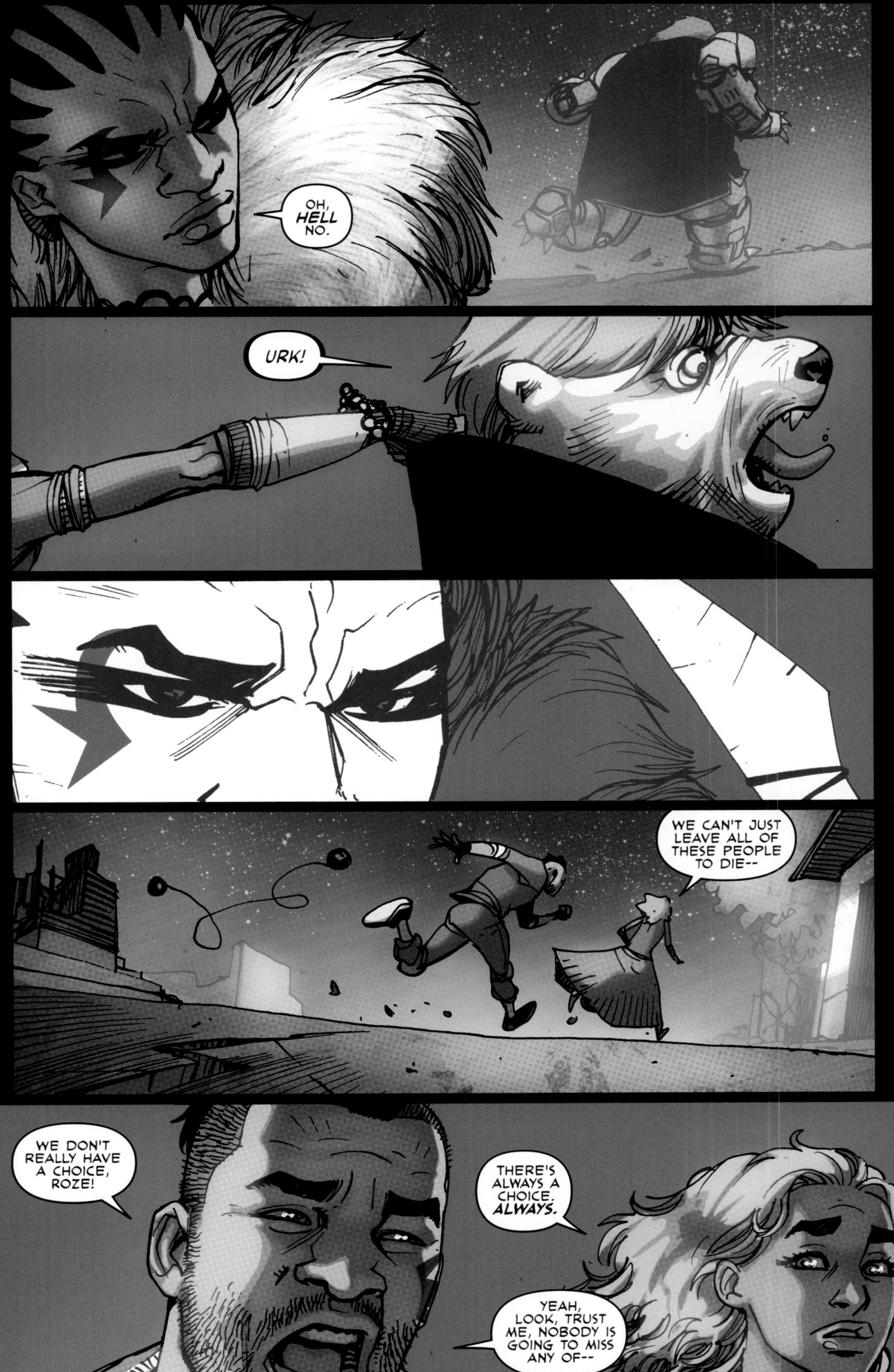
OH, HELL NO.
URK!
WE CAN'T JUST LEAVE ALL OF THESE PEOPLE TO DIE--
WE DON'T REALLY HAVE A CHOICE, ROZE!
THERE'S ALWAYS A CHOICE. ALWAYS.
YEAH, LOOK, TRUST ME, NOBODY IS GOING TO MISS ANY OF--

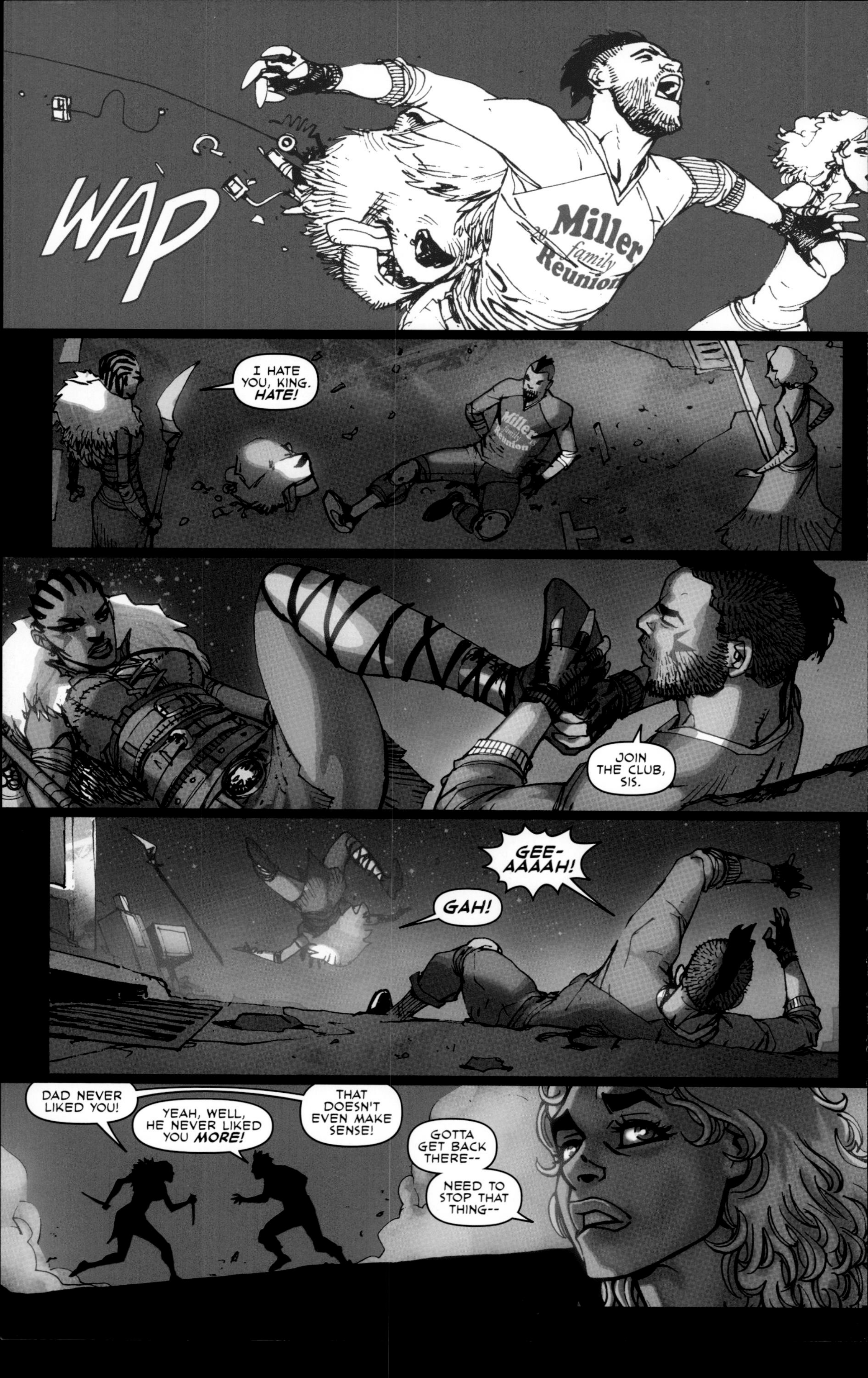
WAP
Miller family Reunion
I HATE YOU, KING. HATE!
Miller family Reunion
JOIN THE CLUB, SIS.
GEE-AAAAH!
GAH!
DAD NEVER LIKED YOU!
YEAH, WELL, HE NEVER LIKED YOU MORE!
THAT DOESN'T EVEN MAKE SENSE!
GOTTA GET BACK THERE--
NEED TO STOP THAT THING--

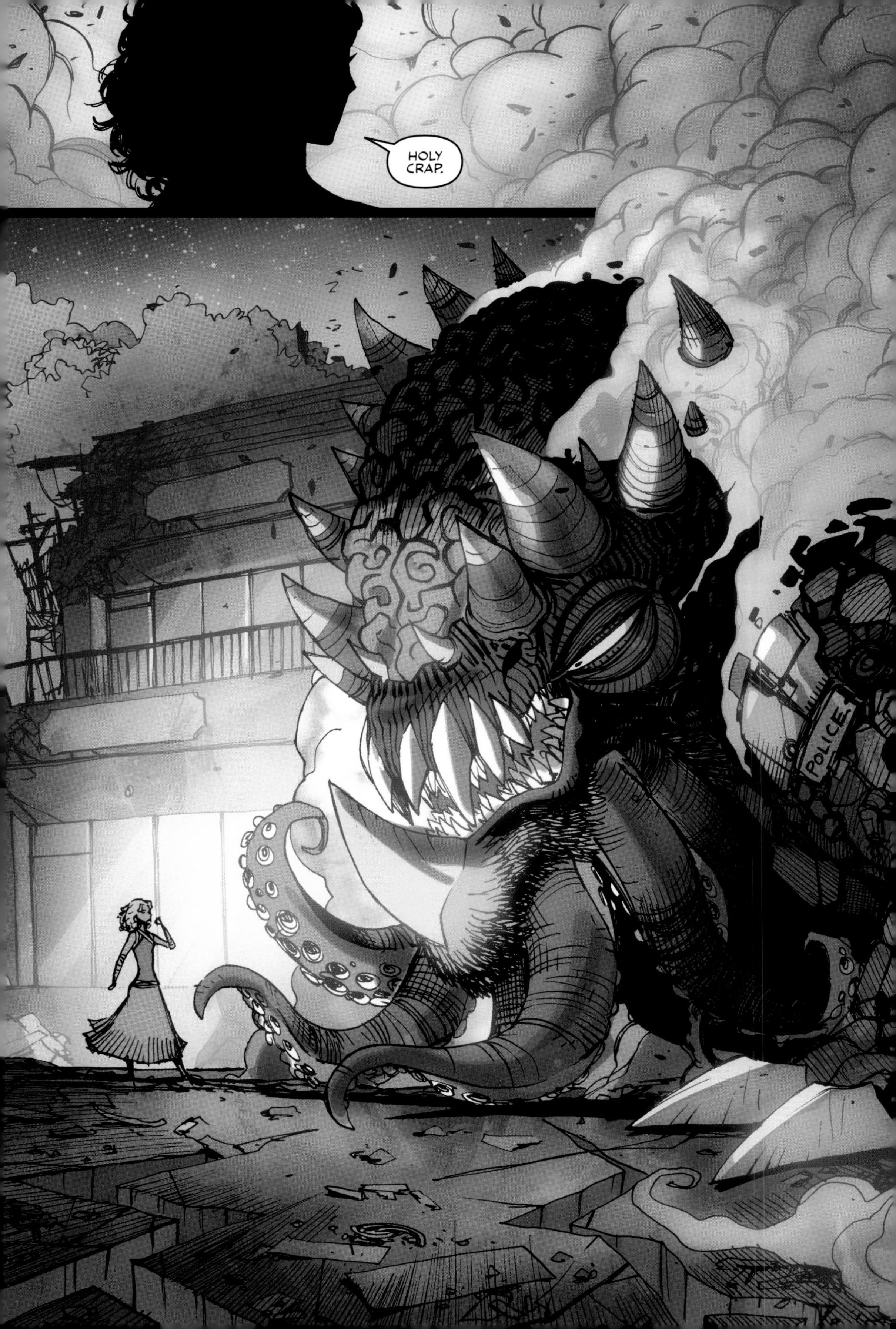
HOLY CRAP.
POLICE
POLICE

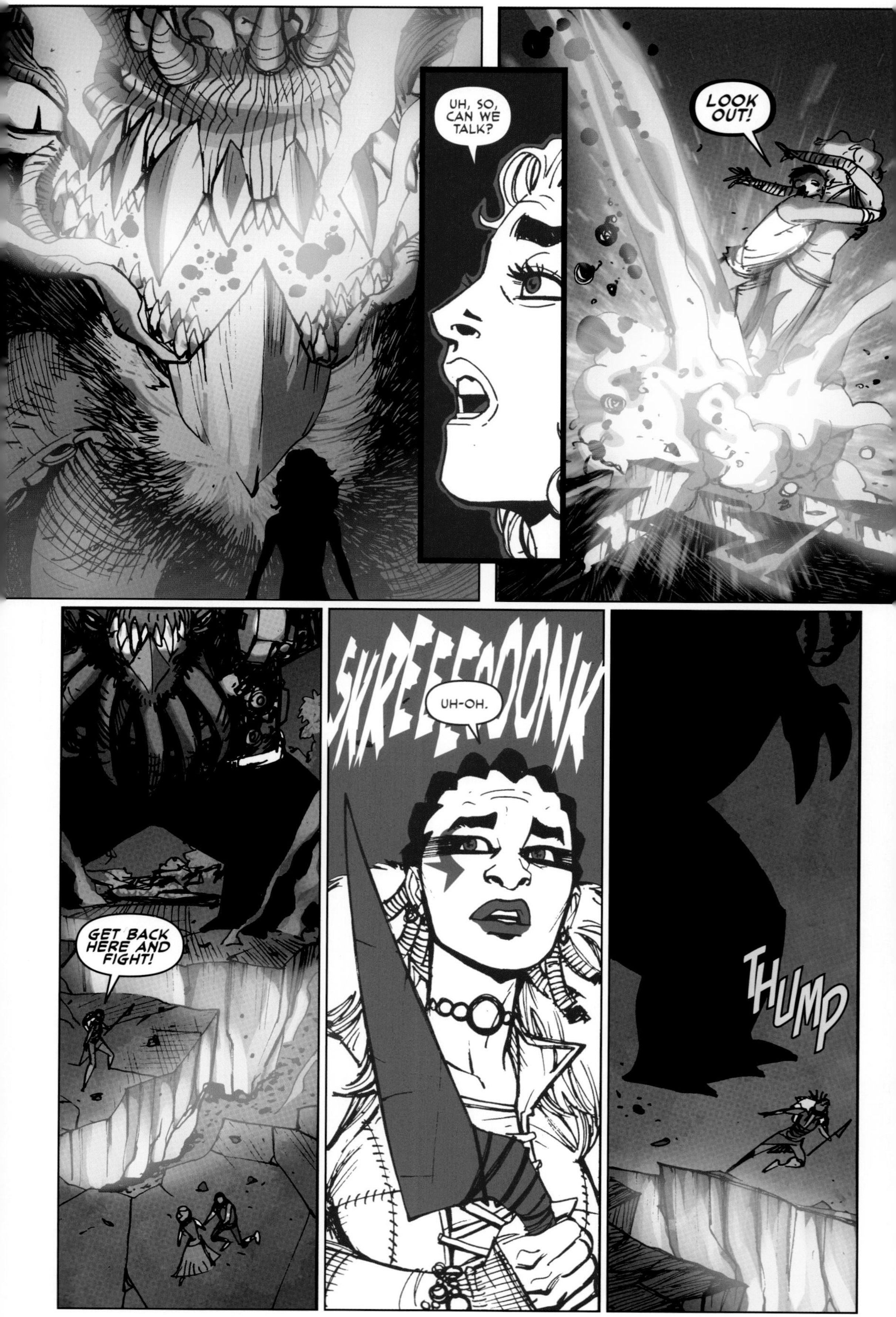
UH, SO, CAN WE TALK?
LOOK OUT!
GET BACK HERE AND FIGHT!
SKREEEEOONK
UH-OH.
THUMP

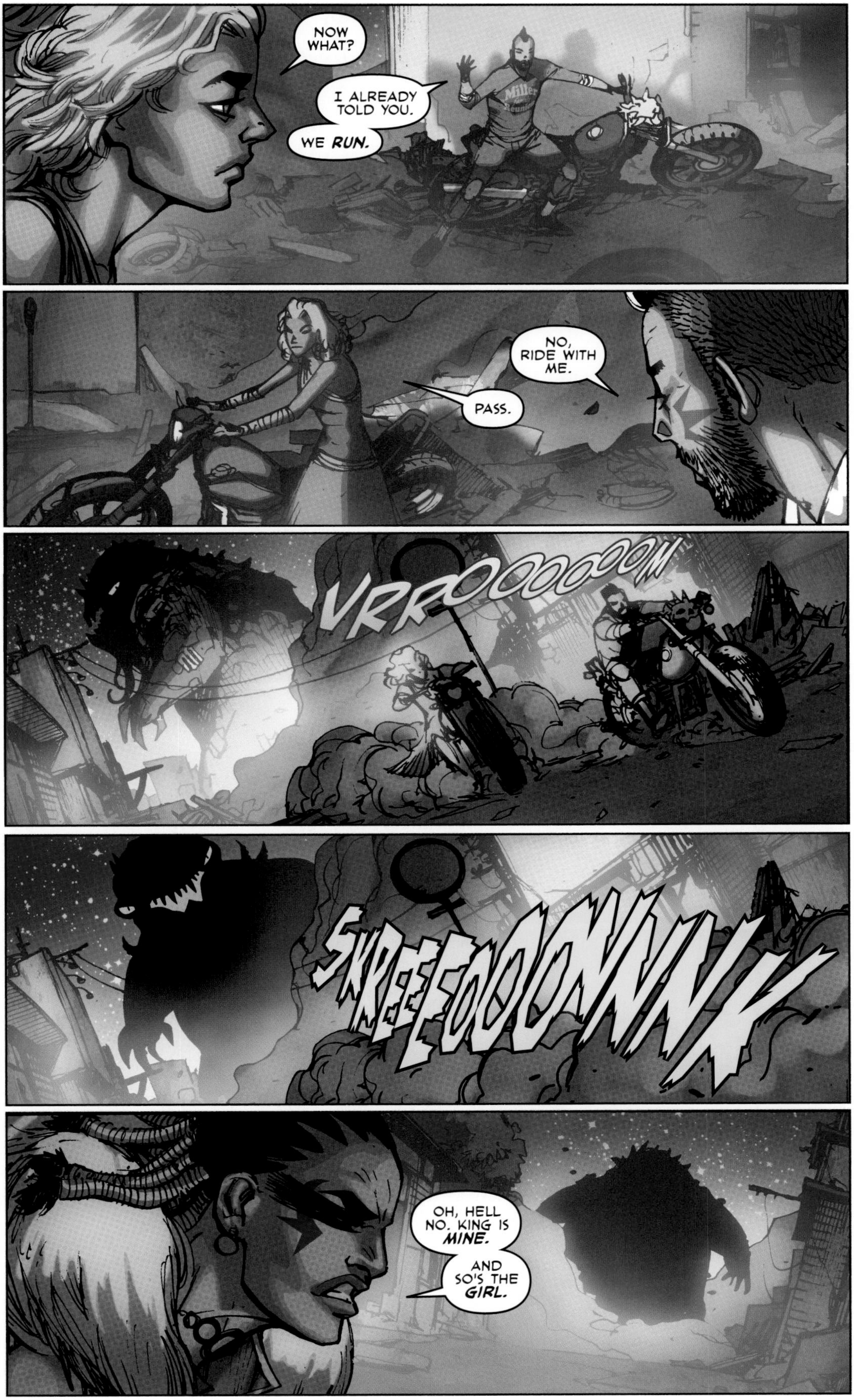
NOW WHAT?
I ALREADY TOLD YOU.
WE RUN.
NO, RIDE WITH ME.
PASS.
VRROOOOOOOOM
SKREEEOOOONNNK
OH, HELL NO. KING IS MINE.
AND SO'S THE GIRL.

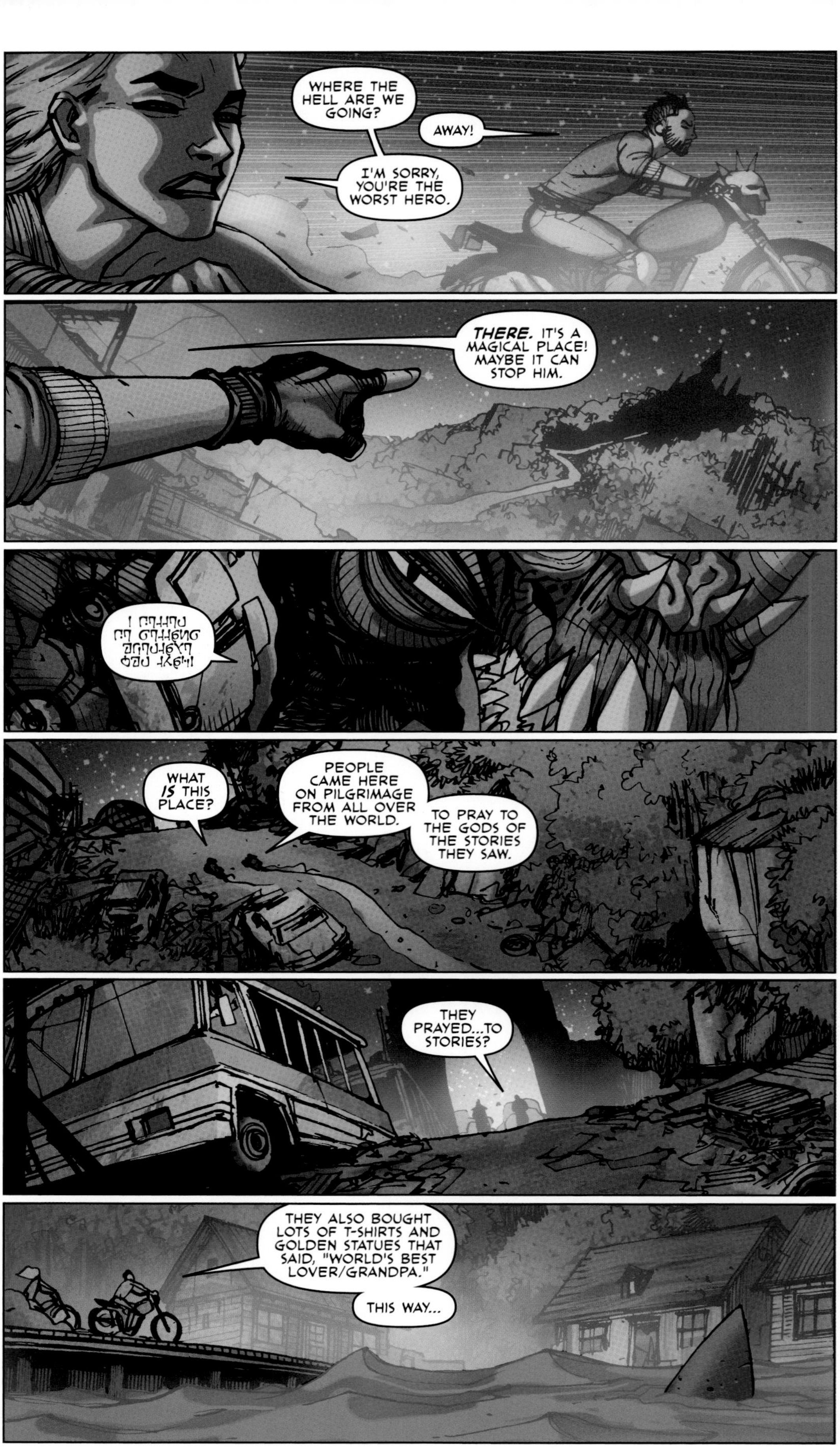
WHERE THE HELL ARE WE GOING?
AWAY!
I'M SORRY, YOU'RE THE WORST HERO.
THERE. IT'S A MAGICAL PLACE! MAYBE IT CAN STOP HIM.
WHAT *IS* THIS PLACE?
PEOPLE CAME HERE ON PILGRIMAGE FROM ALL OVER THE WORLD.
TO PRAY TO THE GODS OF THE STORIES THEY SAW.
THEY PRAYED...TO STORIES?
THEY ALSO BOUGHT LOTS OF T-SHIRTS AND GOLDEN STATUES THAT SAID, "WORLD'S BEST LOVER/GRANDPA."
THIS WAY...

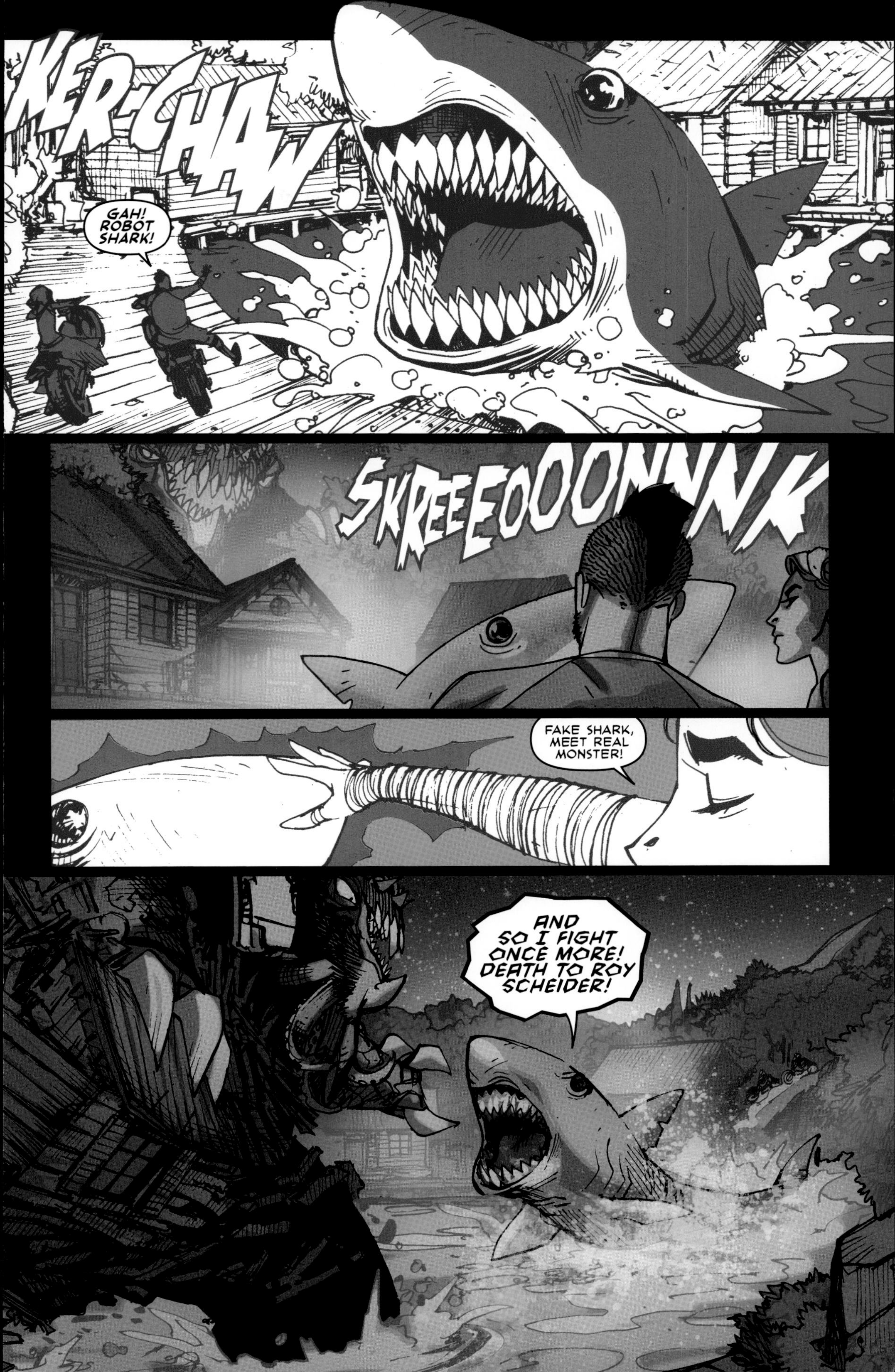
KER-CHAW
GAH! ROBOT SHARK!
SKREEEOOONNNK
FAKE SHARK, MEET REAL MONSTER!
AND SO I FIGHT ONCE MORE! DEATH TO ROY SCHEIDER!

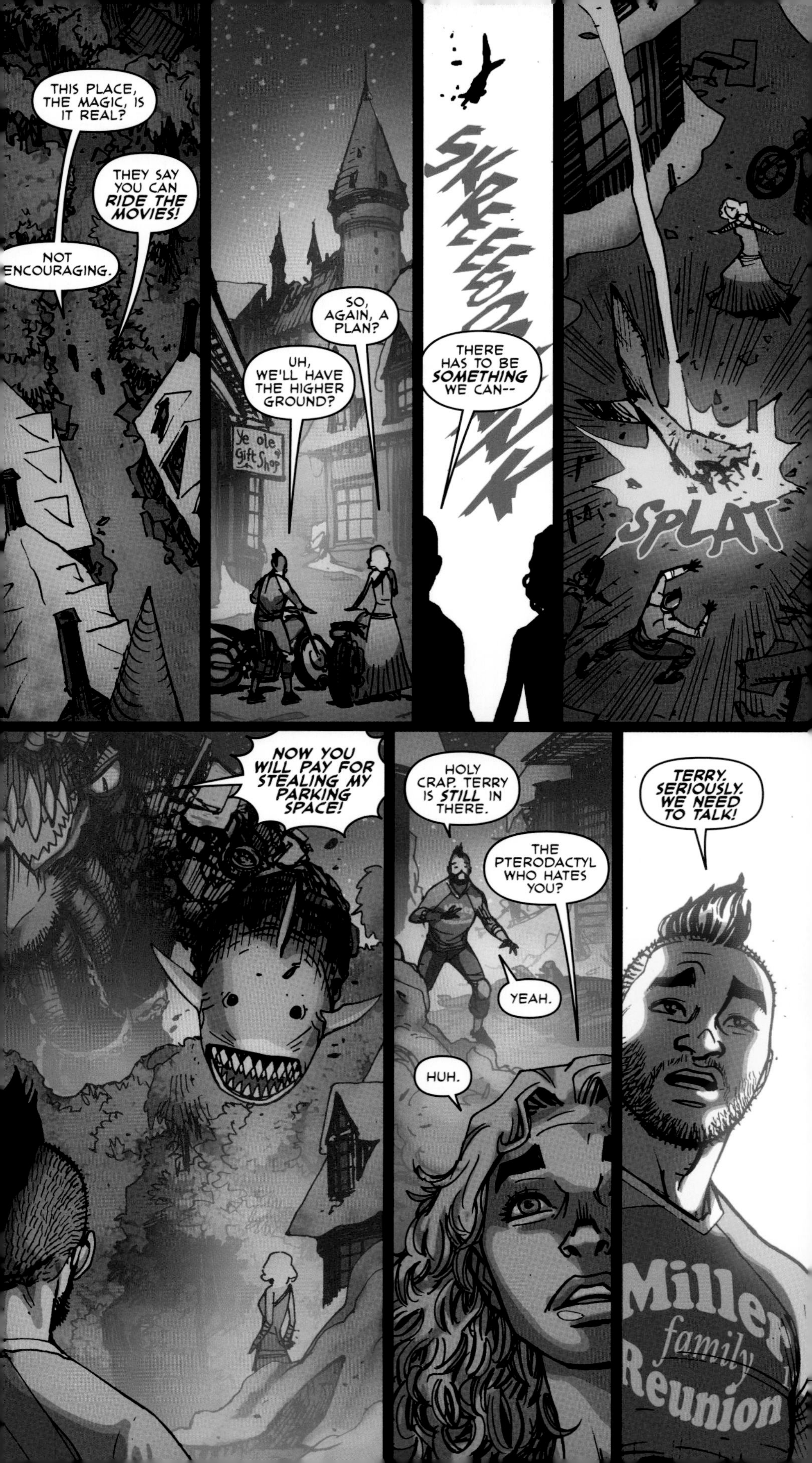

THIS PLACE, THE MAGIC, IS IT REAL?
THEY SAY YOU CAN RIDE THE MOVIES!
NOT ENCOURAGING.
SO, AGAIN, A PLAN?
UH, WE'LL HAVE THE HIGHER GROUND?
Ye ole Gift Shop
SKREEEOONK
THERE HAS TO BE SOMETHING WE CAN--
SPLAT
NOW YOU WILL PAY FOR STEALING MY PARKING SPACE!
HOLY CRAP. TERRY IS STILL IN THERE.
THE PTERODACTYL WHO HATES YOU?
YEAH.
HUH.
TERRY. SERIOUSLY. WE NEED TO TALK!
Miller family Reunion

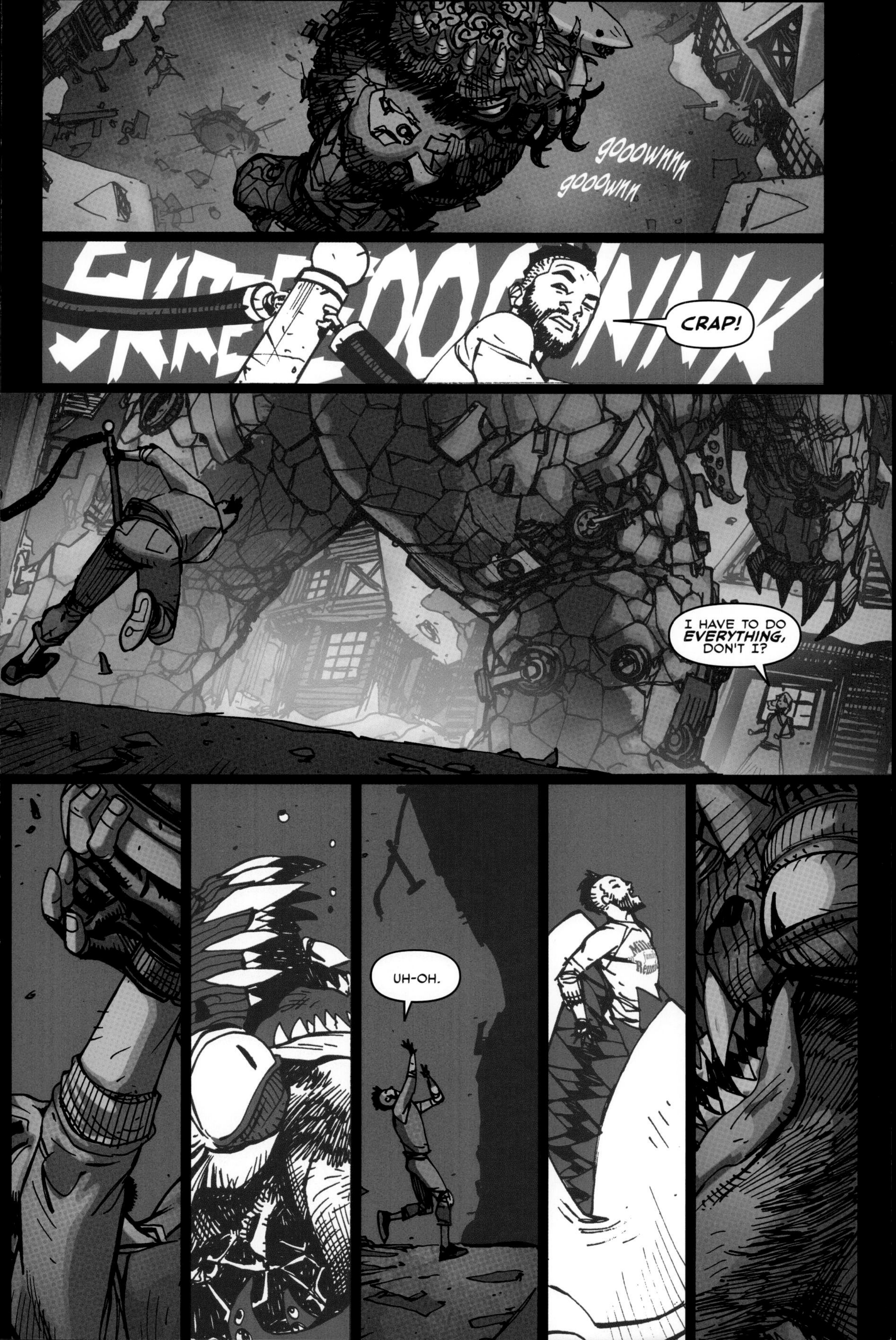
gooowwnnn
gooowwnn
CRAP!
I HAVE TO DO EVERYTHING, DON'T I?
UH-OH.

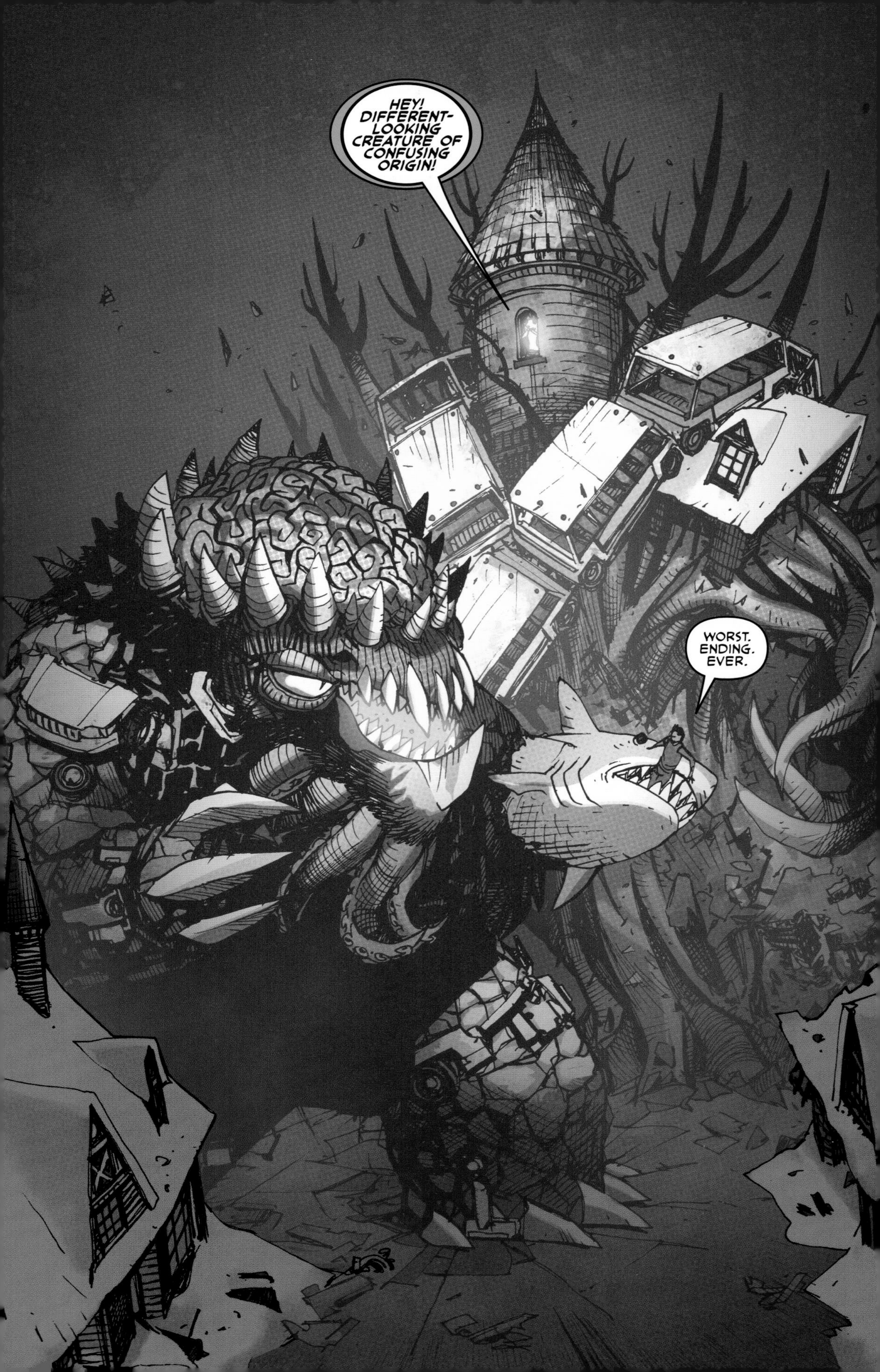
HEY! DIFFERENT-LOOKING CREATURE OF CONFUSING ORIGIN!
WORST. ENDING. EVER.

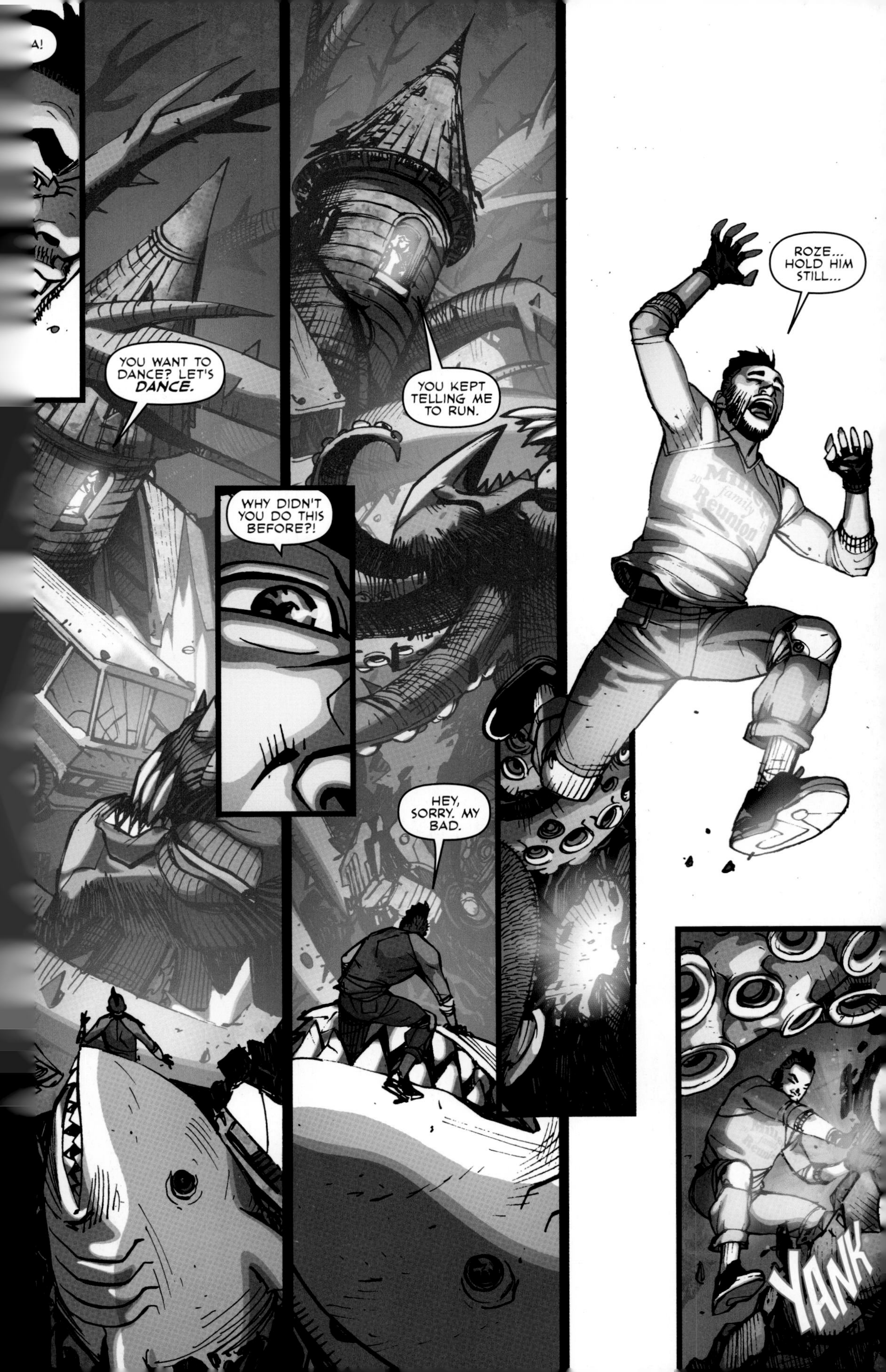
A!
YOU WANT TO DANCE? LET'S DANCE.
YOU KEPT TELLING ME TO RUN.
WHY DIDN'T YOU DO THIS BEFORE?!
HEY, SORRY. MY BAD.
ROZE... HOLD HIM STILL...
YANK

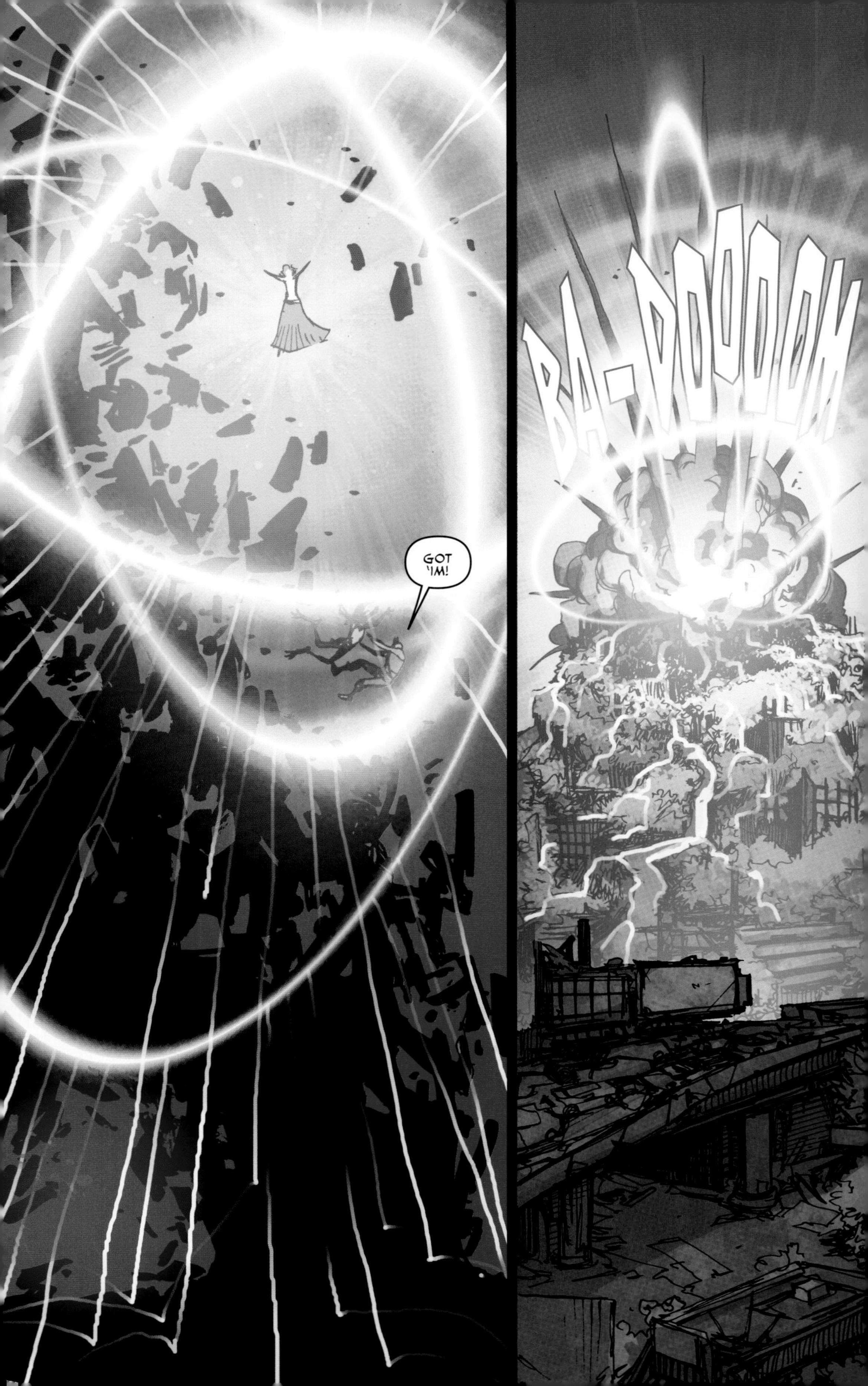
GOT 'IM!
BA-DOOOOM

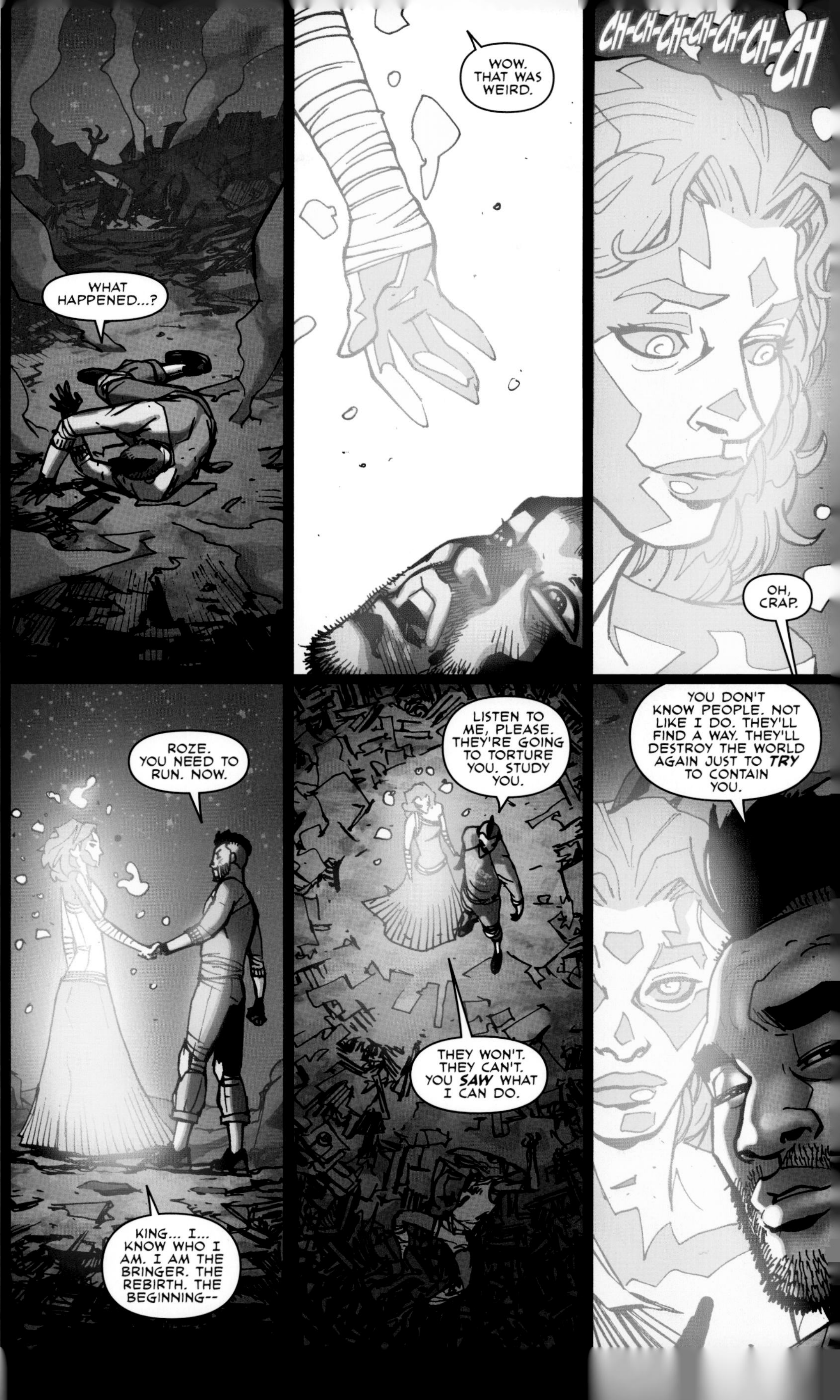
WHAT HAPPENED...?
WOW. THAT WAS WEIRD.
CH-CH-CH-CH-CH-CH-CH
OH, CRAP.
ROZE. YOU NEED TO RUN. NOW.
KING... I... KNOW WHO I AM. I AM THE BRINGER. THE REBIRTH. THE BEGINNING--
LISTEN TO ME, PLEASE. THEY'RE GOING TO TORTURE YOU. STUDY YOU.
THEY WON'T. THEY CAN'T. YOU SAW WHAT I CAN DO.
YOU DON'T KNOW PEOPLE. NOT LIKE I DO. THEY'LL FIND A WAY. THEY'LL DESTROY THE WORLD AGAIN JUST TO TRY TO CONTAIN YOU.

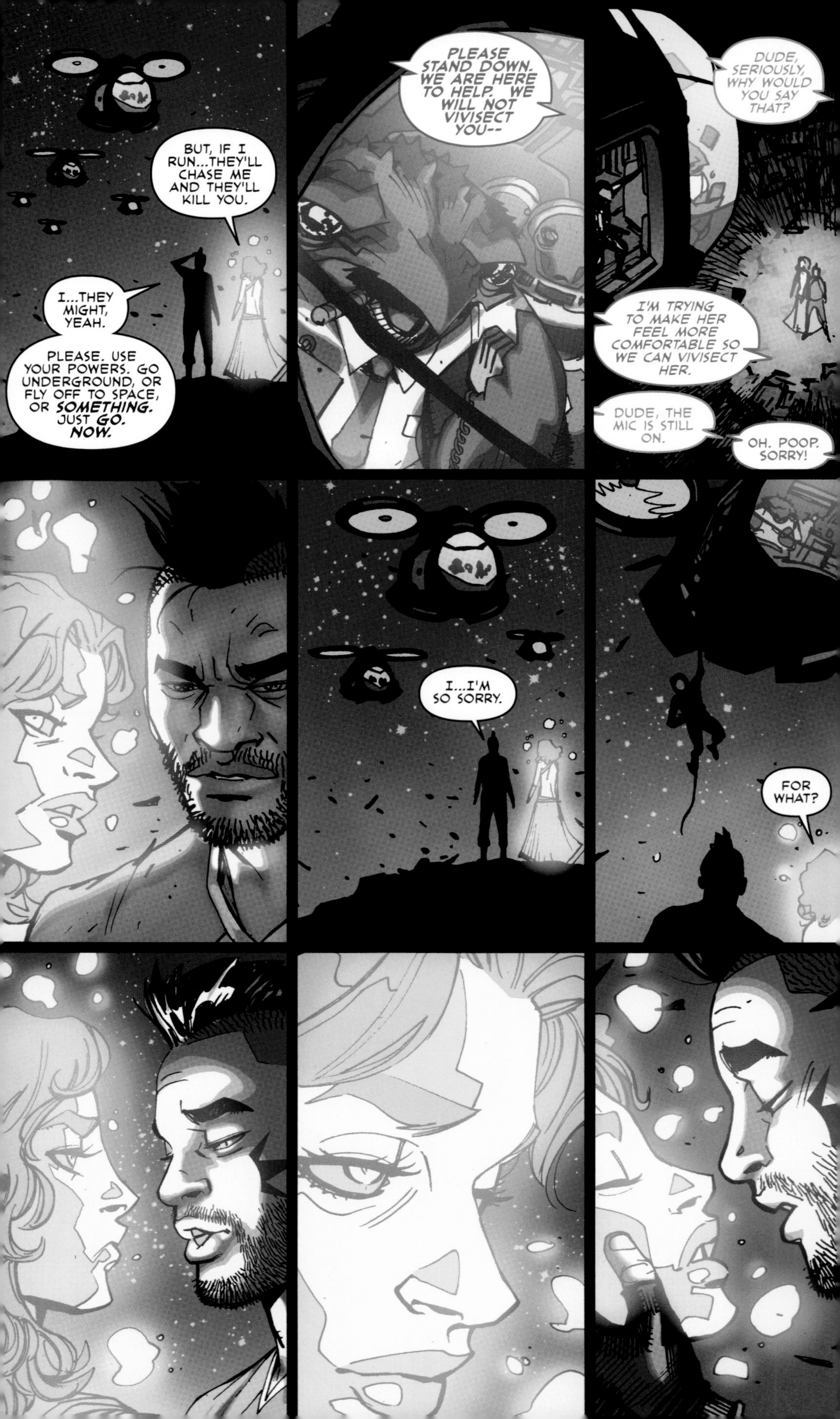
BUT, IF I RUN...THEY'LL CHASE ME AND THEY'LL KILL YOU.
I...THEY MIGHT, YEAH.
PLEASE. USE YOUR POWERS. GO UNDERGROUND, OR FLY OFF TO SPACE, OR SOMETHING. JUST GO. NOW.
PLEASE STAND DOWN. WE ARE HERE TO HELP. WE WILL NOT VIVISECT YOU--
DUDE, SERIOUSLY, WHY WOULD YOU SAY THAT?
I'M TRYING TO MAKE HER FEEL MORE COMFORTABLE SO WE CAN VIVISECT HER.
DUDE, THE MIC IS STILL ON.
OH. POOP. SORRY!
I...I'M SO SORRY.
FOR WHAT?

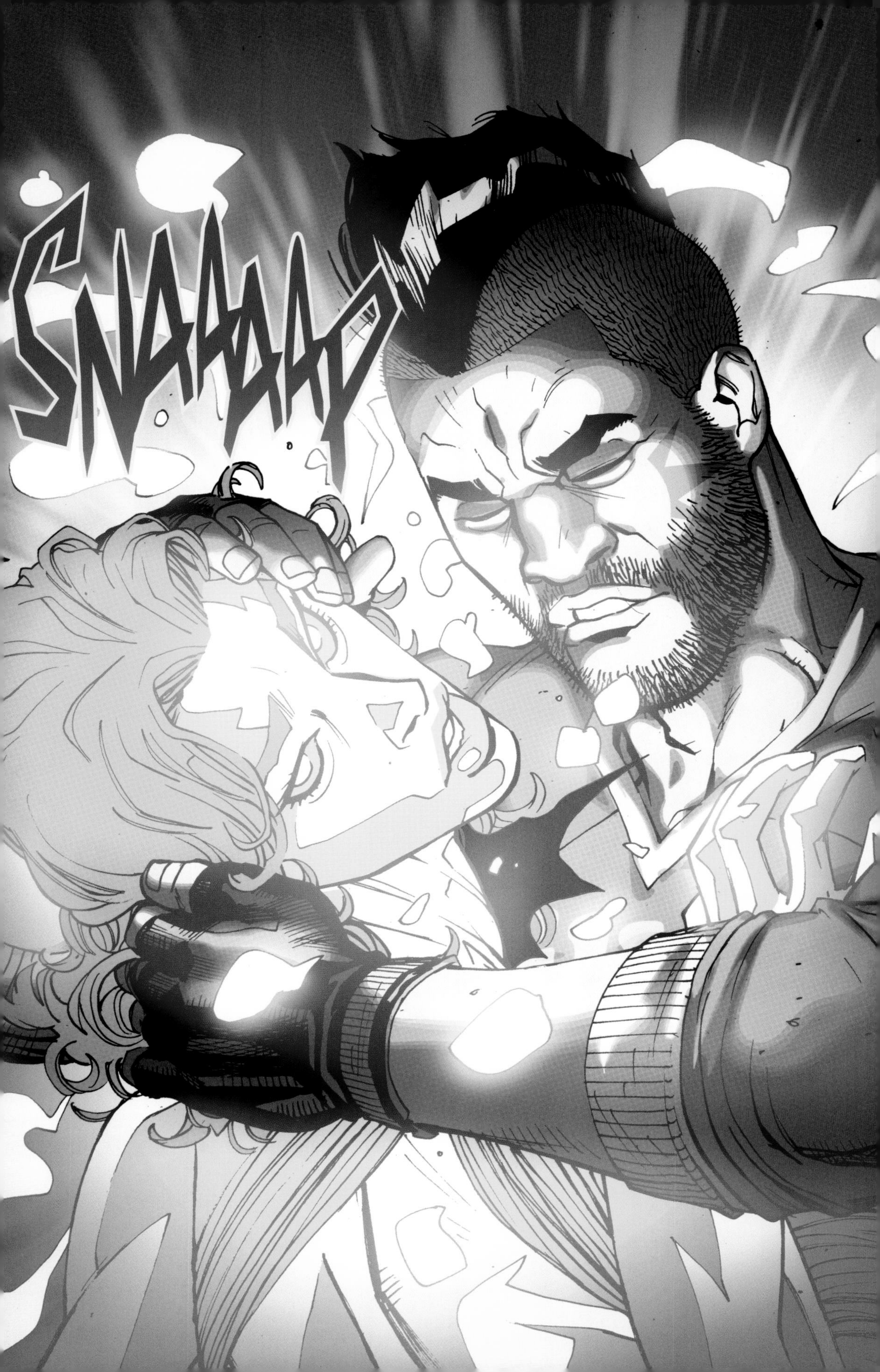
SNAAAAP

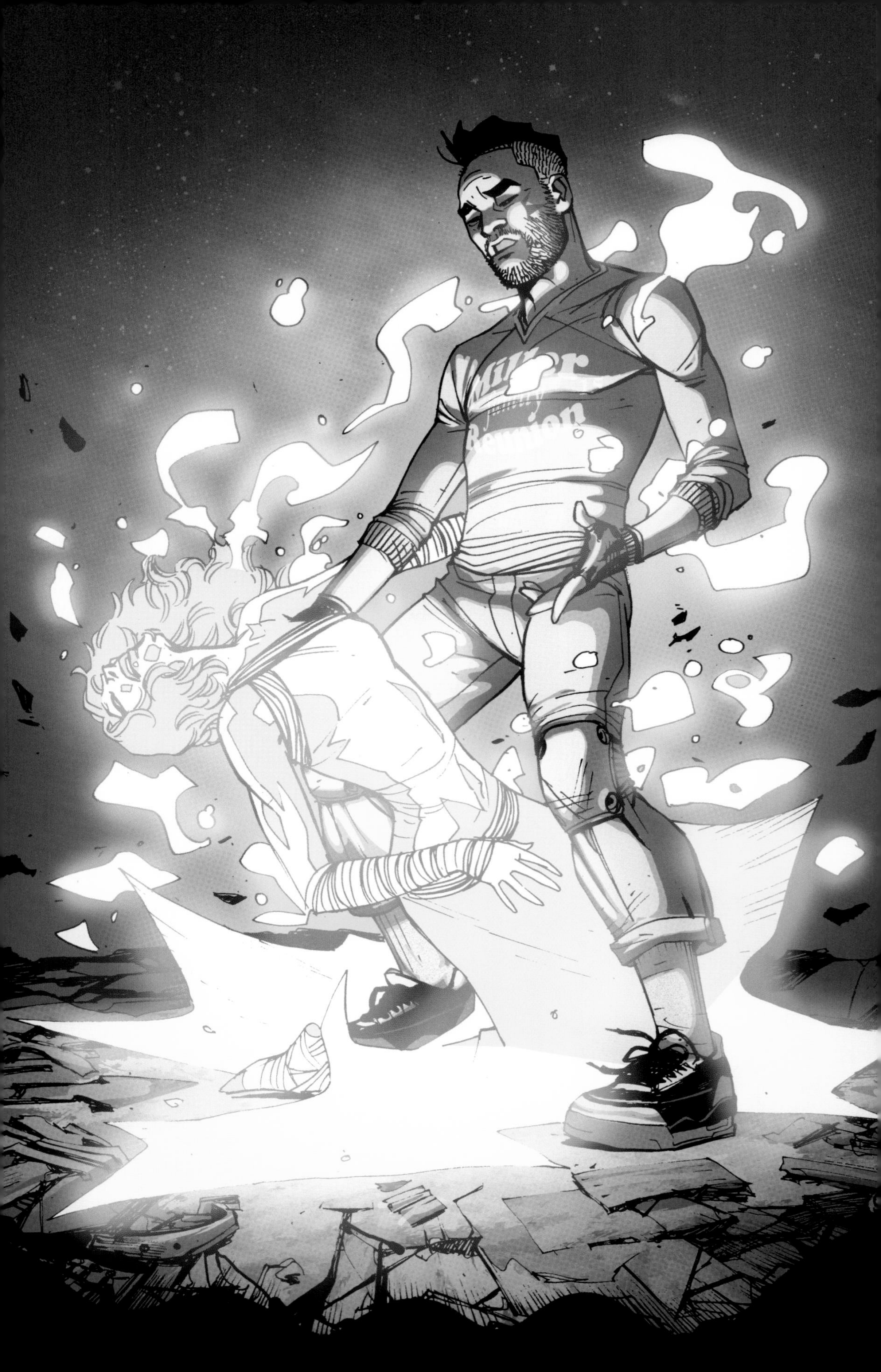
Family

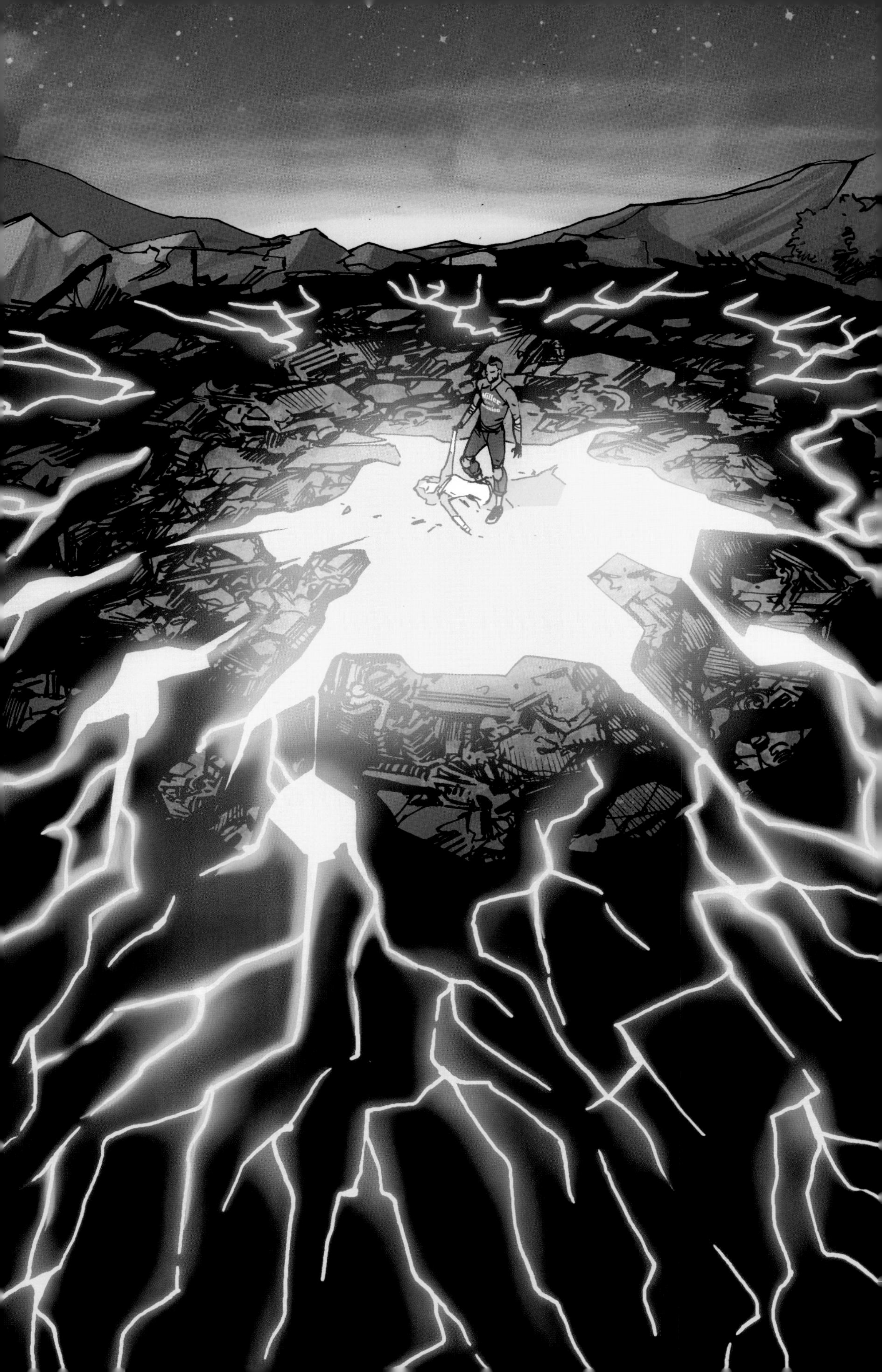

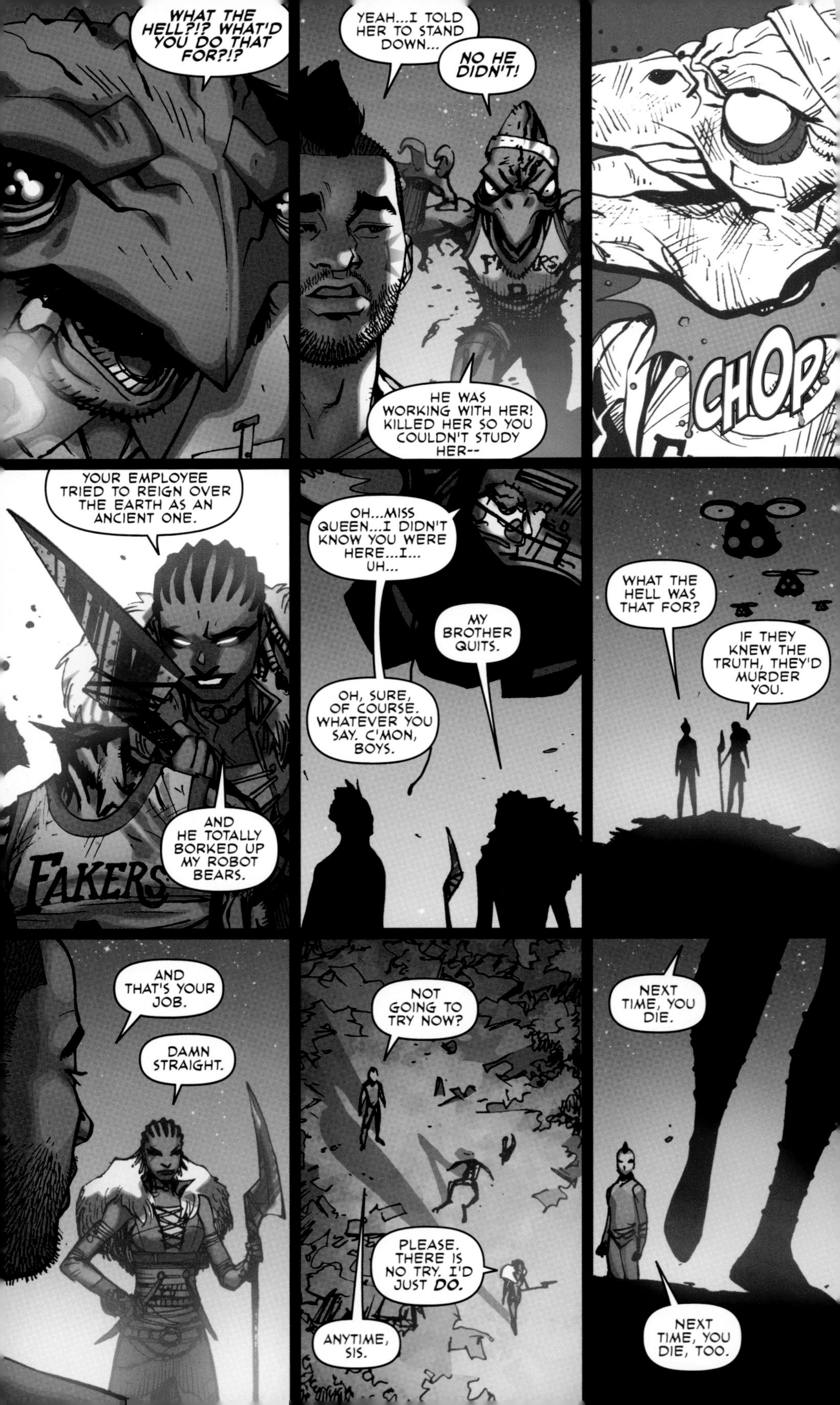
WHAT THE HELL?!? WHAT'D YOU DO THAT FOR?!?
YEAH...I TOLD HER TO STAND DOWN...
NO HE DIDN'T!
HE WAS WORKING WITH HER! KILLED HER SO YOU COULDN'T STUDY HER--
FAKERS
CHOP
YOUR EMPLOYEE TRIED TO REIGN OVER THE EARTH AS AN ANCIENT ONE.
AND HE TOTALLY BORKED UP MY ROBOT BEARS.
FAKERS
OH...MISS QUEEN...I DIDN'T KNOW YOU WERE HERE...I... UH...
MY BROTHER QUITS.
OH, SURE, OF COURSE. WHATEVER YOU SAY. C'MON, BOYS.
WHAT THE HELL WAS THAT FOR?
IF THEY KNEW THE TRUTH, THEY'D MURDER YOU.
AND THAT'S YOUR JOB.
DAMN STRAIGHT.
NOT GOING TO TRY NOW?
PLEASE. THERE IS NO TRY. I'D JUST DO.
ANYTIME, SIS.
NEXT TIME, YOU DIE.
NEXT TIME, YOU DIE, TOO.

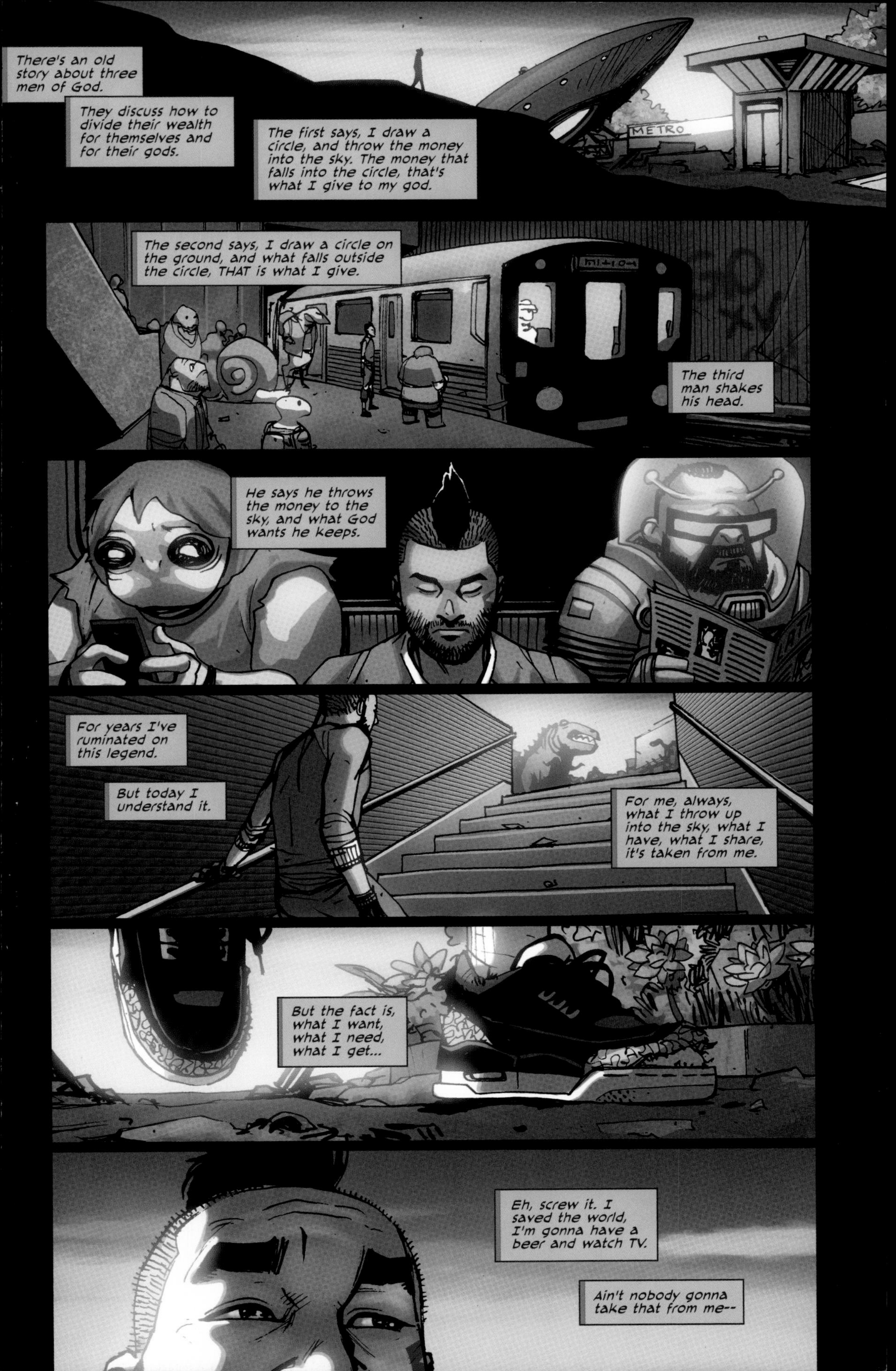
There's an old story about three men of God.
They discuss how to divide their wealth for themselves and for their gods.
The first says, I draw a circle, and throw the money into the sky. The money that falls into the circle, that's what I give to my god.
METRO
The second says, I draw a circle on the ground, and what falls outside the circle, THAT is what I give.
The third man shakes his head.
He says he throws the money to the sky, and what God wants he keeps.
For years I've ruminated on this legend.
But today I understand it.
For me, always, what I throw up into the sky, what I have, what I share, it's taken from me.
But the fact is, what I want, what I need, what I get...
Eh, screw it. I saved the world, I'm gonna have a beer and watch TV.
Ain't nobody gonna take that from me--

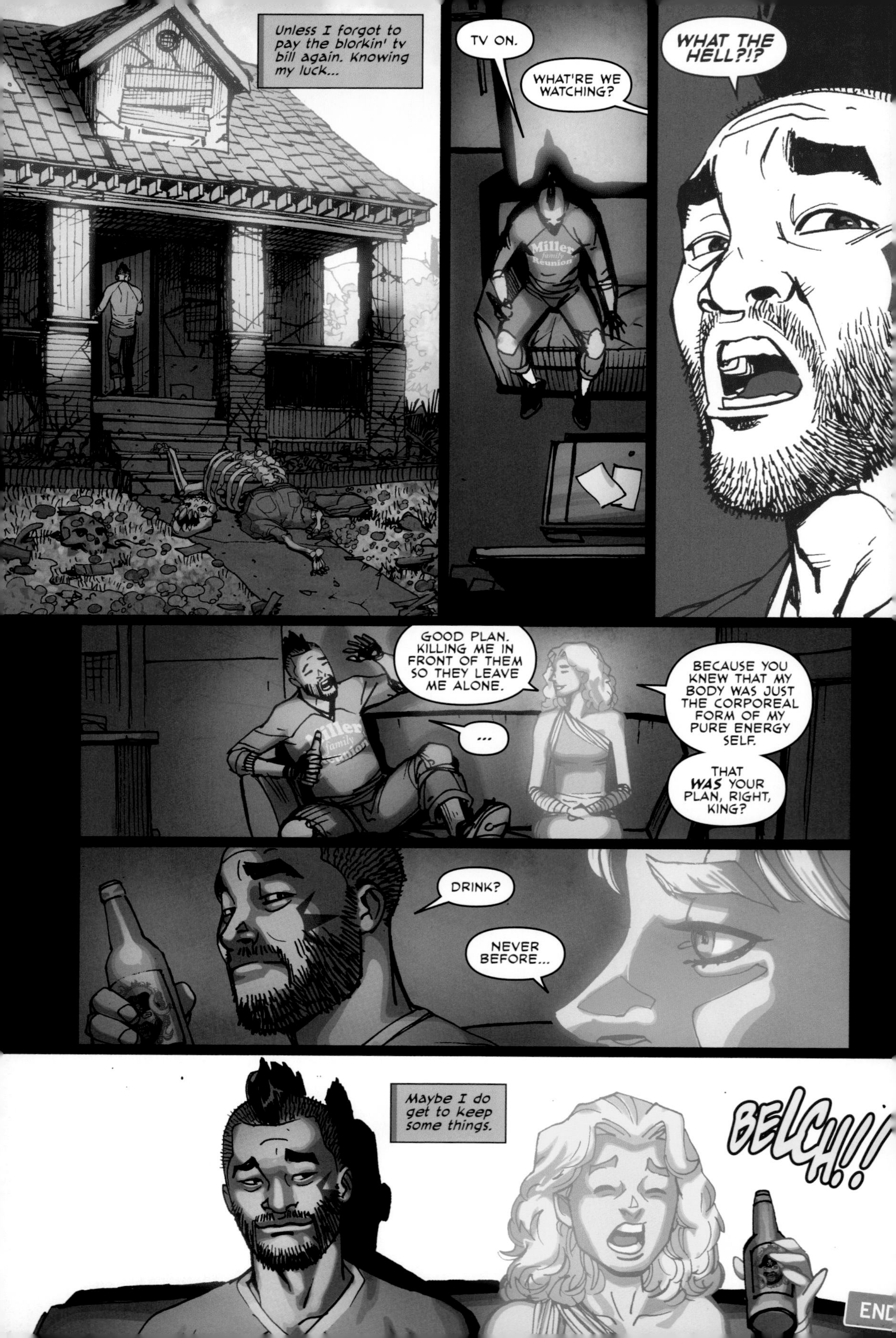

Unless I forgot to pay the blorkin' tv bill again. Knowing my luck...
TV ON.
WHAT'RE WE WATCHING?
Miller family Reunion
WHAT THE HELL?!?
GOOD PLAN. KILLING ME IN FRONT OF THEM SO THEY LEAVE ME ALONE.
...
BECAUSE YOU KNEW THAT MY BODY WAS JUST THE CORPOREAL FORM OF MY PURE ENERGY SELF.
THAT *WAS* YOUR PLAN, RIGHT, KING?
DRINK?
NEVER BEFORE...
Maybe I do get to keep some things.
BELCH!!!

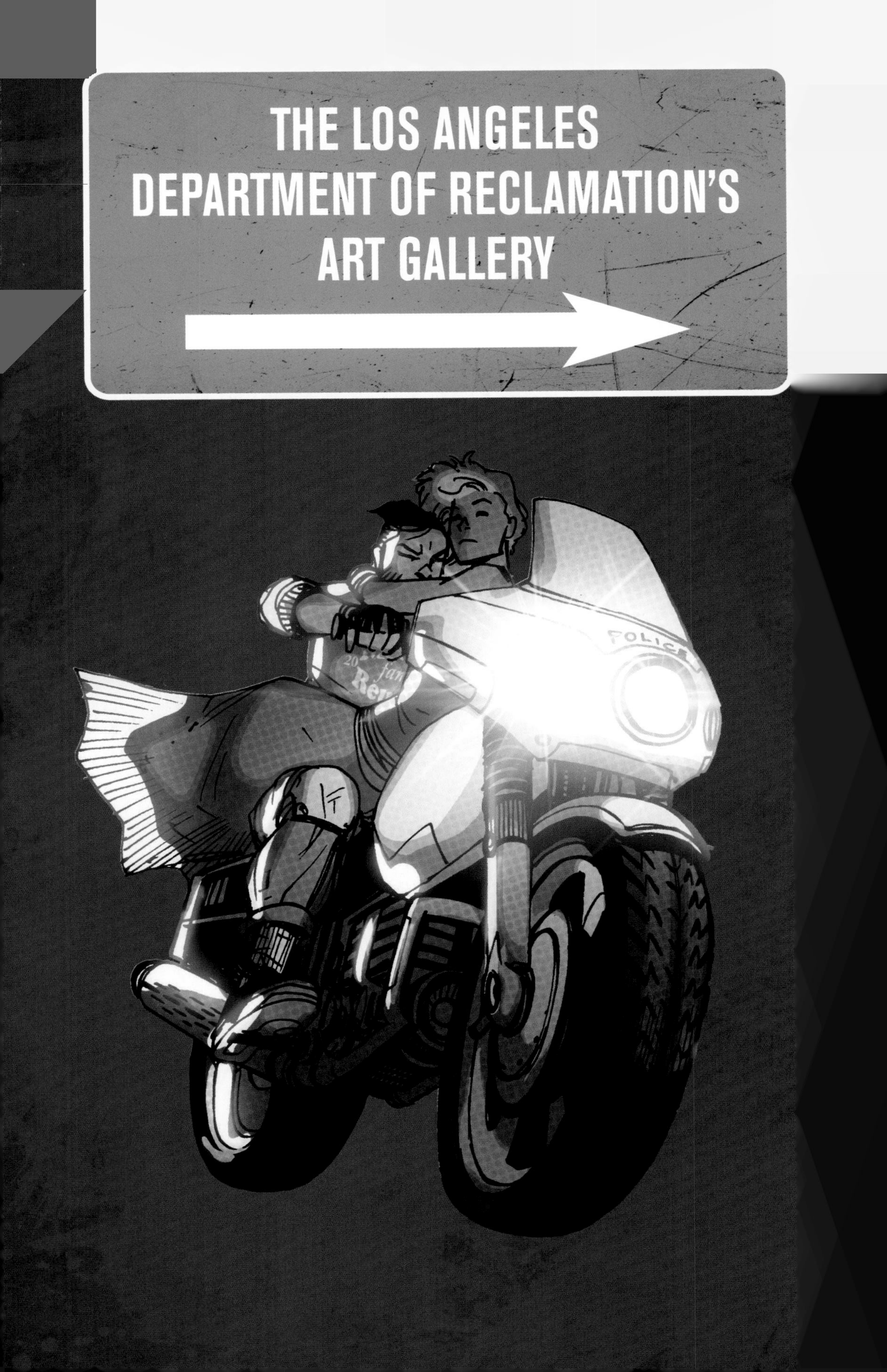
THE LOS ANGELES
DEPARTMENT OF RECLAMATION'S
ART GALLERY
POLICE

COVER GALLERY

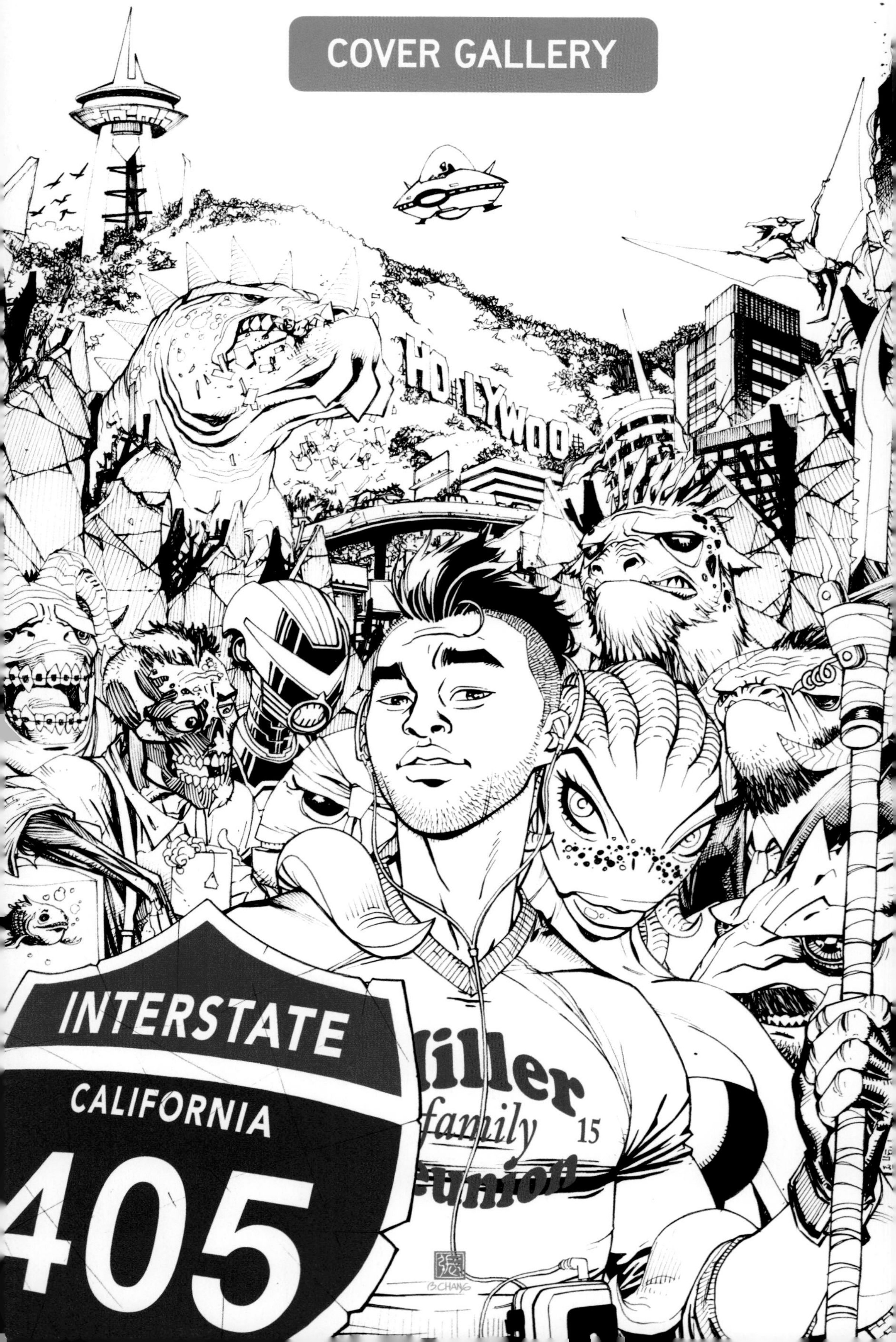
HO LYWOO
INTERSTATE
CALIFORNIA
405
iller
family
15
eunion
B CHANG

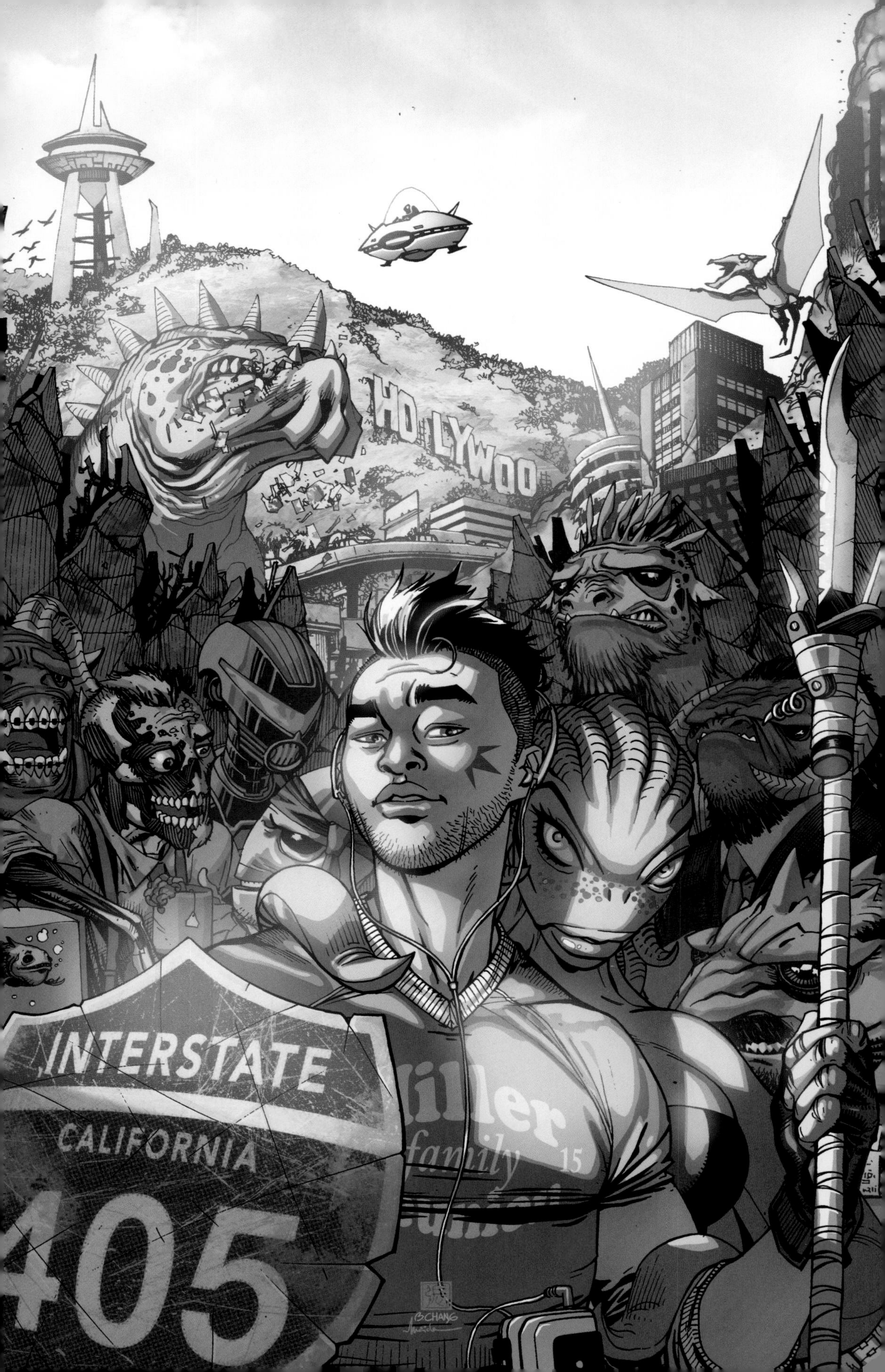
HO LYWOO
INTERSTATE
CALIFORNIA
405
family
15
B CHANG

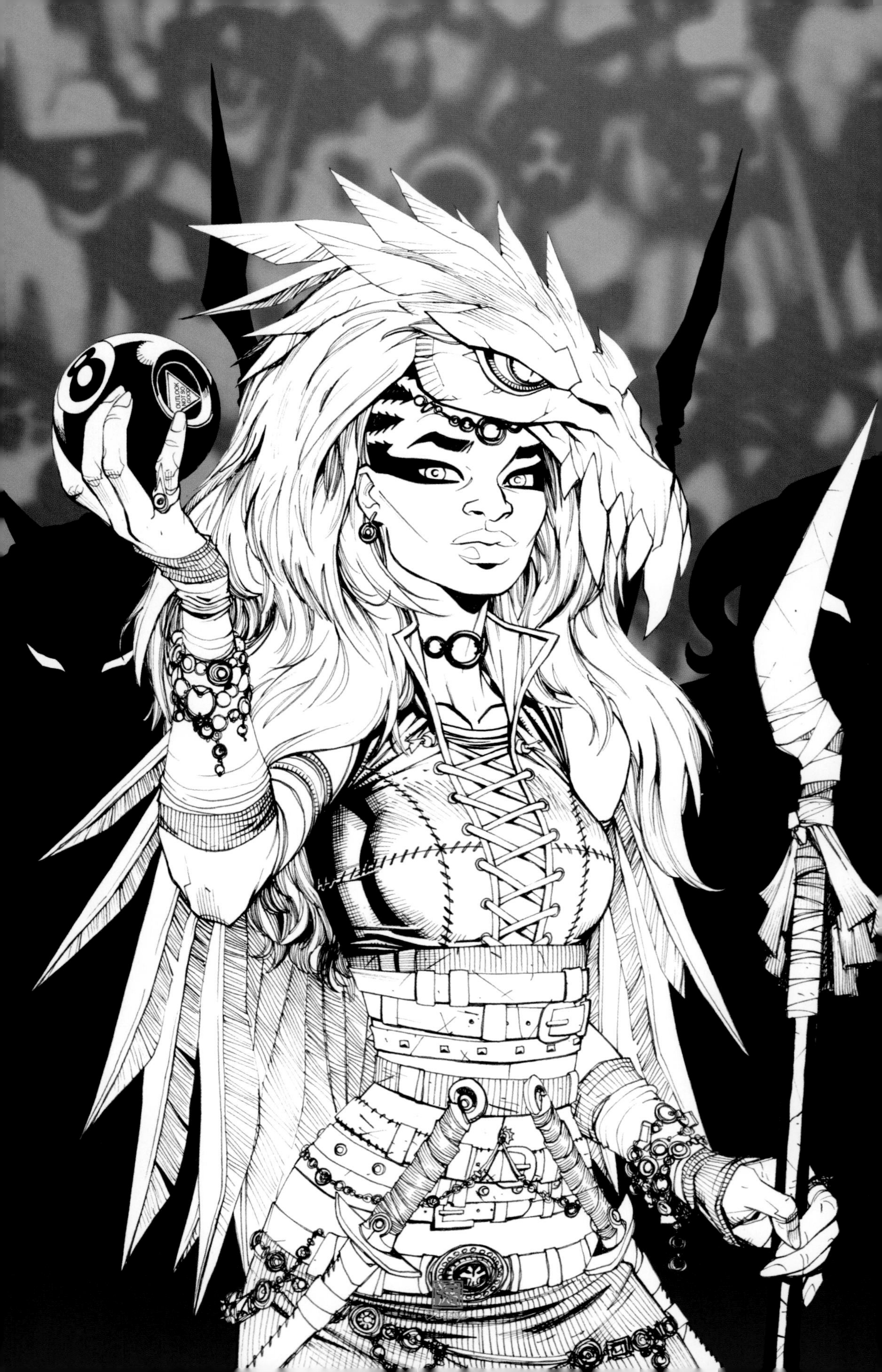
OUTLOOK NOT SO GOOD

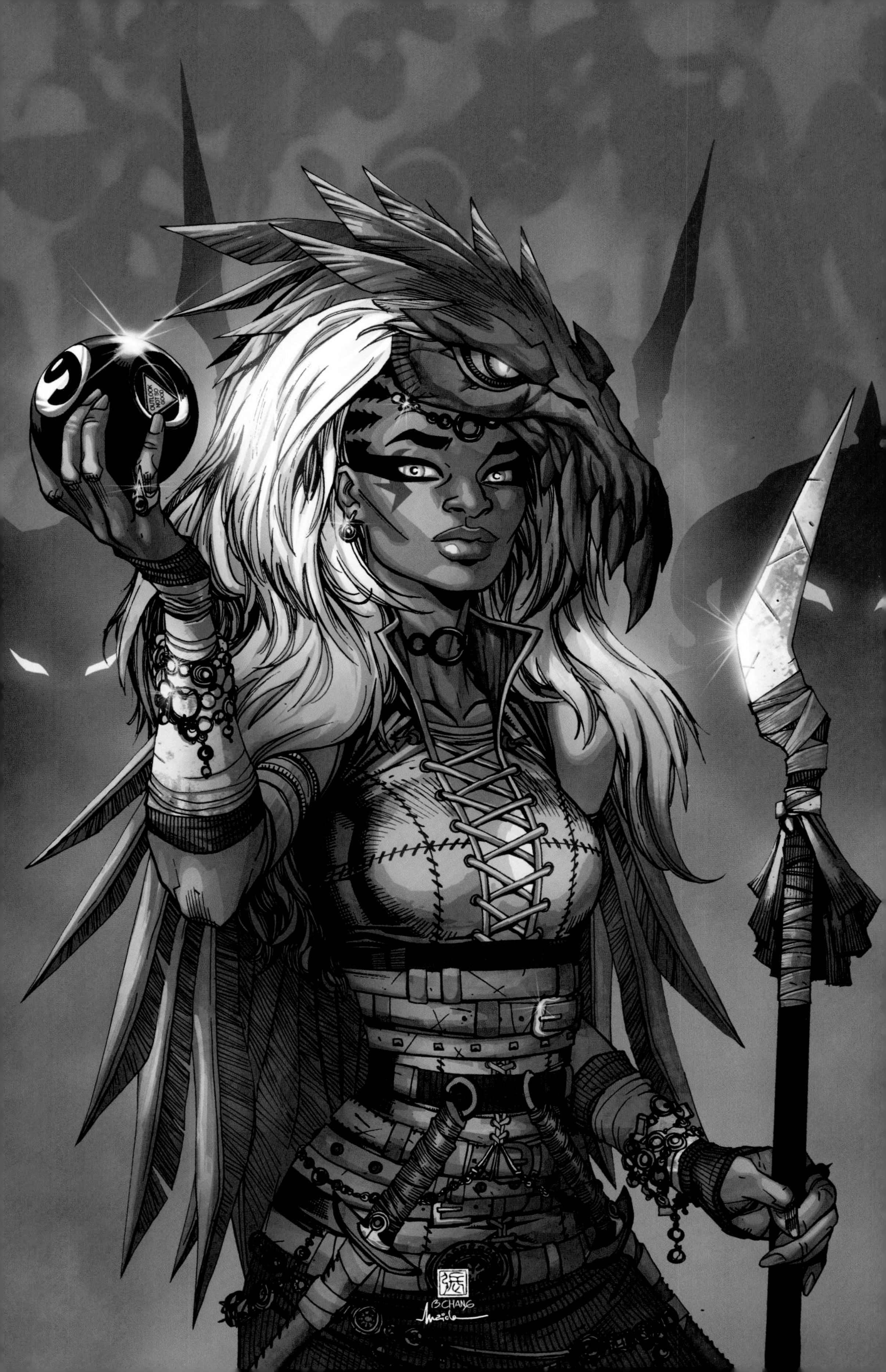
OUTLOOK NOT SO GOOD

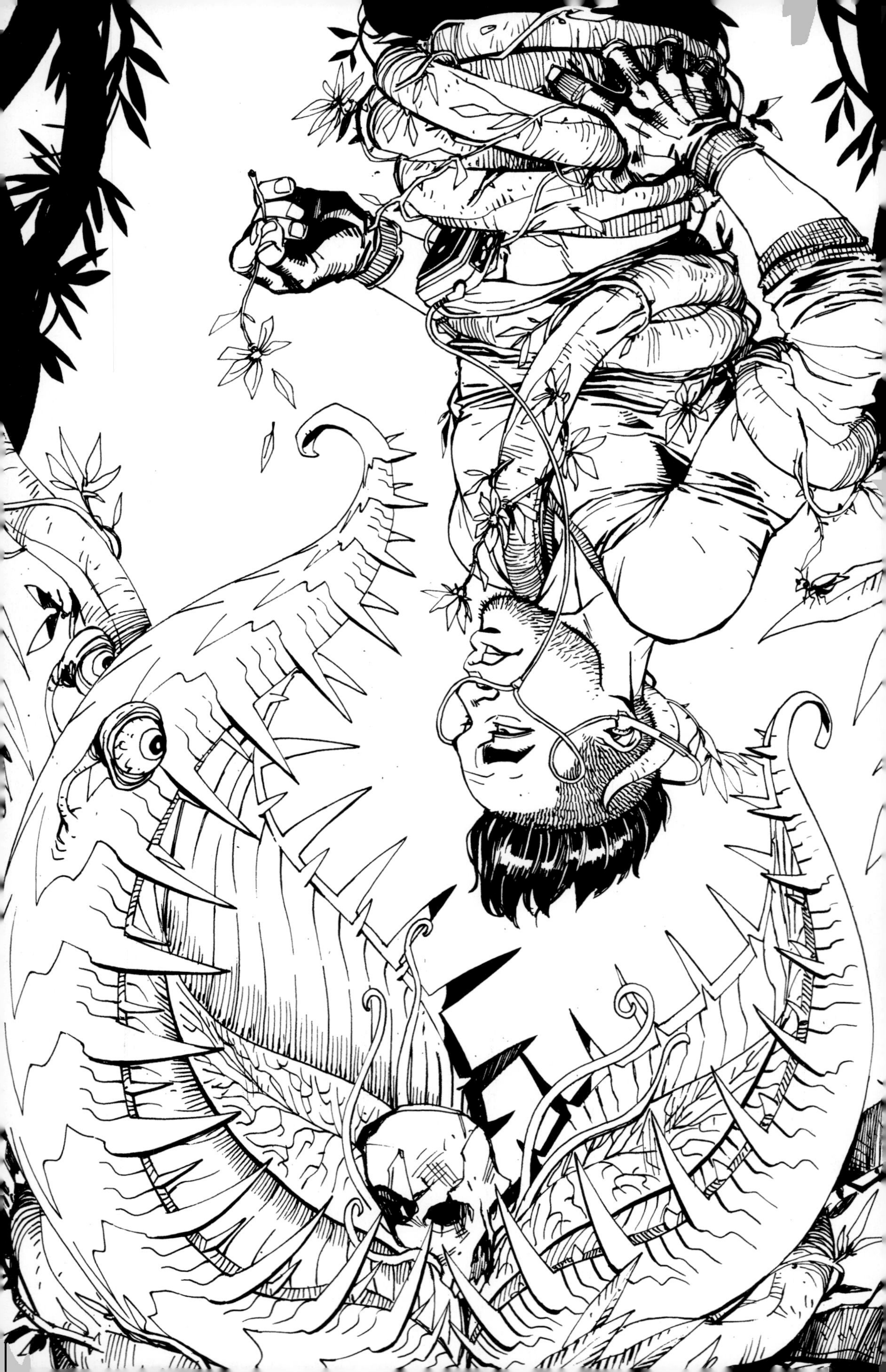

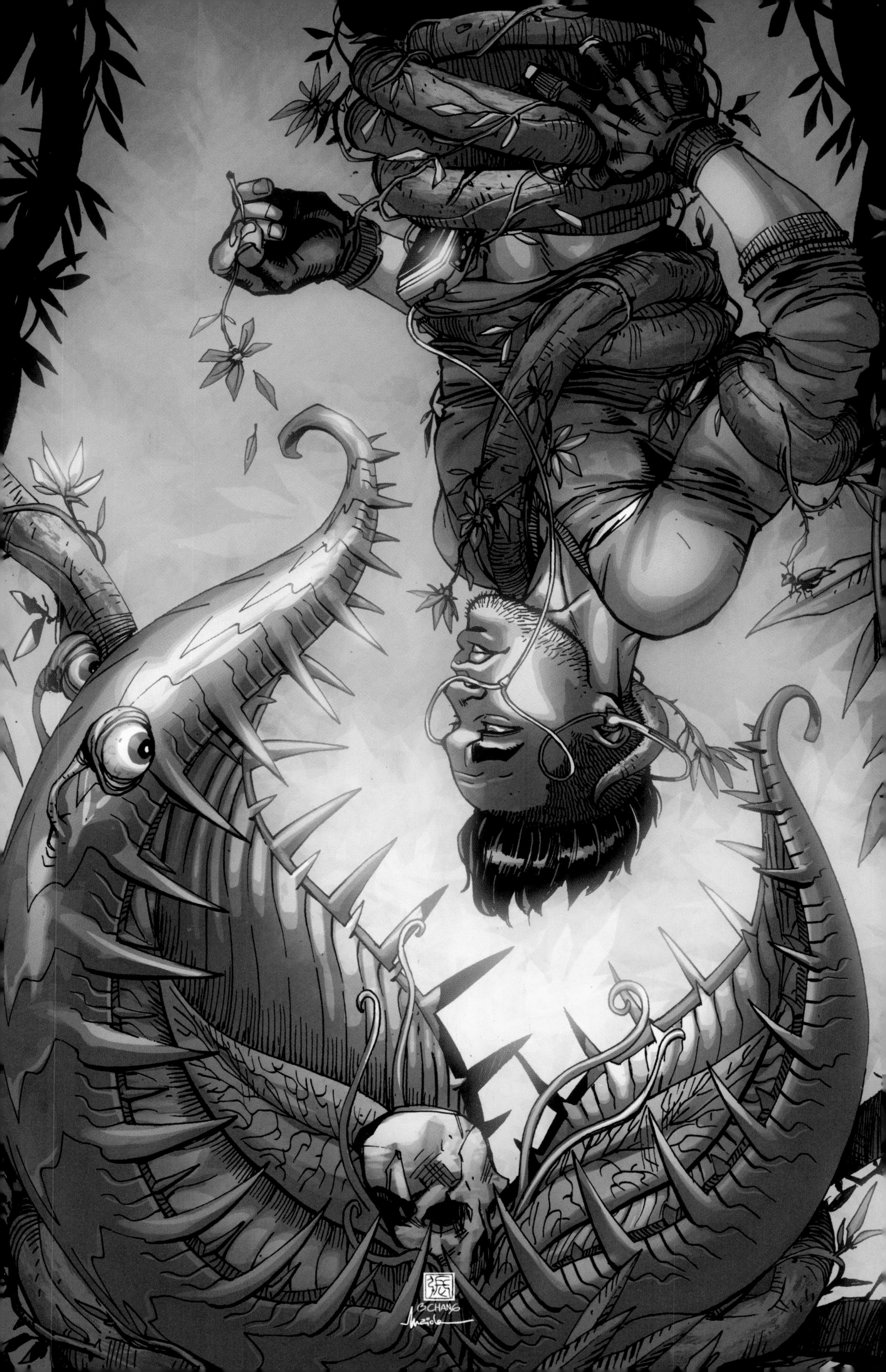
B CHANG

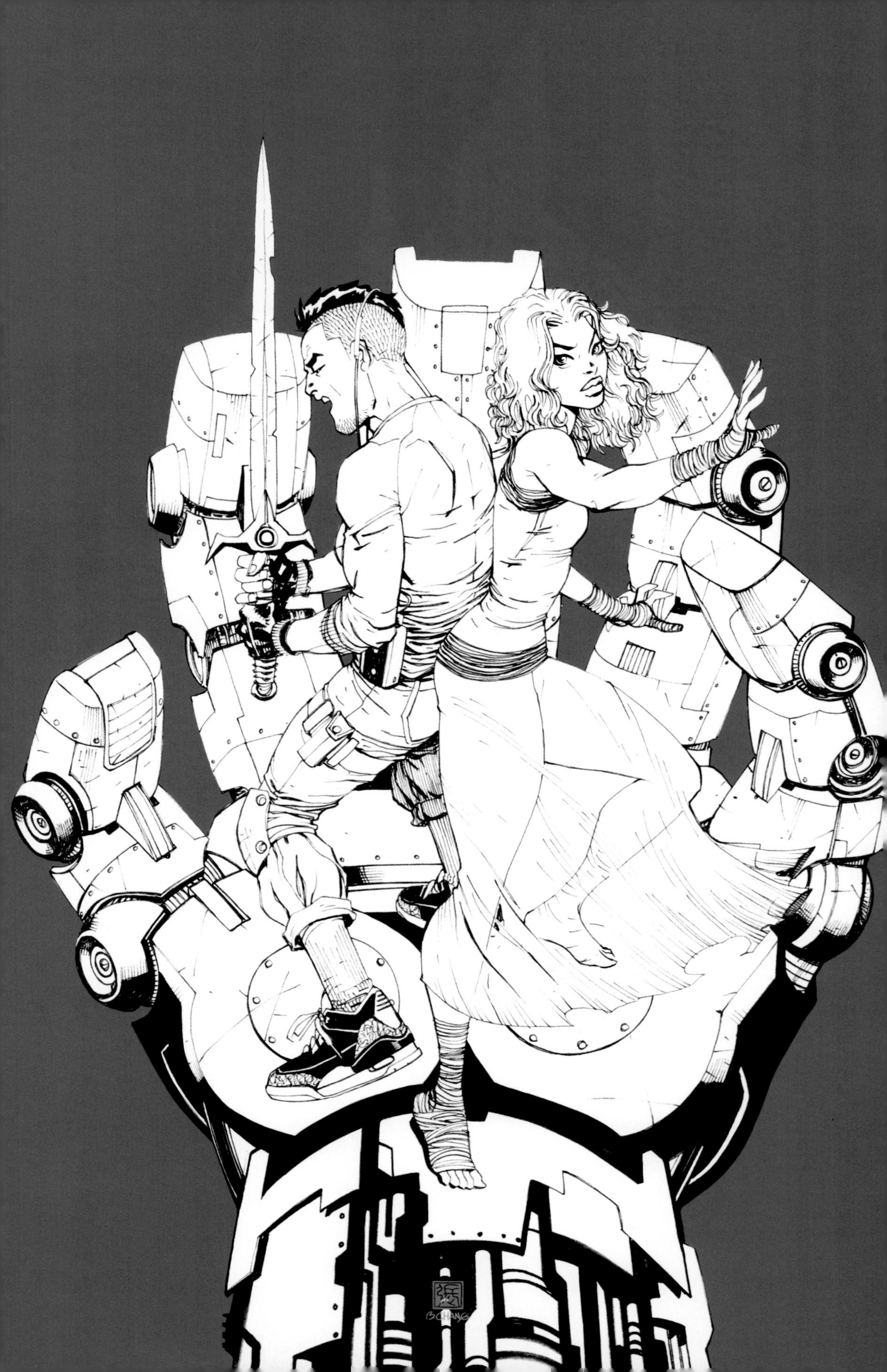
BCHANG

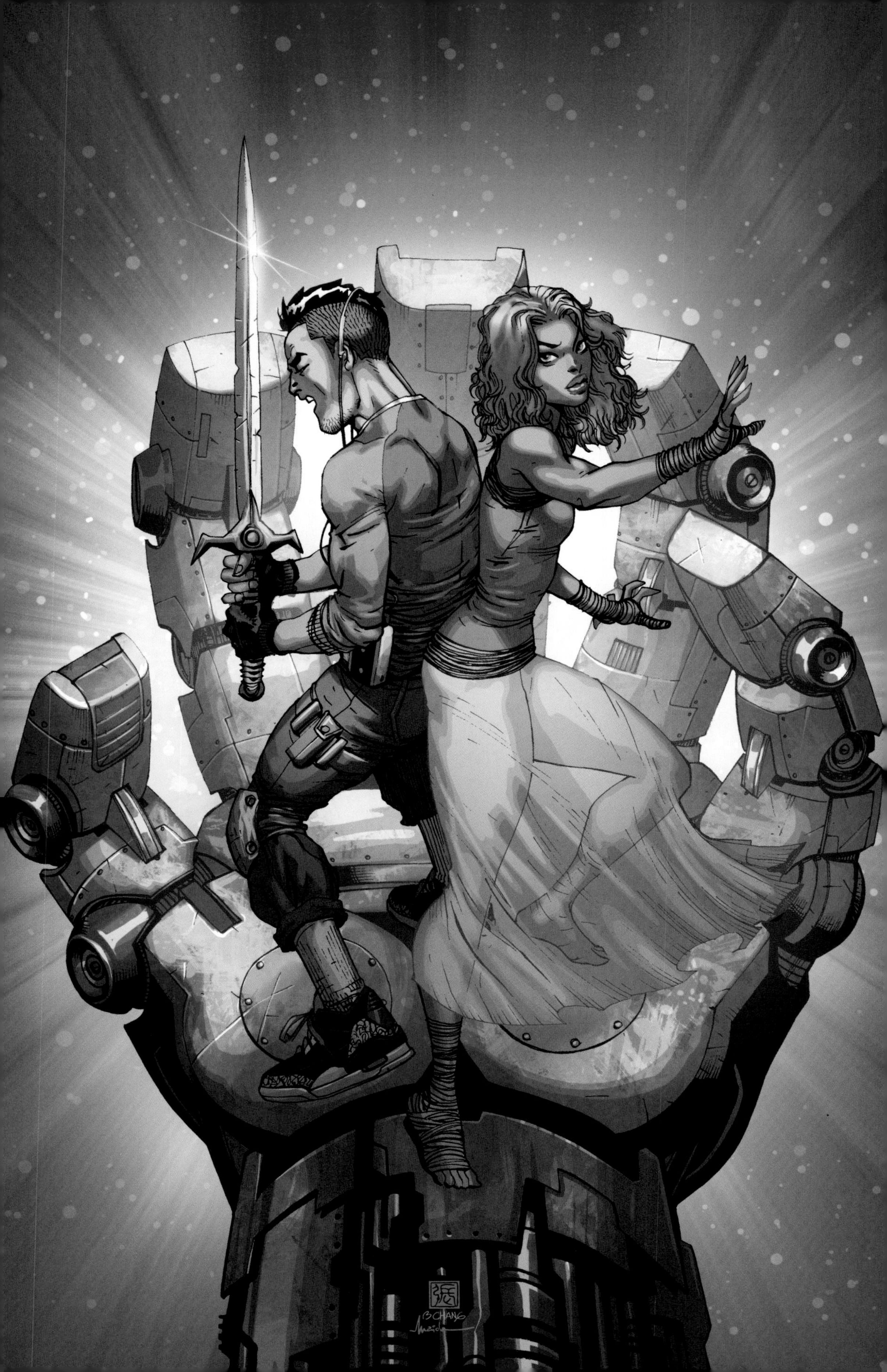
B CHANG

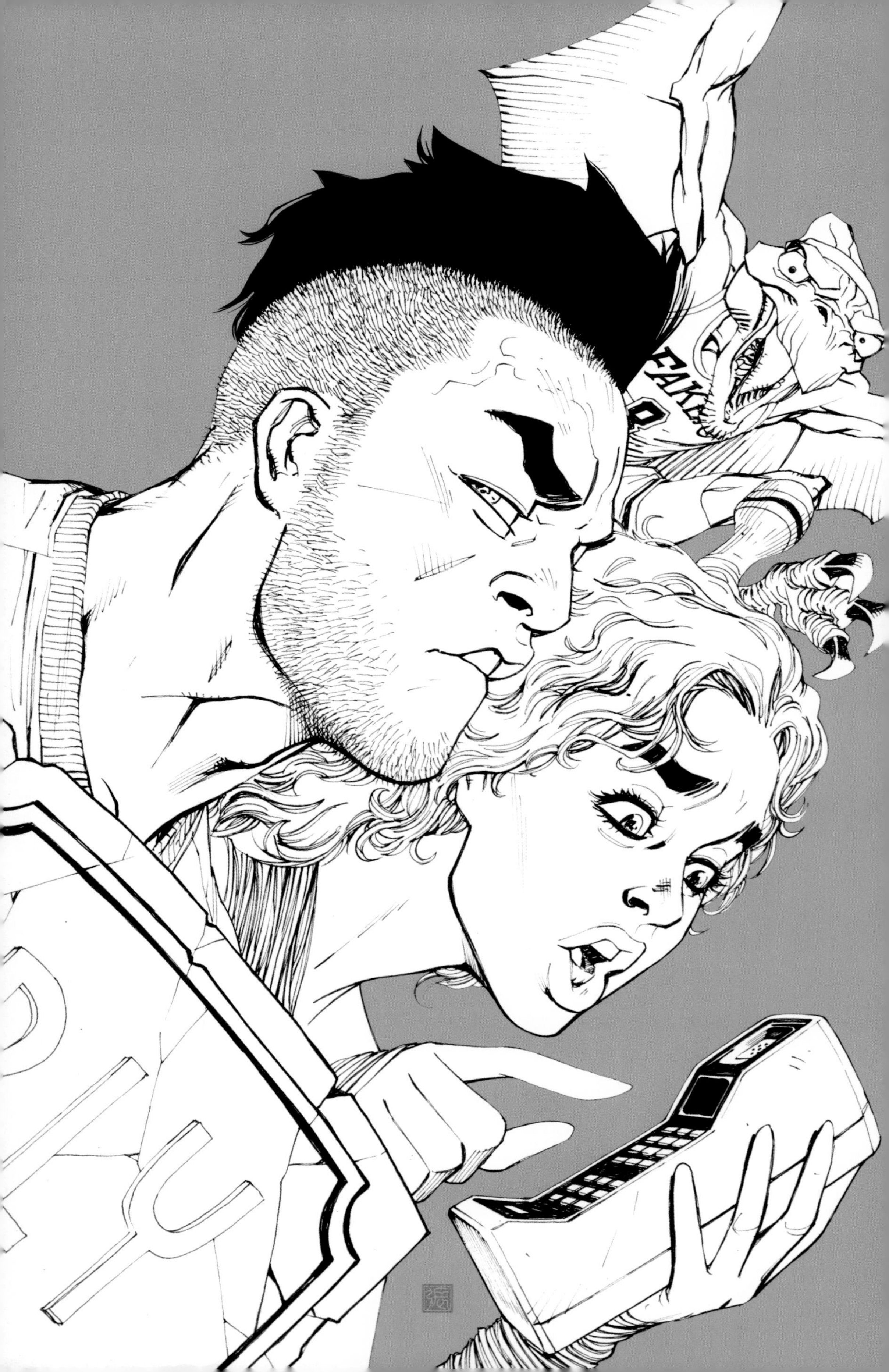

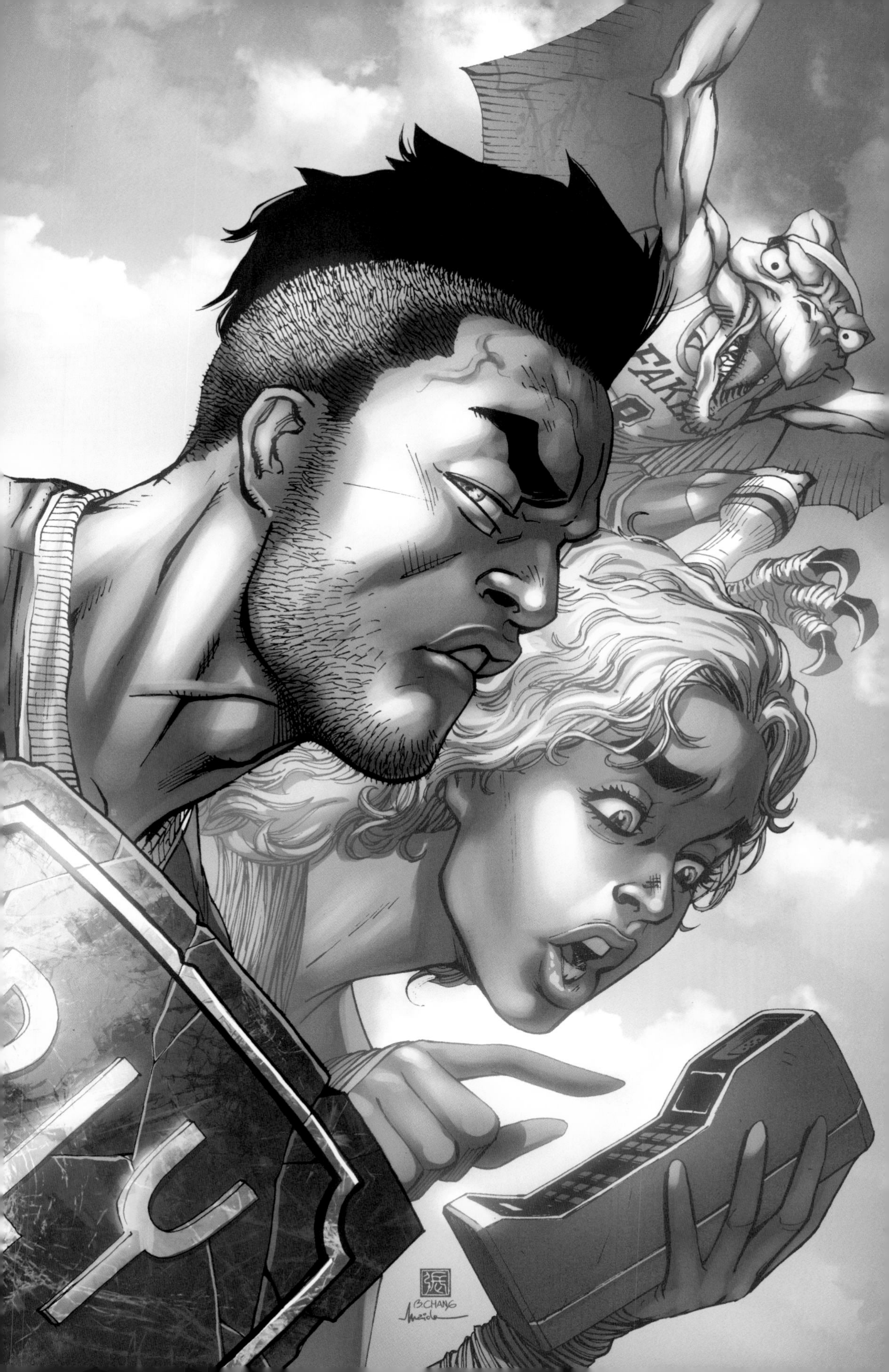
B CHANG

Pin-Up by Rafael de Latorre and Marcelo Maiolo

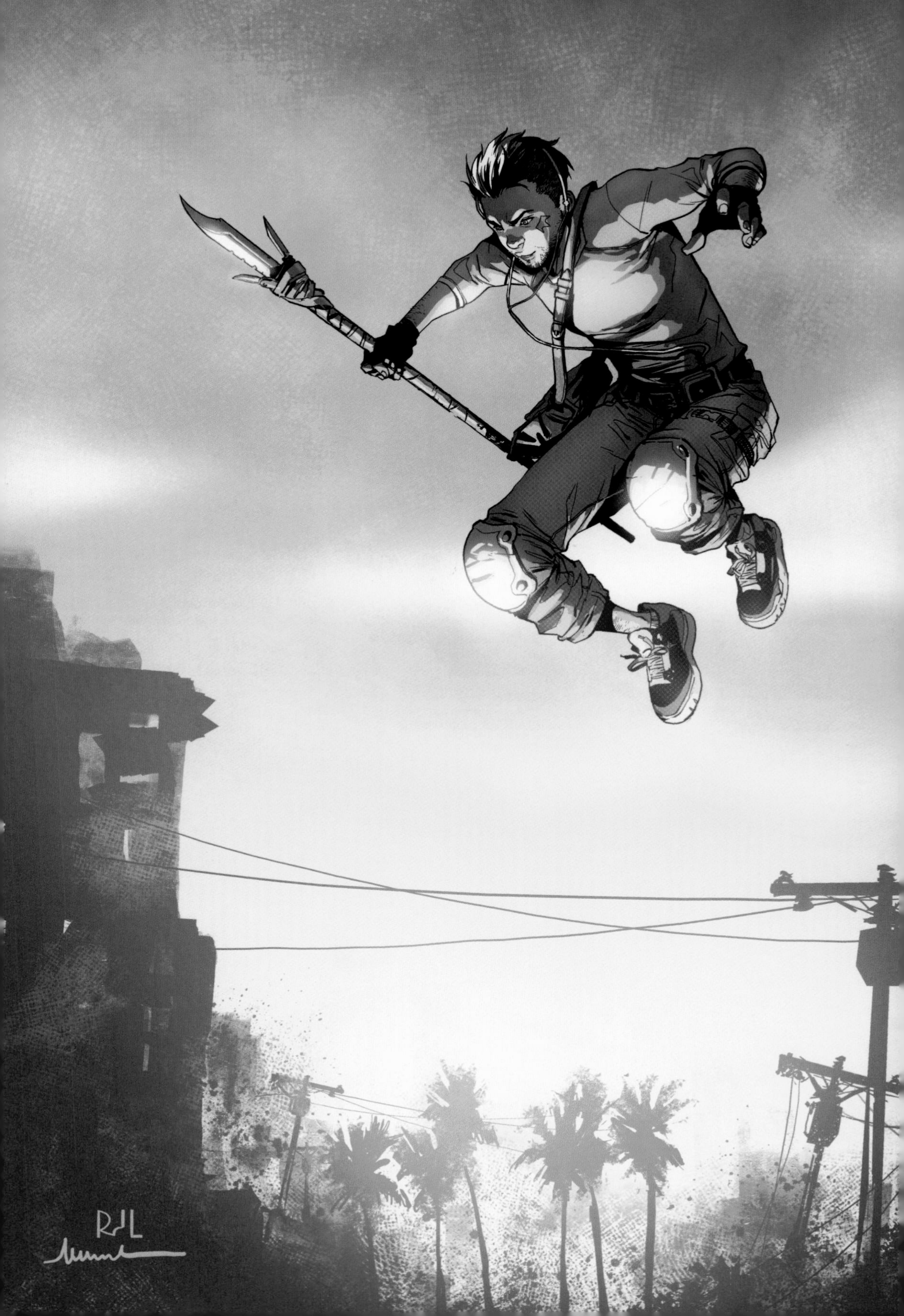

Pin-Up by Marcelo Maiolo

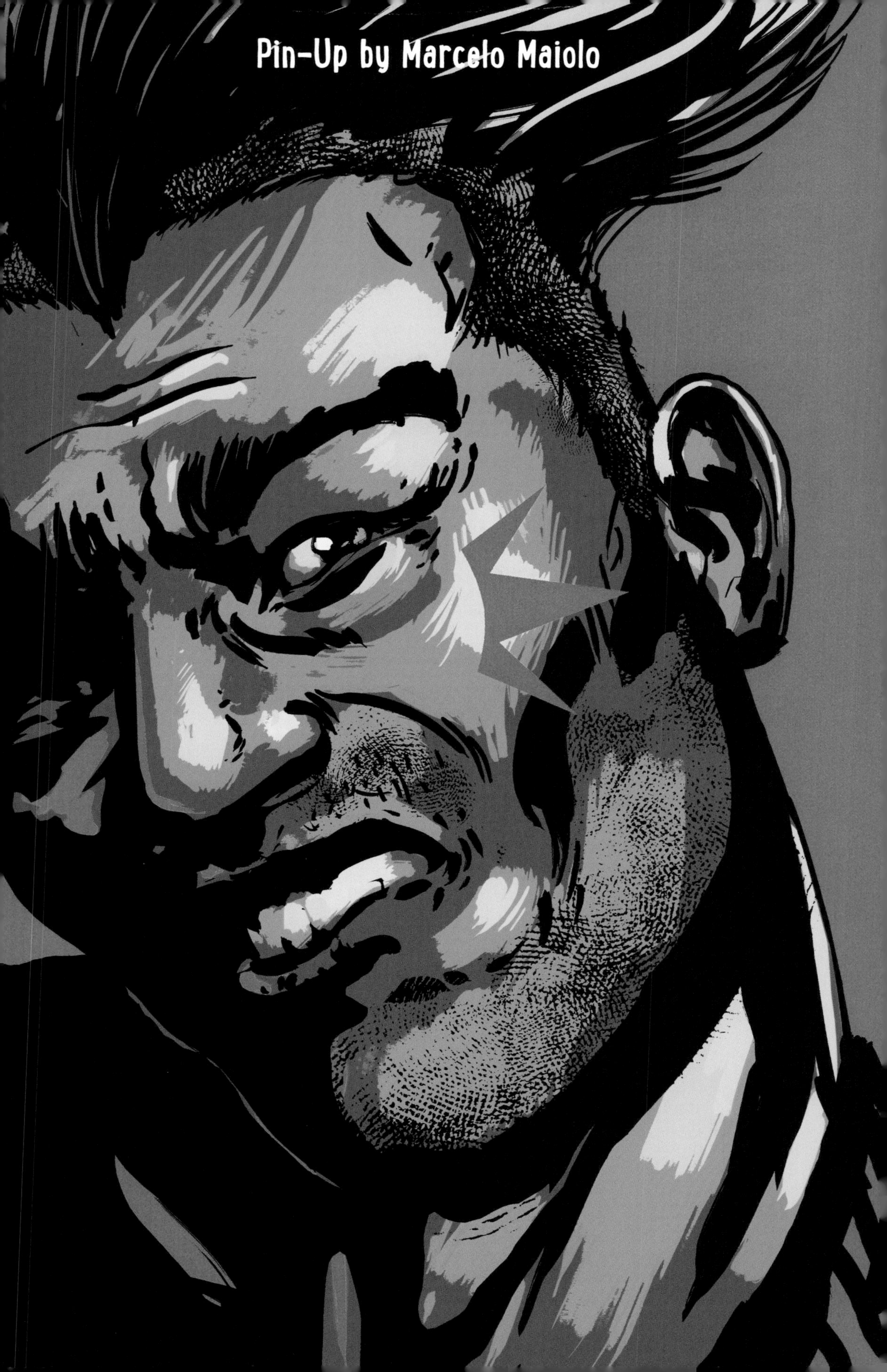

Pin-Up by Marcelo Maiolo

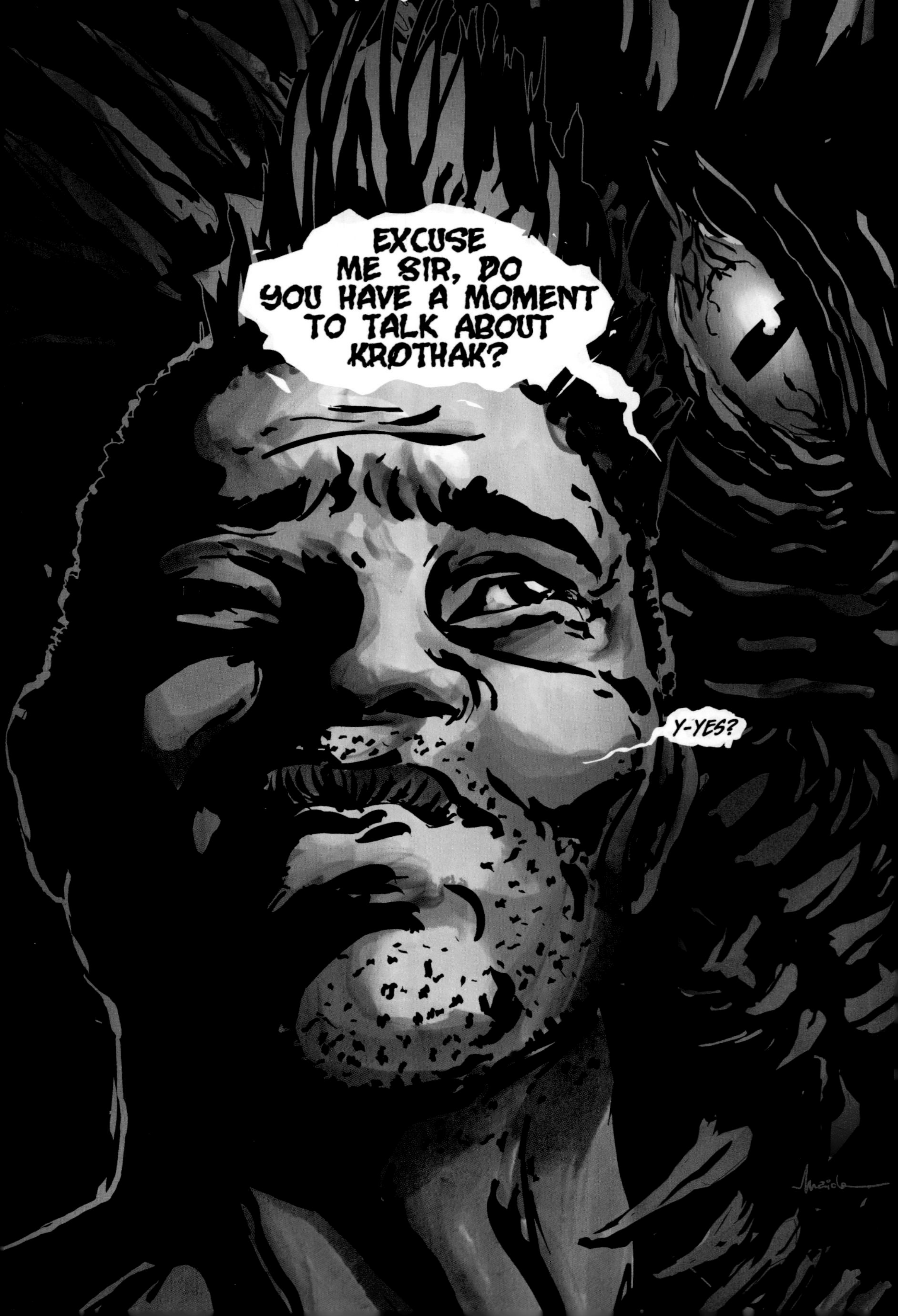
EXCUSE ME SIR, DO YOU HAVE A MOMENT TO TALK ABOUT KRØTHAK?
Y-YES?

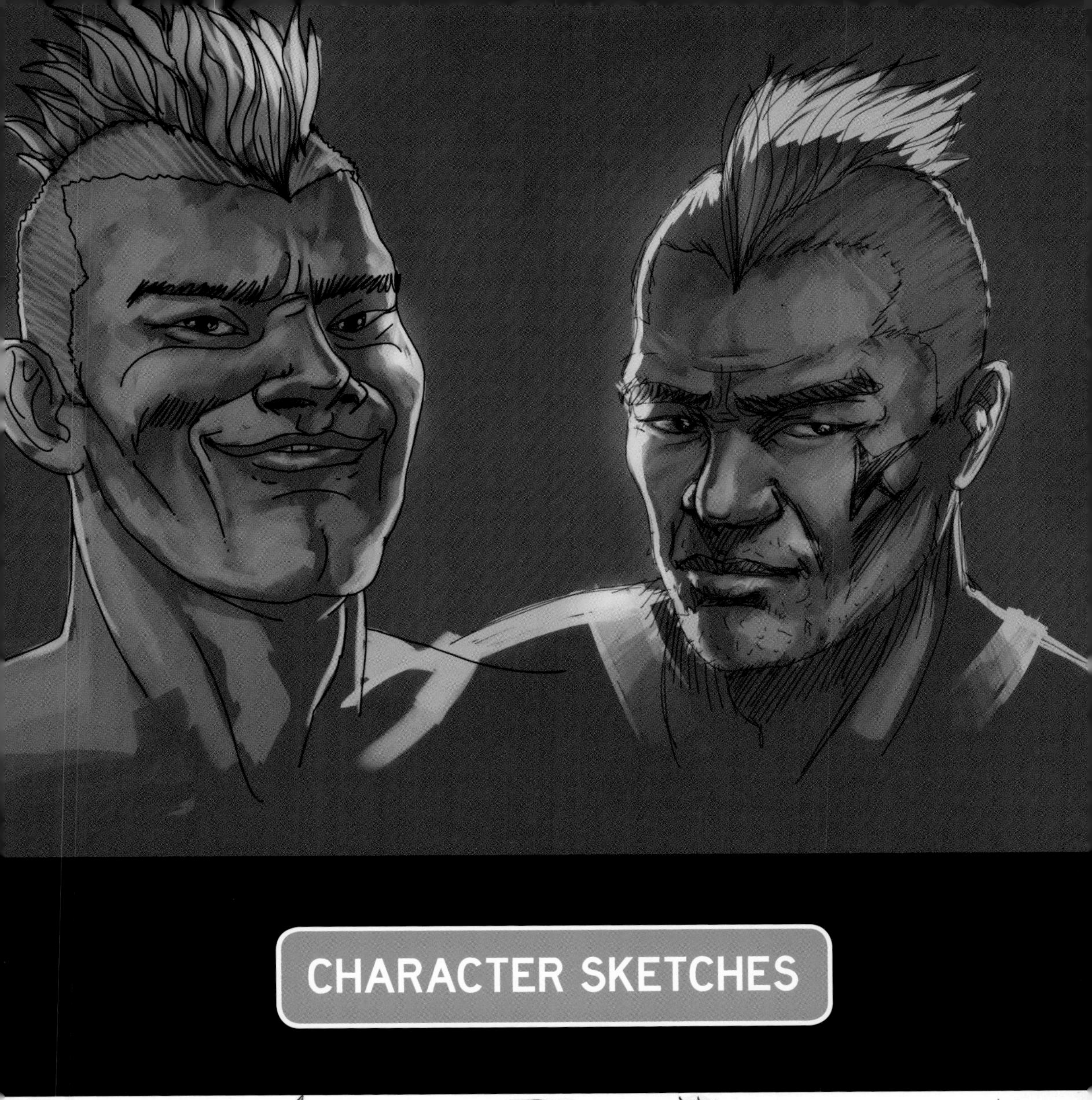

CHARACTER SKETCHES

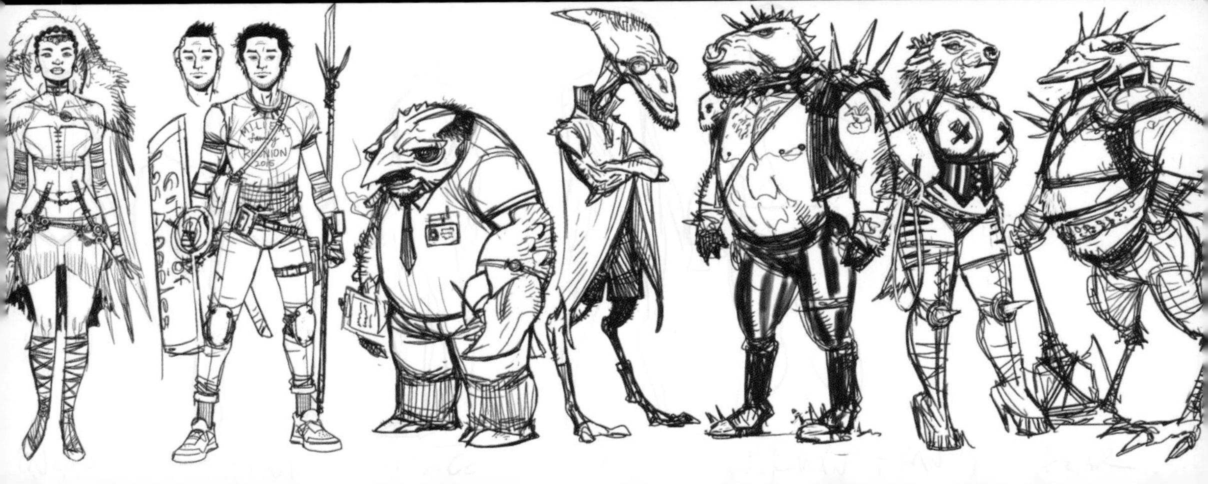

ALTERNATE COVER SKETCHES

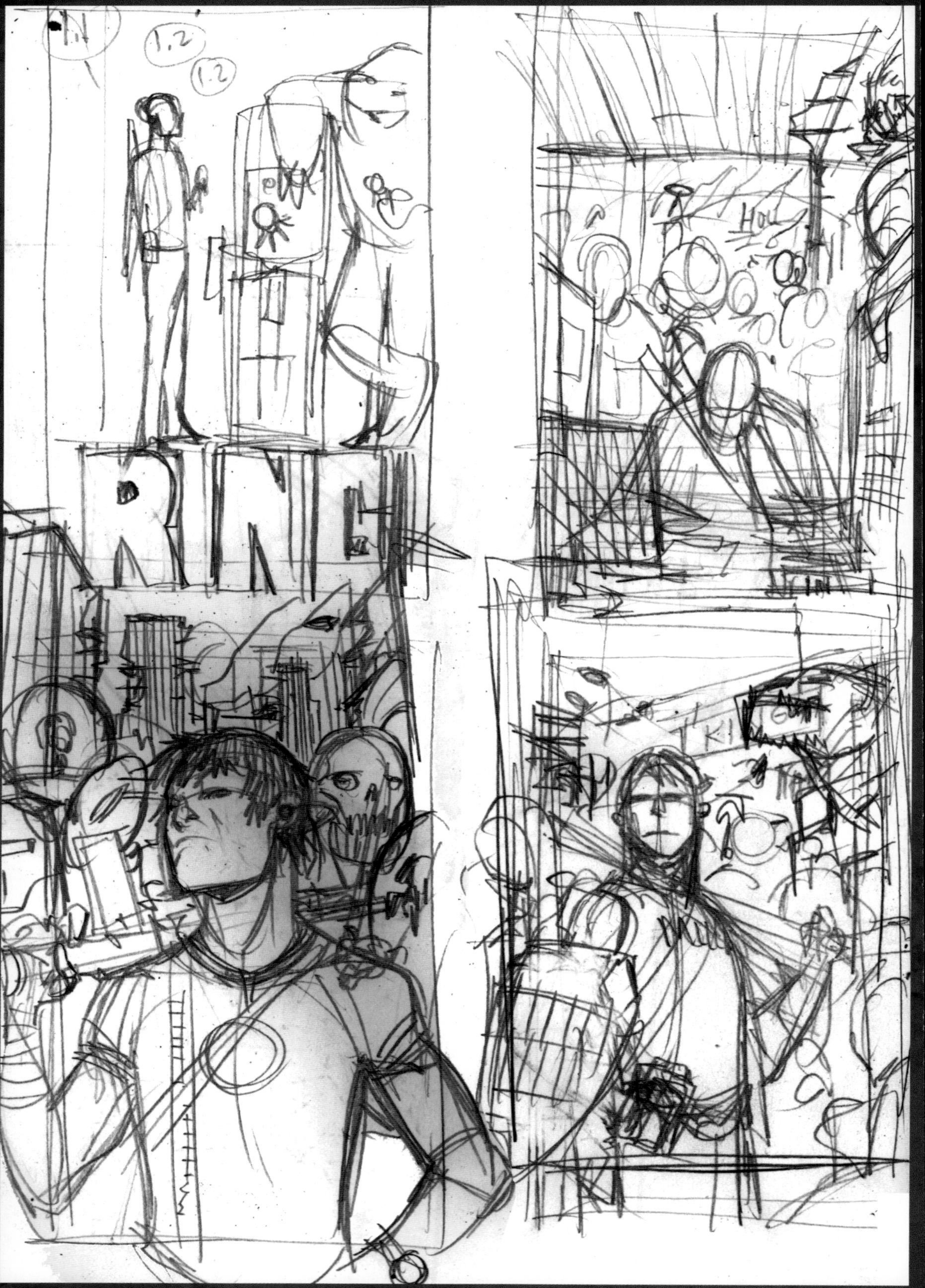

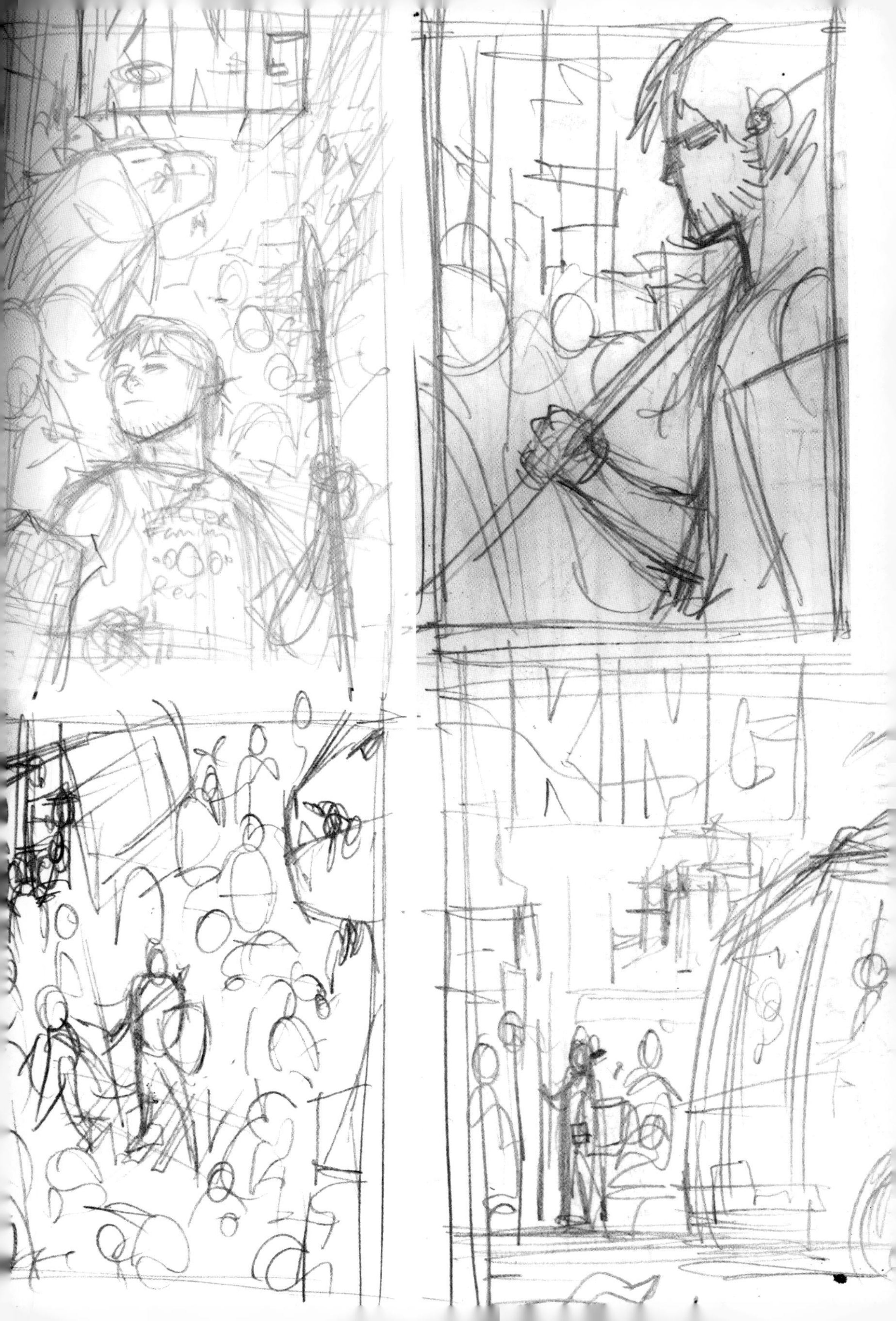

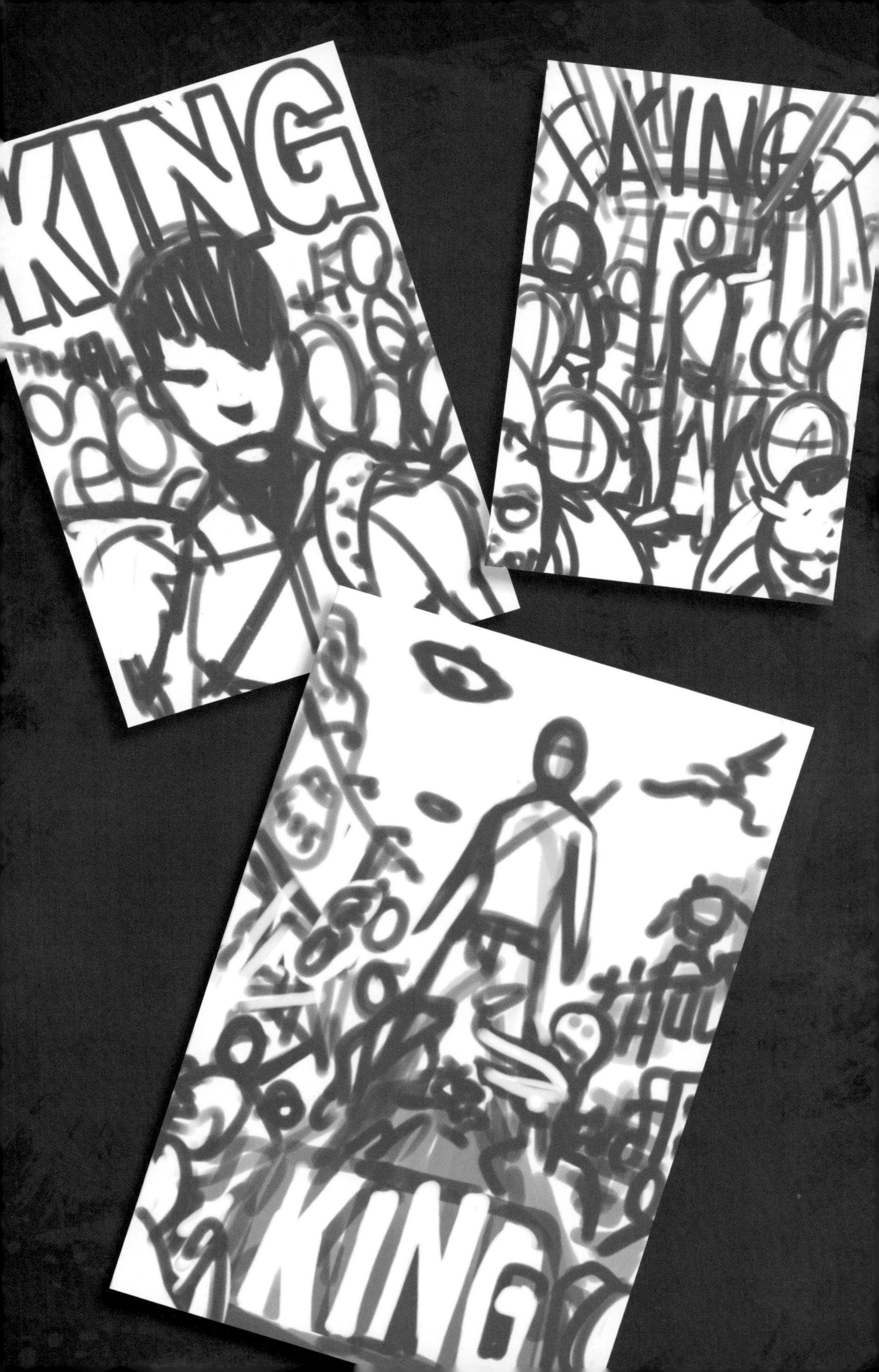
KING
KING
KING

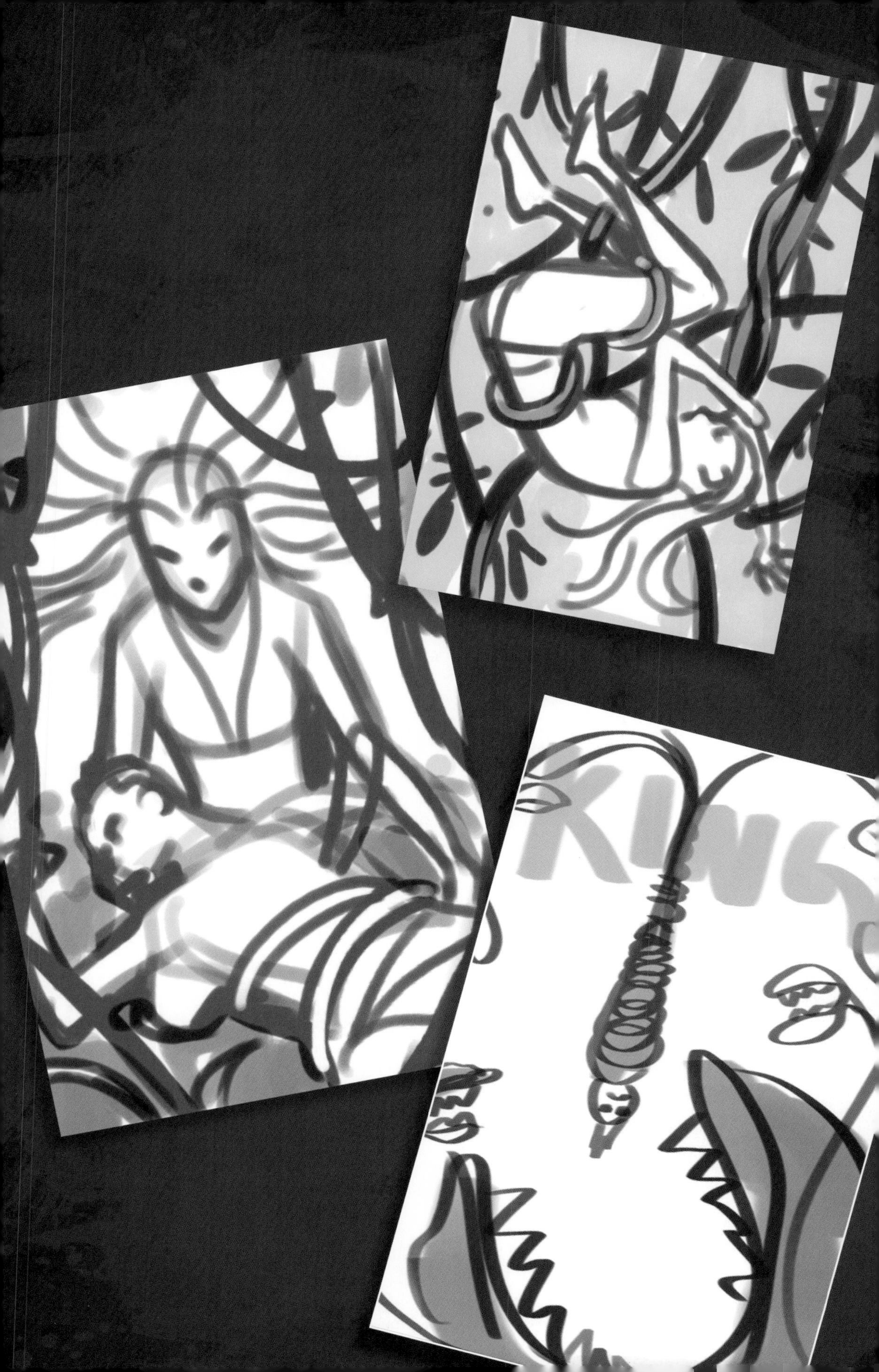

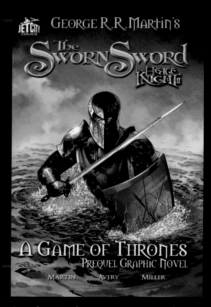

...ALSO FROM JETCITY COMICS

JETCITY COMICS
MUIRWOOD
THE LOST ABBEY
WHEELER STURGES JUSTUS SHEIKMAN JOHN

MUIRWOOD

From renowned fantasy writers
Matt Sturges
(Fables: The Wolf Among Us, Jack of Fables)
and **Dave Justus**
(Fables: The Wolf Among Us)
and **Jeff Wheeler**
featuring stunning art by
Alex Sheikman
(Dark Crystal: Creation Myths)
Lizzy John
(Dark Crystal: Creation Myths)
Cover by **Inaki Miranda**
(Fairest, Coffin Hill)

MAIA, the daughter of the king of Comoros, has been banished, her rank and station taken away. Although magic is forbidden of women in her world, Maia secretly learned...and now her desperate father has sent her on a dangerous quest to save their kingdom. Protected by a hired killer, Maia voyages to another realm—the cursed shores of Dahomey, where an ancient Blight destroyed all the inhabitants. Maia believes she can restore the deadly lands by using her magic medallion, but if she's discovered wielding her clandestine power, she will most certainly be hunted down and killed.

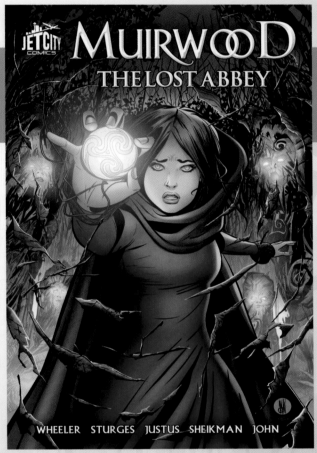

CREATOR BIOS

Joshua Hale FIALKOV

Joshua Hale Fialkov is a creator of graphic novels, including **Elk's Run, The Bunker, The Life After, Punks, Tumor,** and **Echoes.** He also served as a writer on the Emmy Award–nominated animated film **Afro Samurai: Resurrection.**

He has written comics for companies including **Marvel, DC, Legendary, WildStorm, IDW, Dark Horse, Image, Tor Books, Seven Seas Entertainment, Del Rey, Random House, Dabel Brothers Productions,** and **St. Martin's Press.** He also wrote a **Syfy Channel** movie starring Isabella Rossellini and Judd Nelson. Unfortunately, at no point in the film does Judd Nelson punch the sky and freeze-frame.

Joshua grew up in Pittsburgh, Pennsylvania; went to college in Boston, where he got a BFA in writing and directing; and then worked in the New England film industry until finally deciding to move to Los Angeles to do it properly. He lives with his wife, author Christina Rice; their daughter; their dogs, Cole and Olaf (**Twelve Monkeys** and **Frozen,** respectively); and a very unimpressed cat.

Bernard CHANG

Bernard Chang (born 1972 in Montreal, Canada) is an Asian American artist/designer best known for his work in the comic book industry and in entertainment design. Chang started drawing comics professionally in 1992 while attending Pratt Institute in Brooklyn, New York, on a full scholarship for architecture. Within his first year, he was voted onto the **Wizard** magazine Top Ten Artists list for his work on **The Second Life of Dr. Mirage** for **Valiant Comics,** and he was nominated for the Russ Manning Award for Best Newcomer.

After four years at **Valiant,** Bernard went on to illustrate books for **Marvel Comics** and **DC Comics,** including **X-Men, New Mutants, Cable, Deadpool, Superman, Supergirl,** and **Wonder Woman.** His recent credits include **Green Lantern Corps** and **Batman Beyond.**

Marcelo MAIOLO

Marcelo Maiolo is a Brazilian comic book colorist whose credits include **Old Man Logan, X-Men, Green Arrow, Constantine, Superman, Batman Beyond, Green Lantern Corps, Teen Titans, Demon Knights, Pacific Rim,** and **I, Vampire.**